DAVID O. McKAY
BELOVED PROPHET

DAVID O. McKAY

BELOVED PROPHET

MARY JANE WOODGER

Covenant Communications, Inc.

Cover design copyrighted 2004 by Covenant Communications, Inc. Cover photo and all interior
photos courtesy of the Church Archives, The Church of Jesus Christ of Latter-day Saints.

Published by Covenant Communications, Inc.
American Fork, Utah

Printed in Canada
First Printing: November 2004

12 11 10 09 08 07 06 05 04   10 9 8 7 6 5 4 3 2 1

ISBN 1-59156-779-3

PREFACE

Charm . . . is as natural to him as life.
—Emma Ray Riggs McKay[1]

A s the ninth president of The Church of Jesus Christ of Latter-day Saints, David O. McKay endeared himself to members both old and young and to a worldwide populace. His influence was profound, and the magnificent life and personality of David O. McKay has not faded in the memories of Latter-day Saints who knew him as their prophet. This volume pays tribute to that memory by highlighting the stories, ideas, and character traits for which his life is so warmly remembered. As one who has studied the life and administration of President McKay for many years, I hope that the reader will come away as charmed with him as I have been.

In my research, I made every effort to find all available primary sources relating to President McKay's life. One previously unavailable collection has now been cataloged and registered at the University of Utah. This manuscript collection, which I used extensively, includes his personal correspondence and conference notebooks. Another source was the "McKay Scrapbooks," located in the archives of The Church of Jesus Christ of Latter-day Saints. In these scrapbooks, President McKay's secretary, Clare Middlemiss, meticulously documented every talk, address, and activity of the prophet from 1928 to

1970. The work of Stan Larson and Patricia Larson has been invaluable in providing details of Elder McKay's missionary experience in Scotland. I have extensively used some previously published biographies. I also found Keith Terry's interviews with the McKays to be helpful. In addition, I have used many quotes from Francis M. Gibbons's work when discussing incidents involving Church administration; his access to materials as he served as secretary to the First Presidency is unparalleled, and I express my appreciation for his painstaking documentation. President McKay also included much biographical information in his sixty-four years of speaking in general conference and at other venues. Whenever possible, I have used the prophet's own words in describing events. It should be noted that in some quotations the spelling, punctuation, capitalization, and grammar have been standardized.

From the enormous amount of data I have collected over the years I could write several large volumes about David O. McKay and still never completely tell his story. While some readers may expect a fuller, more critical treatment of his life, I have attempted to select experiences that capture the personality, character, and ideals for which he is so lovingly remembered. As you read these experiences and the words of this prophet, you will find that he was an idealist. In every thing he did, he clearly aspired to ideals. His life and his personality became the ideal example to be followed for Church members in the twentieth century. As Elder Henry B. Eyring of the Quorum of the Twelve remembers, "The dominant theme of the way he taught was to hold up before you ideals and make them seem realistic and possible to help you reach higher. . . . He was able to hold up lofty ideals in a way that attracted young people and helped them feel that it is possible to aim very high."[2] It is my intent that the dominant theme of high ideals will become apparent as this much-loved prophet expresses his aspirations for the Church he loved and the Latter-day Saints he led.

NOTES TO PREFACE

1. Quoted in Llewelyn R. McKay, *Home Memories of President David O. McKay* (Salt Lake City: Deseret Book, 1956), 269.
2. Henry B. Eyring, interview by Mary Jane Woodger, August 13, 1996, Salt Lake City, McKay Research Project, College of Education, Brigham Young University, Provo, UT; transcript in author's possession.

ACKNOWLEDGMENTS

I want to thank Dennis A. Wright for his encouragement and assistance. I wish to express my deepest appreciation for Susan Easton Black, whose tireless mentoring continues to bless every aspect of my professional career. A colleague worthy of emulation, I have always found Susan Black as genuine in person as she appears to be from the pulpit. One of Brigham Young University's greatest assets is Paul H. Peterson, chair of the Church History and Doctrine Department. I express gratitude not only for Paul's willingness to provide the necessary secretarial and research staff, but also want to acknowledge his amazing ability to infuse confidence in the scholarly lives of his faculty. Paul's constant encouragement has been a remarkable blessing in my professional career.

I am grateful to my dear friend Christopher D. Searle for reading early drafts of several chapters to make sure that I was not being "too feminine" in my treatment of the prophet's attitudes. I express my thanks to the staff at the LDS Church Archives for their help. I also wish to express thanks to Peter Jasinski for excellent, efficient editing. In producing this book, I am especially indebted to several student assistants who have been involved to varying degrees in the large task of selecting, transcribing, typing, and editing the material included in this manuscript. Jennifer Graham, Valerie Arlene Howes, Ann Johnstun, Britney Schetselaar, and Kevin Whitehead are surely some of the most cheerful, dependable, and intelligent of assistants.

CONTENTS

David O. McKay portrait, 1964.

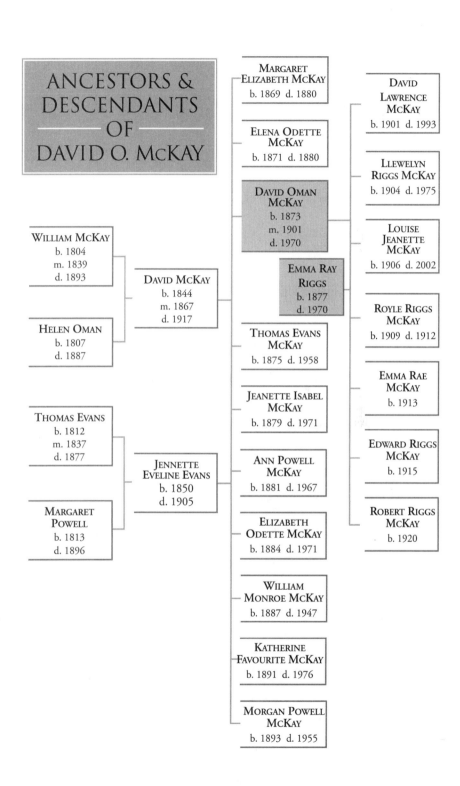

ANCESTORS & DESCENDANTS —OF— DAVID O. McKAY

MARGARET ELIZABETH McKAY
b. 1869 d. 1880

ELENA ODETTE McKAY
b. 1871 d. 1880

DAVID OMAN McKAY
b. 1873
m. 1901
d. 1970

EMMA RAY RIGGS
b. 1877
d. 1970

THOMAS EVANS McKAY
b. 1875 d. 1958

JEANETTE ISABEL McKAY
b. 1879 d. 1971

ANN POWELL McKAY
b. 1881 d. 1967

ELIZABETH ODETTE McKAY
b. 1884 d. 1971

WILLIAM MONROE McKAY
b. 1887 d. 1947

KATHERINE FAVOURITE McKAY
b. 1891 d. 1976

MORGAN POWELL McKAY
b. 1893 d. 1955

WILLIAM McKAY
b. 1804
m. 1839
d. 1893

HELEN OMAN
b. 1807
d. 1887

DAVID McKAY
b. 1844
m. 1867
d. 1917

THOMAS EVANS
b. 1812
m. 1837
d. 1877

MARGARET POWELL
b. 1813
d. 1896

JENNETTE EVELINE EVANS
b. 1850
d. 1905

DAVID LAWRENCE McKAY
b. 1901 d. 1993

LLEWELYN RIGGS McKAY
b. 1904 d. 1975

LOUISE JEANETTE McKAY
b. 1906 d. 2002

ROYLE RIGGS McKAY
b. 1909 d. 1912

EMMA RAE McKAY
b. 1913

EDWARD RIGGS McKAY
b. 1915

ROBERT RIGGS McKAY
b. 1920

EVENTS IN THE
—LIFE OF—
DAVID O. McKAY

1859	Evans and McKay families arrive in Ogden, Utah
1867 Apr. 8	David McKay and Jennette Evans (David O.'s parents) are married by Wilford Woodruff
1873 Sept. 8	Born in Huntsville, Utah, to David McKay and Jennette Evans McKay
1893	Serves as Huntsville Primary School principal
1897	Graduates from University of Utah with a Normal (Teaching) Certificate
1897–1899	Serves a mission to British Isles
1899–1902	Works as a Weber Stake Academy teacher
1901 Jan. 2	Marries Emma Ray Riggs
1902–1906	Works as Weber Stake Academy principal
1906 Apr. 9	Ordained an Apostle
1908	Becomes chairman of the General Priesthood Committee
1918	Becomes superintendent of the Deseret Sunday School Union
1919	Becomes Church Commissioner of Education

1920–1921	World tour of Church missions and schools
1921 Jan. 9	Dedicates land of China for preaching of the gospel
1922–1924	Serves as president of the European Mission
1934–1951	Serves as counselor to Presidents Heber J. Grant and George Albert Smith
1947	Dedicates Pioneer Memorial Monument
1951 Apr. 9	Sustained as President of The Church of Jesus Christ of Latter-day Saints
1955	First President of the Church to tour with Tabernacle Choir in Europe
1955–1964	Dedicates five temples: Swiss (1955), Los Angeles (1956), New Zealand (1958), London (1958), and Oakland (1964)
1958	Dedicates Church College of Hawaii
1961	Announces that members of First Council of the Seventy would be high priests
1963	Dedicates remodeled Salt Lake Temple
1970 Jan. 18	Dies in Salt Lake City, Utah, at the age of ninety-six

David O. McKay, seventeen years old, 1890.

INTRODUCTION

We walk by faith in this world. We are as the little boy who holds his father's hand in the midst of a great city: The little boy is confused by the din and bustle of the crowd, and realizes that if he breaks away he will be lost and may not be able to get back to his father. While he holds that father's hand, however, he is safe. He has an assurance that his father will lead him back to his home.
—David O. McKay[1]

David decided that the time had finally come. Today would be the day. His father had asked him to go hunt for lost cattle; it would be the perfect opportunity to receive a witness.[2] He had waited long enough. He had hungered for it; he felt that if he could get that, all else would be insignificant. Perhaps an angel would appear, though a voice would be sufficient. What better place was there for such an experience than in the solitude of the Ogden Canyon woods? A testimony could come with secret prayer in those lonesome hills.

On countless occasions David O. had listened to his father tell of an experience that had fortified his testimony. It was imprinted so deeply in the boy's heart that he could recite it word for word.

In 1881, while on his mission to Great Britain, his father had found that even mentioning the word "Mormon" brought heated opposition. David Sr. concluded he wouldn't mention anything

Mormon or even the name of Joseph Smith. His message would be about Christian principles: the Atonement, faith, and repentance. There would be no disclosure of a restoration.

In the following weeks, David's father became gloomy, downcast, depressed, and unable to figure out what was wrong. Several weeks passed, and David Sr. concluded, "Unless I can get this feeling removed, I shall have to go home. I can't continue my work thus hampered." After another sleepless night, early one morning before daybreak, he decided to visit a cave near the ocean and take the matter to the Lord. David Sr. was eager to get to the spot, and he started to run so fast he was stopped by a bobby, who wanted to know what in the world was wrong. After a noncommittal but satisfactory answer, the officer let him pass. He finally arrived at the cave and, in the solitude of the sound of the morning tide, poured out his soul to God for relief. He pled aloud, "Oh, Father, what can I do to have this feeling removed? I must have it lifted or I cannot continue in this work." Then it happened. He heard a voice, clear and distinct. It declared, "Testify that Joseph Smith is a prophet of God." Then David Sr. cried out, "Lord, it is enough." David's father left the cave with a sure knowledge that Joseph Smith was a prophet, and the success of the work immediately improved.[3]

Because of that testimony and so many other things, David O. "treasured and honored" his father as "no other man in the world."[4] The story never changed in all the retellings—his father had heard a voice. Now David O. needed to know for himself, to have that same assurance.

It wasn't that he didn't believe the things he had been taught all of his life. As he later recalled, "It has been easy for me to understand and believe the reality of the visions of the Prophet Joseph. It was easy for me in youth to accept this vision, the appearance of God the Father and His Son, Jesus Christ, to the boy praying." David had read the First Vision. He found no difficulty in believing that Moroni appeared to Joseph. He had felt that "Heavenly Beings were real from . . . babyhood on."[5] With time those beliefs were strengthened, but for him they still did not constitute the ideal testimony.

He had staked out a place the week before on his horseback ride to La Plata, a booming mining town where once a week he delivered *The Standard* newspaper.[6] On the long ride to La Plata he often read and memorized favorite passages of literature, but last week he had not read much. Instead he had found his own sacred grove—a serviceberry bush beside a large, wild tree providing needed privacy. He never met many people on the trail out to La Plata, but he wanted to be sure he was not interrupted.

He rode his pony, Mingo, out to the secluded tree. There he jumped off, threw the reins over his horse's head, and then knelt down. The early spring air was crisp, and the sun crept through the leaves of the trees, warming his face. The smell of the wild trees, flowers, and grass scented the air. David focused on the task at hand. It was time to gain a testimony, to stand on his own two spiritual feet. In all the fervor and concentration a teenage boy could muster, he poured out his soul in prayer and asked his Heavenly Father for a testimony of the restored gospel.

After what seemed to have been hours, David finally got up, mounted his horse, and started back over the trail that had brought him to the place he thought would become his sacred grove. As the horse sauntered down the path, David shook his head and said to himself, "No spiritual manifestation has come to me. If I am true to myself, I must say I am just the same 'old boy' that I was before I prayed."[7]

Now what was he to do? The scriptures promise, "Ask, and ye shall receive; knock, and it shall be opened unto you" (D&C 4:7). "If any of you lack wisdom, let him ask of God, . . . and it shall be given him" (James 1:5). He had asked, and as far as he could tell, he had received no answer.

Although disappointed, David made a decision. Just because the answer hadn't come today, it didn't mean that it would never come, and it didn't mean it wasn't true. He would do what he had always done. He would just have to hang on to his father's testimony and hope that someday the Lord might see fit to give him the same assurance he felt in his father's witness.[8] Words he spoke many years later apply to the situation he found himself in then: "We walk by faith in this world. We are as the little boy who holds his father's hand in the midst of a great city: The little boy is confused by the din and bustle of the crowd, and realizes that if he breaks away he will be lost and may not be able to get back to his father. While he holds that father's hand, however, he is safe. He has an assurance that his father will lead him back to his home."[9]

While such an anticlimactic experience is hardly considered the stuff that prophets are made of, unbeknownst to David, this moment and a myriad of others were shaping an obscure young man growing up in the small, rural town of Huntsville, Utah, for an extraordinary future. He could not have known then that as a young missionary in Scotland, ten years later, he would receive the witness he had asked for as a teenager. In just another ten years, he would be ordained a member of the Quorum of the Twelve Apostles. And on April 9, 1951, at the age of seventy-seven, David Oman McKay would become the ninth president of The Church of Jesus Christ of Latter-day Saints. Standing over six feet tall, with a full head of wavy white hair, he would be an imposing figure who many said *looked* like a prophet. He would see great changes in the world and the Church during his lifetime, his life extending from the era of the horse and buggy to that of man walking on the moon. As a Church leader during World War I, World War II, the Korean conflict, and the Vietnam War, his enlightened messages would bring peace and hope to generations that faced a war-torn world. Church membership during his presidency would grow from 1.1 to 2.9 million, with two-thirds of Church membership having known no other prophet. David's odyssey, from kneeling at a tree in Ogden Canyon to becoming a prophet of the Lord, is a remarkable tale of preparation, guidance, and living ideals that prepared him to lead an entire church.

NOTES TO INTRODUCTION

1. "Keep the Faith," *Improvement Era,* June 1951, 397.
2. See David O. McKay, *Cherished Experiences from the Writings of President David O. McKay,* comp. Clare Middlemiss (Salt Lake City: Deseret Book, 1955), 16.
3. David O. McKay, *Gospel Ideals* (Salt Lake City: Deseret News Press, 1957), 21–22; also found in David O. McKay, *Cherished Experiences,* 22–24; see also Henry D. Moyle, Conference Report, April 1961, 93.
4. David O. McKay, *Gospel Ideals,* 22.
5. Conference Report, October 1951, 182–83.
6. Jeanette McKay Morrell, *Highlights in the Life of David O. McKay* (Salt Lake City: Deseret Book, 1966), 147.
7. David O. McKay, *Cherished Experiences,* 16.
8. Richard McKay, interview by Mary Jane Woodger, 1995, Salt Lake City, McKay Research Project, College of Education, Brigham Young University, Provo, UT; transcript in author's possession.
9. "Keep the Faith," 397.

CHAPTER 1

THE IDEAL CHILDHOOD

Next to eternal life, the most precious gift that our Father in Heaven can bestow upon man is his children. Ideals that relate to God and his little children are indispensable elements to happiness and eternal life.

—David O. McKay[1]

In the spring of 1859, with a good team of horses to pull the wagon and a cow tied behind to furnish milk, the Evans family headed west. Jennette, just nine years old at the time, walked most of the way across the plains. Her story was similar to that of many other pioneer children. She was born August 23, 1850, in Cefn Coed, Wales, where her well-to-do parents, Thomas and Margaret Powell Evans, joined The Church of Jesus Christ of Latter-day Saints. Disowned as a result by their relatives, they followed the call to gather to Zion, selling their possessions and sailing from Liverpool on May 25, 1856. The family reached Iowa in July and took three years to earn enough to purchase supplies for the long journey. They arrived in Salt Lake City on August 18, 1859, and, after a short stay, moved on to Ogden.[2]

It was on the very day of Jennette's arrival in Ogden that David McKay, age fifteen, first saw his future wife. Her father had come to make arrangements to buy farmland. Jennette was seated on the tongue of the family wagon and was wearing a gingham dress. When David Sr. first looked into Jennette's big, brown eyes, peeking out from beneath a pink sunbonnet, he was mesmerized. At that young age, "there would appear to have been little in the way of female allurement to evoke feelings of matrimony," but he later remembered "that at this moment he knew that Jennette Evans was to be his bride."[3]

David, the youngest son of William and Ellen Oman McKay, was born May 3, 1844, in Janetstown (Thurso), Scotland. Like Jennette's family, the McKays were among those who converted to the Church in the British Isles in 1850. They faced similar trials as well. While preparing to emigrate to Utah, the McKay children became sick with the measles, delaying the family's departure. The children recovered by April 1856, and the McKays left for Liverpool, where they joined 764 other Mormons who sailed aboard the *Thornton* on May 4, 1856. After spending forty-one days on the ocean and landing at Castle Garden, New York, the McKays found that a "friend" who had borrowed money in Scotland did not appear with the promised repayment. Lacking the funds necessary for their journey west, the McKays were now stranded at the port of entry in a strange, new land. It took the family two long years to earn enough money for the train fare to Iowa. In Iowa, the family worked for another year to prepare for the journey to Utah. Joining an LDS company at Florence, Nebraska, on June 14, 1859, David McKay's family set off for a thousand-mile walk across the plains.[4]

Matured beyond his years by the hardships he had endured, David reached Ogden, Utah, in 1859, and after his first meeting with Jennette, he moved to Huntsville and started farming. Despite a lack of a formal education, he taught himself the necessary skills to later be elected to the Utah legislature and serve three terms in the Utah senate. He also joined the newly organized Utah militia under Commander Samuel Glascow.

By the time Jennette was ready to be courted, David McKay Sr. sported a dark, well-trimmed "General Grant" beard. Jennette, now a grammar school teacher, had become one of the prettiest girls in Weber County, with "straight dark hair" that she "parted and tied in a bun at the nape of her neck."[5]

As the relationship between Jennette and David became more serious, her parents insisted that she wait until she was eighteen years old to wed. However, after much coaxing from Jennette, they gave permission in the spring of her seventeenth year. Almost eight years from the time they met, David and Jennette traveled to the Salt Lake Endowment House and were sealed for time and all eternity by President Wilford Woodruff on April 9, 1867.

GROWING UP IN HUNTSVILLE

The young couple was among the first settlers in the growing town of Huntsville. Located thirteen miles east of Ogden in the northern Ogden Valley, Huntsville soon grew to a population of one thousand[6] and became a "well-organized, thriving, . . . self-sustaining community. Although its residents traced their ancestry to several different countries, the town was surprisingly homogenous, resulting from the influence of the Church."[7] One member of the congregation was Mary Heathman Smith, also known as Grandma Smith. Nearly an institution in the town, she had received medical training in England and was the midwife who ushered most of Huntsville into the world, including a baby boy given his father's first name—David Oman McKay.[8]

David O. was the first son and third child born to David and Jennette McKay. He was preceded by two sisters, Margaret and Ellena. For the most part, his early childhood was happy and peaceful. He was supported by a strong and devoted mother. When he was just learning to walk, one of his uncles visited the McKay home and directed a teasing remark toward him. Jeanette, pressing her cheek against her baby, corrected this relative: "Don't talk like that to him. . . . You do not know, he may be an Apostle some day!"[9] That kind of statement didn't seem at all out of place to David later, as his mother was always expressing her confidence in her son.

One of David's aunts observed early on that Jennette had her hands full with the energetic little boy. During one harvest, Jennette asked her sister to watch David while she cooked for the threshers.

Feeding the men who came to help with a harvest was one of the biggest jobs for frontier wives, as the six to twelve men required to operate the threshing machines expected three hearty meals a day. While so much cooking was arduous labor, after a few hours with David, Jennette's sister offered to trade jobs—she had decided that cooking for all the threshers would be an easier task than watching David.[10]

In 1878, when David was five years old, the LDS Church established its Primary Association. Moiselle Hammond Halls became the first president of the Huntsville Primary, which was organized on October 20, 1880, with David as one of its first members.[11] "One of his early experiences with Primary imbedded the importance of teaching into his young mind. One afternoon there was a terrible storm and the water level on the hitching posts outside the school indicated a dangerous situation. On that day, Sister Hall swam on horseback across a river to teach David and the rest of his classmates."[12] Even as a little boy, David realized his teacher's sacrifice and ever after listened attentively to what she told him.

When his mind would wander during a long church meeting, David would look above the pulpit of the Huntsville meetinghouse, where there hung a large photograph of President John Taylor. Underneath the photo, in what appeared to David to be gold letters, was the phrase: "The Kingdom of God or Nothing." Those words made an impression on little David from the time he was able to read.[13]

By 1880, the McKays lived in a twelve-room house, which had wide, cool porches, and decks surrounding the second floor.[14] The yard included a rhubarb patch, fruit trees, towering poplars, a barn, an old "tithing yard," and a high board fence that enclosed a half block.[15] The McKay home was brimming with family. David's sister Margaret was eleven, Ellena was nine, and David O. was seven at the time. David also had a five-year-old brother, Thomas Evans, and a three-year-old sister named Jeanette. Extended family living close to the McKay household visited often and knew almost as much about David as his immediate family.

David O. McKay, five years old.

David McKay holds David O. (five years old), and Jennette McKay holds Thomas E. Elena (left) and Margaret (right) later died in a diphtheria epidemic.

David's pleasures were those every little boy of the era sought. "He owned a dog, pigeons, rabbits, and a magpie he taught to talk,"[16] and though he loved all the animals on the farm, the horses were his favorite. Kate and Puss (a gray team), Prince and Charlie (spanking sorrels), and Old Kate (a large white circus horse) were "more than farm animals—they were friends."[17]

While David would have had to learn hard work on the farm, some were dubious about his potential. For instance, one day a "neighbor, visiting with David's mother on the front porch, noticed a stray cow in the McKay's pasture." David's mother asked David to "drive the animal from the field."

> In response, David ran to the pasture, leaped onto his horse without a saddle or bridle, and chased the cow away. Then the young man galloped up to the front porch, "coming precariously close to the visitor, and announcing the job completed. He then galloped back to the pasture, jumped off his horse and turned him loose." The neighbor, somewhat startled at the exhibition and near collision, turned to Jeanette and shook her head, warning, "Mark my words, that boy will come to no good end!"[18]

Jennette McKay begged to differ with that conclusion. However, when she thought David's behavior warranted correction, she would switch her little boy's behind with a willow shoot. As the oldest son, David was held to a high standard. He later discovered that he was the only child she ever switched.[19] Despite occasional spankings, looking back on his childhood David would later say it was his mother's love and confidence that gave him "power more than once during fiery youth to keep [his] name untarnished and [his] soul from clay."[20] It was that love and confidence that also got him through the year that changed his family's lives.

Though the climate of Ogden Valley had been known for being "exceedingly healthful," David had begun, even as a little boy, to sense worry in the eyes of the adults during the winter of 1877–1878.

Huntsville was visited by a "severe epidemic of diphtheria," with influxes of cases continuing on and off for the next year and a half. Hardly a family in Huntsville escaped a visit from the dreaded malady.[21] The *Deseret News* reported in March 1878 that Huntsville had lost about twenty children from scarlet fever and diphtheria since January.[22] Luckily, the McKay household seemed to dodge ill health until the fall of 1879, when Margaret contracted rheumatic fever. The illness prevented her from attending school the entire year, and doctors were unable to heal her. At the same time, Ellena, the second oldest, came down with a cold which turned worse until it bloomed into full-blown pneumonia. Margaret passed away on March 28, 1880. Four days later, Ellena joined her sister in death.[23] The two sisters were buried in a common grave, and sorrow infused the McKay household.

FATHER'S MISSION

During the next year, the house must have seemed empty to David, who now faced the responsibilities of oldest child. But further trials lay ahead for the boy and his family. On March 25, 1881, a year after Margaret and Ellena passed away, David's parents received a letter with a return address that simply said, The Church of Jesus Christ of Latter-day Saints, Box B. A letter from that address could mean only one thing. There was look of apprehension on his mother's face as his father read out loud the call for David McKay Sr. to serve in the British Isles Mission. At that time, Jennette was a few weeks away from delivering another child. In the two days that followed, David Sr. could not eat or sleep. He finally "decided that he would ask for a postponement."[24] When his father told his mother of his decision, David O. saw his parents argue in front of him for the first and only time.[25] Jennette turned to her husband and adamantly said, "David, you go on that mission. You go now. The Lord wants you now, not a year from now, and he will take care of me."[26] "You need not worry about me. David O. and I will manage things nicely."[27] His father then sat down and wrote to President John Taylor:

Yours of the 25th inst I received and as you wish to know my
feelings concerning the call mentioned therein, I have this to say
(in short) that with the help of the Lord I will try to respond to
the Call.

Your Brother in the Gospel[28]

David's father left just twelve days later, on April 7. He would not see
his family again until his return on April 30, 1883.[29]

We can imagine the scene in the McKay household the night
before David Sr. left. It would have been natural for him to have led
his family in prayer. Father McKay's prayers were always thorough,
giving "complete reports on the well-being of the family, the community, the Church, and the nation." One phrase always signaled that
his prayer was coming to an end: ". . . for thou hast said that we are
the salt of the earth, and we know that if the salt loseth its savor . . ."[30]
That night his voice likely cracked as he said the familiar line in
closing. Gaining his composure, Father McKay may have taken
Tommy and Jeanette on his knee, as he so often had done, and sung
to them "Billy Boy, Billy Boy."[31] Before retiring for the night, David
Sr. put his hands on young David's shoulders, and, looking intently
into his eyes, he said, "While I am away on this mission you will be
the man of the house. It will be up to you to see that no harm comes
to your mother or to any of the family."[32] With that request, David's
childhood abruptly ended.[33] Later that year, David would be baptized
in his father's absence by Peter C. Geertsen, a family friend.[34]

The tasks facing David and his mother were difficult and discouraging. Prior to his departure, David's father had tried to provide help
for his family while he was gone by arranging "for a man to take
responsibility for the cattle and other heavy outside work."
Unfortunately, that help was short-lived and actually only added to
the family's troubles.

[The man] came, bringing with him a yoke of oxen, which only
became an additional barnyard worry. He had not been there

long when he went away to visit distant relatives, leaving the oxen to young David to attend. One evening when David and his mother were feeding the animals in the barnyard, they came to the discouraging task of carrying sufficient hay to satisfy the huge bovines, who always seemed to eat faster than they could be supplied. With tears in his eyes, David hefted the heavy hay, and said to his mother, "Now, let's give them two large armfuls of hay and run to the house before they eat it."[35]

Still, the McKays were not entirely left to themselves during David Sr.'s mission. Ten days after his departure, Jennette gave birth to a baby girl she named Ann. The baby was born during the spring planting. Neighbors helped plant the grain, and by summer the farm had a fine crop of hay.[36] That autumn grain prices fell, and "upon good advice," Jennette held onto the grain until spring. The spring price was high enough that the profits allowed Jennette to have a new addition built onto the house, a surprise for David Sr. The addition included a staircase, a welcome new convenience for Jennette.[37] "Many a winter night before this . . . she had dressed warmly, gone outside, and climbed a ladder up the side of the house into the second story to tuck her children in bed and have evening prayers."[38]

During the two years of his father's absence, David became increasingly closer to his mother. Later, holding her up as the ideal of motherhood, he would recall:

> I cannot think of a womanly virtue that my mother did not possess. . . . To her children, and all others who knew her well, she was beautiful and dignified. Though high-spirited she was even-tempered and self-possessed. Her dark eyes immediately expressed any rising emotion which, however, she always held under perfect control. In the management of her household she was frugal yet surprisingly generous . . . in providing for the welfare and education of her children. . . . In tenderness, watchful care, loving patience, loyalty to home and to right, she

seemed to me in boyhood, and she seems to me now after these years, to have been supreme.[39]

On another occasion David said of his mother: "Her influence and beauty entwined themselves into the lives of her sons and daughters as effectively as a divine presence."[40]

Father McKay returned in April 1883. Finally united once again, the family gathered in the living room to catch up on the last two years. After listening attentively, one of the children, wanting to hear of more spectacular happenings from his father's mission, asked if he had performed any miracles. Looking at the new addition on the house, David Sr. replied, "Your mother is the greatest miracle that one could ever find!"[41]

A FATHER'S EXAMPLE

The next morning David remembered his father had returned when he heard the old pump under the sleeping porch where he slept squeak promptly at four o'clock in the morning. That was his father's irritating form of an alarm to wake him up. Sleeping longer was impossible because of the noise—and guilt—that would result from sleeping while dad was working.[42] Sometimes, before the boys got up, their father would have already weeded the garden or made a milk stool or gate.[43] The McKay brothers—David, Tommy, William, and Morgan—worked side by side with their father, who always wore a white shirt even as he worked in the soil.[44] It was from him that the children acquired their idea of perfection, even being perfect in farm chores.[45]

They also learned from him that the tenth load of crops was to be given as a tithing offering to the Church. One day, as the McKay boys were out collecting hay, Father McKay told the boys to get the tenth load from a better spot than they had been gathering. David said, "No, let us take the hay as it comes." "No, David," said his father, "that is the *tenth* load, and the *best is none too good for God.*" Later David said that was the "best sermon on tithing I ever heard in my life."[46]

Just a year after David Sr. returned from his mission, the bishop of the Huntsville Ward, Francis A. Hammond, was called to settle the San Juan Stake of Zion. At a sacrament meeting held on March 22, 1885, David's father became the new bishop, a position he held for the rest of David's youth and early adulthood, until 1905.[47]

EARLY RELIGIOUS EXPERIENCES

With such committed parents, it is not surprising that as David grew up he had a sense of his own religious duties. Being the bishop's son carried a weight of responsibility, which David expressed to his younger siblings. One day as they walked home from church, they passed a park and saw some boys playing baseball. Thomas said, "Come on, David! Let's play ball." David replied, "Tommy, it's the Sabbath, and our father is the bishop. We're going home."[48]

David had additional responsibilities at church that helped him grow spiritually. In Sunday School, David was given experience bearing his testimony and delivering talks.[49] At the age of twelve, he was called to his first priesthood responsibility as a counselor in the deacon's quorum presidency. According to minutes kept by the secretary of the quorum, David told the group of six boys that he "'felt his inability to fill his position when he could see others that were more capable to occupy it than himself,' but 'he felt to press on with the help of the Lord.'"[50] He worked with the other boys in fulfilling responsibilities such as "keeping the chapel clean, seeing that chopped wood was always available for the chapel's stoves, and also going two by two to chop wood for the widows of the ward."[51] Responsible and diligent, he attended 100 percent of his church meetings as early as 1889.[52]

That same year, on January 27, David was made secretary of the Huntsville Sunday School at the age of sixteen. He served in this position until August 20, 1893, when he was called, at the age of nineteen, to serve as a Sunday School teacher for the next three years, along with playing the piano for priesthood meetings.[53]

David's first time blessing the sacrament as a priest was a humbling experience. During this time the sacramental prayers were not printed on a card as they are today. Instead, the bishop would stand right over the priest blessing the bread and water. He later recalled,

> I thought I knew the prayer. But I had memorized it privately, and when I knelt and saw the audience before me, I became flustered. I remember when I got to "That they are willing to take upon them the name of Thy Son," everything went blank, and I said, "Amen." Father said, "And always remember Him . . ." I was half rising from my knees, but I knelt down again and said, "And always remember Him. Amen." Father said, "And keep His commandments which He has given them." I knelt down again. "And keep His commandments which He has given them. Amen." [Father said,] "That they may always have His Spirit to be with them. Amen."[54]

David repeated the line and sat down in humiliation. Fortunately, such discouragements must have been more than compensated for by the ample opportunity David had to rub shoulders with great Church leaders.

When visiting Huntsville, Church leaders often stayed with the McKays, as there was no hotel or restaurant in town. Guests at the McKay household included President Wilford Woodruff and his counselors, George Q. Cannon and Joseph F. Smith, and other Church leaders. "At times when there were many guests for dinner, Jennette had a special code, 'FHB,' which stood for 'family hold back.' The children were encouraged to 'hold back' from taking too much food, to be sure everyone at the table got enough."[55]

Some of the Church leaders who visited Huntsville made statements that would prove to be prophetic in David's life. One such leader was general Relief Society president Eliza R. Snow, who came to Huntsville to speak at a conference. David and some other deacons sang a song for the meeting at which she was speaking. In her address she prophesied: "I can see in that group of boys bishops of wards, presidents of stakes, Apostles, and some of you will live to see the Savior."[56]

Sister Snow was not the only visitor to prophesy about David's future. When David was thirteen years old, Church patriarch John Smith visited the McKay home. At the time David had been much more interested in the patriarch's horse than in a blessing.[57] Nevertheless, Elder Smith gave David his patriarchal blessing, which included the following prophetic statements: "The eye of the Lord is upon thee; He has a work for thee to do in which thou shalt see much of the world, assist in gathering scattered Israel, and also labor in the ministry. It shall be thy lot to sit in council with thy brethren and to preside among the people and exhort the Saints to faithfulness." Thus the blessing indicated that "at an early day" David should prepare "for a responsible position."[58] After the blessing, the patriarch put a hand on David's shoulder and looked intently into his eyes. "My boy," he said, "you have something to do besides play marbles." David then went into the kitchen and said to his mother, "If he thinks I'm going to stop playing marbles, he is mistaken."[59]

YOUTHFUL EXPLOITS

Like most other youth, David was more concerned with having fun than such things as "a responsible position." One of David's many enjoyments was playing baseball. Though David and Tommy's father discouraged playing ball on the Sabbath, he did place some importance on the game. After he was made the bishop, "he suggested that the farmers set aside Saturday afternoons for baseball, and after the noon meal all the youngsters in town hurried to the public square for this activity."[60] As part of the Huntsville team, David played second base, and Tommy traded between first base and catcher.[61]

One game, against the neighboring rival Eden team, landed David in the position of a local hero and a leader among his peers. During the seventh inning, one of the Huntsville players was forced to leave the game because of an injury, and David took his place. When David came to bat, the score was tied. The umpire called two strikes, but the pitcher on the Eden team, a large boy with a quick temper, claimed that it was the third strike. One account relates that the boy took a baseball bat and came up to David.

> He waved the bat menacingly and demanded, "Get out of there, kid, or I will crack this on your head!"

> Immediately a hush came over the spectators who anxiously awaited the outcome. [David's brother] Thomas E. claims that he was shaking in his boots to see [him] in such a predicament. . . . In a cool tone [David] said, "The umpire called only two strikes; so go back to your pitcher's box and try to get me out; you have one more chance!" . . . The pitcher looked at the determination on David O.'s face . . . and decided to continue the game. His next throw was a swift straight ball. David O. connected and made a two-base hit. The next batter hit a single, and [David] was able to make home plate safely. This brought a thunderous applause from the spectators because this was the deciding run of the game.[62]

David's youth was marked by an irrepressible enthusiasm. Thomas E. McKay recalled that one spring he, David, and a group of friends went to their favorite swimming hole. Though the ice and snow had melted on the south bank, the north bank was still frozen. Thomas E., speaking in 1953, said,

> I dipped my toes in the water, then my fingers, and stepped back on the bank shivering. Two or three of the others did the same thing. We each decided that it was too cold. . . . There was one in that group, however, that didn't put his fingers nor his toes in; he just ducked under. He said, "Come on in, boys; the water's fine." He enjoyed the swim. He's the president of the Church today.[63]

Like any other boy growing up in rural America near the turn of the nineteenth century, his impetuousness sometimes got him into trouble. One time the Democrats in Huntsville were holding a convention in the ward chapel. David and one of his buddies climbed up into the belfry. Each time the crowd applauded, the boys rang the bell. The boys hid, but one of Bishop McKay's counselors found them, took the boys down, and reprimanded them. The counselor never told David's father.[64] This was fortunate, for usually if David was disciplined at church or in school, he would be punished again at home.[65]

INTELLECTUAL PURSUITS

As David matured, he also enjoyed intellectual and artistic endeavors, such as music, drama, and debate. One debate pitted David and Fred Wood against Donald D. McKay and Chris Mortenson. "Was George Washington greater than Napoleon Bonaparte?" served as the question for the night's discussion. David spent many evenings at the neighboring Pass home studying several volumes Brother Pass had about Bonaparte. The hours of study must have paid off, because David's team won.[66]

In addition to being an excellent debater, David showed some talent in acting and music. He was usually chosen to play the hero in local dramatic productions.[67] The Huntsville school had a movable stage that was used for plays in the evenings and as a pulpit on Sunday. On occasion, David also played the piano in the Huntsville town band for dances "held on the second floor above the village mercantile store."[68] Eventually his parents decided it was inappropriate for him to be out so late and asked him not to play in the band anymore. He told his parents that he had made a commitment to play on Saturday but would discontinue after that, and he was allowed to play one more night.[69]

David was also an avid learner and a successful student. His mother, who had taught at the Second Ward School, had infused the ideal of education in her young son, encouraging him to obtain as much schooling as possible. In 1889, after finishing his course work and passing his graduation exams, the fifteen-year-old "had advanced as far as the Huntsville school could promote him."[70] Most of David's peers in Huntsville and the rest of America discontinued their formal education with primary school at the age of sixteen. But David wanted more schooling, and he set his sights on attending the Weber Stake Academy in Ogden, which would require him to leave home. He would do so well prepared by his parents, Church members, and the Huntsville community, who had furnished him with ideals that would serve him well for the future events of his life. Later, as the prophet, David would conclude, "My home life from babyhood to the present time has been the greatest factor in giving me moral and spiritual standards and in shaping the course of my life."[71]

NOTES TO CHAPTER 1

1. General Sunday School Conference, October 2, 1949, McKay Scrapbook, no. 14, MS 4640, LDS Church Archives, Salt Lake City.
2. Jeanette McKay Morrell, *Highlights in the Life of David O. McKay* (Salt Lake City: Deseret Book, 1966), 8–9.
3. Ibid., 10; and Francis M. Gibbons, *David O. McKay: Apostle to the World, Prophet of God* (Salt Lake City: Deseret Book, 1986), 3.
4. See Llewelyn R. McKay, *Home Memories of President David O. McKay* (Salt Lake City: Deseret Book, 1956), 19–20; and Keith Terry, *David O. McKay: Prophet of Love* (Santa Barbara, CA: Butterfly, 1980), 8–9.
5. Terry, *Prophet of Love*, 12, 14.
6. Laverna B. Newey, *Remember My Valley: A History of Ogden Canyon, Huntsville, Liberty, and Eden, Utah, from 1825 to 1976* (Salt Lake City: Hawkes Publishing, 1977), 70.
7. Gibbons, *Apostle to the World*, 8.
8. Morrell, *Highlights*, 22.
9. Marie F. Felt, "David, a Boy of Promise," *The Instructor*, September 1969, 329.
10. Ernest L. Wilkinson, "David O. McKay Building Dedication," *BYU Speeches of the Year* (Provo, UT: Brigham Young University, 1954), 2.
11. Extracts from an Address of President David O. McKay, n.d., Huntsville, UT, Loris F. Allen Scrapbook; copy in author's possession.

12. Ibid.

13. David O. McKay, *Cherished Experiences from the Writings of President David O. McKay,* comp. Clare Middlemiss (Salt Lake City: Deseret Book, 1955), 30.

14. Description taken from a drawing of the McKay home in Huntsville, UT, by Dale W. Bryner of Weber State College, *Ogden Standard-Examiner,* September 9, 1971, 8B. See also photos in David Lawrence McKay, *My Father, David O. McKay* (Salt Lake City: Deseret Book, 1989), 58; and Gibbons, *Apostle to the World,* 9.

15. David O. McKay to Lou Jean McKay, aboard the SS *Tofua,* May 5, 1921, McKay Papers, MS 668, box 1, folder 5, Manuscripts Division, University of Utah Marriott Library, Salt Lake City; this letter is reproduced in part in David Lawrence McKay, *My Father,* 130–32. The barn was destroyed by fire in 1905.

16. Morrell, *Highlights,* 22; see also Wilkinson, "David O. McKay Building Dedication," 2.

17. Morrell, *Highlights,* 292; Elizabeth McKay Hill, "Memories of the Old Home," *The Instructor,* March 1959, 85.

18. Terry, *Prophet of Love,* 25.

19. Susan Arrington Madsen, "'No Prophet Is Greater than His Mother': Jennette Eveline Evans McKay, 1850–1905," in Barbara B. Smith and Blythe Darlyn Thatcher, eds., *Heroines of the Restoration* (Salt Lake City: Bookcraft, 1997), 229.

20. Leonard J. Arrington and Susan Arrington Madsen, *Mothers of the Prophets* (Salt Lake City: Deseret Book, 1987), 146.

21. Richard L. Evans, "The Fields of McKay," *Improvement Era,* September 1943, 530.

22. Cited in ibid., 530–31.

23. Gibbons, *Apostle to the World,* 10.

24. Thomas E. McKay, Conference Report, April 1952, 24.

25. See Madsen, "'No Prophet Is Greater than His Mother,'" 223.

26. Thomas E. McKay, Conference Report, April 1952, 24.

27. Madsen, "'No Prophet Is Greater than His Mother,'" 223.

28. David McKay to President John Taylor, March 27, 1881, film CR1/168, reel 1, p. 937, Church Archives.

29. Missionary Index, CR 301 44, Church Archives.

30. David Lawrence McKay, *My Father,* 68.

31. See Llewelyn R. McKay, *Home Memories,* 23.

32. Felt, "David, a Boy of Promise," 330.

33. See Morrell, "Boyhood of President David O. McKay," *Relief Society Magazine,* October 1953, 657; Gibbons, *Apostle to the World,* 10; and Morrell, *Highlights,* 24.

34. Andrew Jenson, *LDS Biographical Encyclopedia: A Compilation of Biographical Sketches of Prominent Men and Women in The Church of Jesus Christ of Latter-day Saints* (1901; repr., Salt Lake City: Western Epics, 1971), 3:761.

35. Morrell, *Highlights,* 24; see also Thomas E. McKay, Conference Report, April 1952, 25.

36. Gibbons, *Apostle to the World,* 11.

37. See Llewelyn R. McKay, *Home Memories,* 6.

38. Madsen, "'No Prophet Is Greater than His Mother,'" 224.

39. Arrington and Madsen, *Mothers of the Prophets,* 146.

40. David O. McKay to Lou Jean McKay, May 5, 1921, McKay Papers.

41. Llewelyn R. McKay, *Home Memories,* 6.

42. Gibbons, *Apostle to the World,* 16.

43. Llewelyn R. McKay, *Home Memories,* 23.

44. Lavina Fielding Anderson, interview by Mary Jane Woodger, October 24, 1995, McKay Research Project, College of Education, Brigham Young University, Provo, UT; transcript in author's possession.

45. Llewelyn R. McKay, *Home Memories,* 23.

46. David O. McKay, "The Temple Ceremony," *Address at the Salt Lake Temple Annex,* September 25, 1941, 4 (original emphasis).

47. Evans, "The Fields of McKay," 531. David McKay was first called to be bishop of the Eden Ward, assuming that calling on November 20, 1883; he served until March 29, 1885, when he was called to succeed Bishop Francis A. Hammond in the Huntsville Ward.

48. Gunn McKay, interview by Mary Jane Woodger, June 28, 1995, Huntsville, UT, McKay Research Project; transcript in author's possession.

49. Richard N. Armstrong, *The Rhetoric of David O. McKay, Mormon Prophet* (New York: Peter Lang, 1993), 4.

50. Minutes cited in Leland H. Monson, "David O. McKay Was a Deacon, Too" *The Instructor,* September 1962, 299.

51. Morrell, *Highlights,* 28.

52. David O. McKay file, 1955, International Society of the Daughters of Utah Pioneers, reading room, Salt Lake City.

53. Morrell, *Highlights,* 28, 58; David Lawrence McKay, *My Father,* 88.

54. David O. McKay, address given at the dedication of the Aaronic Priesthood Monument on Temple Square, October 10, 1958, Salt Lake City (some punctuation, capitalization, and language of the prayer standardized).

55. Madsen, "'No Prophet Is Greater than His Mother,'" 228.

56. John C. Peterson to President David O. McKay, December 19, 1955, McKay Scrapbook, no. 188.

57. Terry, *Prophet of Love,* 23.

58. Patriarchal blessing, given by John Smith, patriarch, to David Oman McKay, September 8, 1873, Huntsville, UT, Historian's Office, Patriarchal Record, vol. 52, 864, McKay Scrapbook, no. 188.

59. Morrell, *Highlights,* 26.

60. Ibid., 20.

61. J. Earl Felt, comp., "Brief History of David O. McKay," Huntsville, UT, in Loris F. Allen Scrapbook; copy in author's possession.

62. Llewelyn R. McKay, *Home Memories,* 163; see also Llewelyn R. McKay, "When He Was a Boy," *The Children's Friend,* September 1960, 30.

63. Thomas E. McKay, "Standards for LDS Youth," in *Address to the Brigham Young University Student Body* (Provo, UT: BYU Extension Division and Delta Phi, 1953), 2.

64. Edward and Lottie McKay, interview by Mary Jane Woodger, July 30, 1995, Salt Lake City, McKay Research Project; transcript in author's possession.

65. Informal conversation with Melba Hill by Mary Jane Woodger at the McKay home in Huntsville, UT.

66. Josie Allen Pass, interview, in Newey, *Remember My Valley,* 202.

67. Ibid.

68. David Lawrence McKay, *My Father,* 88.

69. George R. Hill, interview by Mary Jane Woodger, October 28, 1995, Salt Lake City, McKay Research Project; transcript in author's possession.

70. Terry, *Prophet of Love,* 30.

71. Llewelyn R. McKay, *Home Memories,* 213.

CHAPTER 2

AN AWAKENING MIND

The skill of the able teacher is shown not in the imparting of instruction, but in the awakening in the mind of the student a desire for learning and in directing him how to obtain it.

—David O. McKay[1]

L ate in the summer of 1889, David set out to attend Weber Stake Academy. As he looked back at his childhood home he somehow sensed things would never be the same. He would be living with his Grandmother Evans on Twenty-Eighth Street and Lincoln Avenue in Ogden, Utah. He had visited his grandparents often, but visiting and living somewhere were not the same thing. He wished now that he had taken advantage of his mother's offer to teach him the Welsh language since his grandmother slipped from English into Welsh constantly, leaving him to wonder what she had said. As he approached Lincoln Avenue he could smell the apple orchard and currant bushes that covered almost the entire block. Though it wasn't home, it was familiar.

WEBER STAKE ACADEMY

The Church had encouraged each stake to provide an academy of learning for its youth, which would serve as the equivalent of today's high schools. One of the stake-sponsored schools was the Weber

The family of David McKay and Jennette Evans McKay, 1897. *Front row, left to right:* David McKay, William McKay, Katherine McKay (Ricks), Morgan McKay, Elizabeth McKay (Hill), Jennette Evans McKay. *Back row, left to right:* Jeanette McKay (Morrell), David O. McKay, Thomas E. McKay, Ann McKay (Farr). This photo was taken by C. R. Savage of Salt Lake City when the four children standing were students at the University of Utah.

Stake Academy, which was only in its second academic school year when David enrolled as one of just seventy students on August 19, 1889. He paid $3.25 in tuition for a five-week course in the academic department. At Weber "there were no pencils or ink . . . for students to use," so David brought a slate to write on and a bottle of soap suds with which to erase.[2] He soon discovered that the ward building, where the academy was housed, was "hot and oppressive" and that many of his classmates "left about as fast as new ones came."[3] There was a shortage of desks, tables, and school materials, and rooms were not designed for school instruction.[4]

Even with such limitations, David was mesmerized by the teachers at Weber. He especially enjoyed Professor Richard Haag, who taught German, French, Greek, and Latin; and Professor Anton Pederson, who taught vocal and instrumental music.[5] But more than any other person at Weber, Principal Louis F. Moench was a mentor to young David, who first learned from him as a student, then as a colleague; eventually David would become his successor. David felt he had finally met what he called a "true teacher," and it was Moench's influence that solidified David's desire to become a teacher as well.[6] David found his mind enlightened and was delighted with the opportunity to sit at the feet of this wonderful teacher. He especially liked studying English classics, and it was during this time that he learned to love Robert Burns and William Shakespeare and memorized passages that he remembered for the rest of his life.

During the next year, David grew surer of his life's mission to become an educator. After completing courses in the academic department, David taught as a professional teacher for the first time at the Huntsville Primary School during the year of 1893–1894. That winter, he also served as the principal of the school, though he was barely twenty years old.[7] David loved being a teacher and decided he should qualify for a state teaching certificate at the University of Utah. Unfortunately, money was so tight in the McKay household that this goal seemed impossible. Then David's mother received a gift of $2,500 from David's Grandmother Evans. Jennette's siblings, who

David O. McKay (upper left) with classmates at the University of Utah.

Members of the first official University of Utah football team, 1894. *Front row:* A. B. Sawyer, Fred J. Mayes, Captain Harry Kimball, Fred Eccles, and Seth Thomas. *Middle row:* Ernest Van Cott, F. W. Reynolds, H. E. Hyde, Joseph W. Strongfellow. *Back row:* Paul Kimball, David O. McKay, F. N. Poulsen, Bernard J. Stewart, I. E. Willey, and Theodore Nystrom.

received the same sum, suggested that Jennette put the money in stocks, but she had already decided where to invest it: "Every cent of this," she said, "goes into the education of our children."[8] David's dream of getting a teaching certificate suddenly seemed obtainable. His years at Weber had awakened his mind and kindled a desire for learning, and with the means available David sought an opportunity few young men in the late 1800s ever experienced.

UNIVERSITY LIFE

In 1894 David set out again in the late summer, this time with his father, brother Thomas E., and sisters Jeanette and Annie. They "rolled over the sand ridge from Huntsville with horse and wagon, a cow in the trailer, . . . a sack of flour milled from wheat [they] had grown, [and] jars of fruit their mother had bottled," on their way to a great adventure.[9] Their destination—the University of Utah.

Upon arriving in Salt Lake City, the McKays set about looking for housing. David's father rented a small house near campus for the children; it was "located on what was then called Union Square, a site now occupied by Salt Lake City's West High School on north Third West."[10] After taking a quick tour of campus, Father McKay left with Tommy and Annie the next day, feeling a bit relieved that his two oldest children would at least have shelter, bread, milk, and fruit.[11]

David soon was fully immersed in college life. He registered for a three-year course in the Normal Department (or education department), with an emphasis in English literature.[12] Outside the classroom, he was a popular piano player at dances and became the class president. He also became a tackle and guard on the first official University of Utah football team, which won high honors. Although the team had no coach, a Russian student named Maximilian Lipenov, who understood the basics of the game, volunteered to "teach them what he knew." Maximilian tried "to give the team a psychological edge by organizing what was descriptively called a 'yelling brigade,' the forerunner of the modern 'pep club.'"[13] During football practices, David also became acquainted with and grew to love a custodian, August A. Nordvall, who, as David later recalled, "helped us with the football suits" and even "helped us with some of our lessons. He was unassuming, unostentatious, but did his duty well," and David felt he had as much influence in his education as any of his professors.[14]

During his first year at the university, David joined the Zeta Gamma Fraternity. Fellow fraternity member George Q. Morris became one of David's best friends. One night on the way home from a fraternity meeting, the two freshmen had a conversation that stayed with David for years. As young men often do, the two were discussing how they would know when they fell in love. George turned to David and informed him, "My mother once told me that when I met a girl who awakened in me the highest and noblest feelings of manhood, who inspired in me a desire to be worthy of a woman such as she, then that would be a feeling of true love."[15] Such ideas prepared David to meet someone whom he would later consider the "most important aspect of his schooling."[16] She was Emma Ray Riggs.

Emma Ray was born to Emma Louisa Robbins Riggs and Obadiah H. Riggs on July 23, 1877. Obadiah and Emma decided to name their daughter Emma Ray, for they felt she was a "ray of sunshine."[17] In 1882, Obadiah took a second wife in plural marriage, and he and his first wife, Emma, separated.[18] Therefore, at an early age, Emma Ray was raised by her single mother. As a little girl, she played marbles and ball games and became better at them than her five brothers. She also learned homemaking skills from her mother and grandmother. Filling the oil lamp and doing the weekly washing and ironing were some of her chores. In her spare time she had two hobbies. One was reading. Like her future husband, "she was an avid reader of Dickens, Scott and Shakespeare." She once said that as a child she was "never lonely" because she "always had the companionship of good books." Her other hobby was playing the piano, and she often accompanied her family.[19] As she matured she proved herself capable of considerable responsibility. At the age of seventeen Emma Ray took a Sunday School course, and shortly thereafter she directed ninety children in her ward's Sunday School.[20]

During David's second year at the University of Utah, he and his siblings made arrangements with Emma Ray's mother, Emma Louisa Riggs, to rent a cottage in the back of her house on Second West. As David and Thomas walked up to the house on the first day, Sister Riggs called her daughter to the window and observed, "There are two young men who will make some lucky girls good husbands. See how considerate they are."

Though engaged to another young man at the time, Emma Ray looked at David, the darker of the two, and replied, "I like the dark one."[21]

As the McKays got settled in their cottage, David announced to his siblings that Emma Ray Riggs possessed every virtue with which he thought a sweetheart and wife should be endowed. David's siblings roared with laughter, and his sister Jeanette adamantly told David he was a poor country lad and "there was no chance."[22] It was then and there that he decided that, despite what he had been told, he would one day make her his wife.

Because Emma Ray was not taking the Normal course, she didn't have any classes with David. The only time she saw him was when she came for the rent or accidentally ran into him. One day at the end of the 1896 school year, she was walking down a hall past a room where the Normal Society was meeting. As Emma Ray passed the door, she heard a voice and stopped, realizing it was David speaking. She stayed and listened to what she felt was "the most beautiful talk." When David closed his remarks, Emma Ray thought, "Well, there is a young man who is going to amount to something someday." She had loved every word. She later recalled, "I wanted to go up and shake hands with him and congratulate him because of that lovely talk. But I was very shy, and I did not do it. . . . He was surrounded by beautiful girls all the time. I did not dare to do it."[23] Some months later she broke off her engagement.[24]

As graduation loomed for David in the spring of 1897, the plan for supporting the rest of the McKay siblings in their education came to the forefront of his mind. David and Jeanette were to graduate, teach, pay the debts, and keep Tommy and Annie in school.[25]

University of Utah's graduating class of 1897. David O. McKay: third row center between two mustached classmates.

David O. McKay and his sister Jeanette McKay (Morrell)
at the time of their graduation from the University of Utah, 1897.

According to plans, David graduated from the University of Utah with a teaching certificate that June. As valedictorian, he gave the oration to the graduating class, declaring that "an unsatisfied appetite for knowledge . . . is the state of the normal mind."[26] David was offered a teaching job in Salt Lake County and made arrangements to begin teaching in the fall, allowing him to help his siblings complete their education.[27] However, before school ended in June, a letter came to the McKay home from Box B addressed to David. Thomas E. later recalled the episode:

> [Our sisters] had already gone to school that morning. I was writing a composition. The doorbell rang, and David O. answered. The mailman handed him the letter, and as [David] read, I glanced up and saw that he was quite agitated. I said, "What is the matter? Is somebody sick at home?"
>
> He threw the letter across the table in disgust and said, "Isn't that heck?" He used a stronger word.

David's well-laid plans had suddenly reached a detour that would take him far from his teaching career and far from a girl he had decided to marry—but still had never dated.

NOTES TO CHAPTER 2

1. David O. McKay to Walter A. Kerr, February 5, 1951; cited in Walter A. Kerr, *The Life of Louis Frederick Moench* (Ogden, UT: Weber State College, 1953), 77.
2. See Walter A. Kerr, *The History of the Weber Stake Academy: The Period of Struggle, 1889–1894* (Ogden, UT: Weber College, 1953), 15.
3. Ibid., 24.
4. See ibid., 15.
5. Llewelyn R. McKay, *Home Memories of President David O. McKay* (Salt Lake City: Deseret Book, 1956), 26; and Clarisse H. Hall, *The Development of the Curricula at Weber State College: 1889–1933* (Ogden, UT: Weber State College, 1969), 18.

6. David O. McKay to Walter A. Kerr, in Kerr, *Moench,* 77.

7. Richard N. Armstrong, *The Rhetoric of David O. McKay, Mormon Prophet* (New York: Peter Lang, 1993), 4.

8. Jeanette McKay Morrell, *Highlights in the Life of David O. McKay* (Salt Lake City: Deseret Book, 1966), 31.

9. Llewelyn R. McKay, *Home Memories,* 9.

10. Francis M. Gibbons, *David O. McKay: Apostle to the World, Prophet of God* (Salt Lake City: Deseret Book, 1986), 28. The University of Utah campus "was not moved to its present location on the east bench until several years after David O. McKay completed his studies."

11. Llewelyn R. McKay, *Home Memories,* 9; see also Preston Nibley, *The Presidents of the Church* (Salt Lake City: Deseret Book, 1971), 312.

12. I express my appreciation to Kirk Baddley at the University of Utah Archives for supplying this information.

13. Gibbons, *Apostle to the World,* 30.

14. David O. McKay, *Secrets of a Happy Life*, comp. Llewelyn R. McKay (Englewood Cliffs, NJ: Prentice-Hall, 1960), 145; David O. McKay doesn't mention the name of the custodian, but in the University of Utah Archives, August A. Nordvall is the only custodian listed that worked during those years. Phone conversation with University of Utah archivist, February 5, 2004.

15. "Services for Elder George Q. Morris," *Deseret News,* May 5, 1962, Church News section; cited in Gibbons, *Apostle to the World,* 33.

16. David O. McKay file, 1955, International Society of the Daughters of Utah Pioneers, reading room, Salt Lake City.

17. See LaRue Sneff, "Mrs. McKay Is 'Ray of Sunshine,'" *Deseret News,* January 22, 1950.

18. Newell G. Bringhurst and Frederick S. Buchanan, "The Forgotten Odyssey of Obadiah H. Riggs: Early Utah Crusader for Education Reform," *Utah Historical Quarterly* (1998): 26.

19. Emma Rae McKay Ashton, "Emma Ray Riggs McKay," *Relief Society Magazine,* June 1960, 351.

20. Sneff, "Mrs. McKay Is 'Ray of Sunshine.'"

21. David Lawrence McKay, *My Father, David O. McKay* (Salt Lake City: Deseret Book, 1989), 1–2; see also "Tribute to Emma Ray McKay" (Salt Lake City: International Society of the Daughters of Utah Pioneers).

22. David O. McKay to Emma Ray McKay, January 2, 1921, McKay Papers, box 1, folder 4, LDS Church Archives, Salt Lake City.

23. Emma Ray Riggs, September 8, 1957, Quarterly Conference, Salt Lake City, McKay Scrapbook, no. 131, MS 4640, Church Archives; see also "Tribute to Emma Ray McKay."

24. "Tribute to Emma Ray McKay."

25. Thomas E. McKay, Conference Report, April 1952, 25.

26. Nibley, *The Presidents of the Church,* 312.

27. Gibbons, *Apostle to the World,* 35.

CHAPTER 3

OBEDIENT TO THE CALL

The Latter-day Saints throughout the world find confirmation of their testimony in every performance of duty. They know that the gospel teaches them to be better individuals; that obedience to the principles of the gospel makes them stronger men, and truer women.

—David O. McKay[1]

Ever since the call, David had wrestled with a wide range of emotions: anger, guilt, relief, confusion, and determination. His feelings constantly shifted. He had good reason to be upset. If he was to serve a mission, he would want to wait for two years while Tommy and Annie finished at the university. Besides the worries of his financial commitment to his brother and sister, there were also constant thoughts of Emma Ray Riggs.

He could kick himself for not doing something about her sooner. Why hadn't he asked her out? There were a myriad of excuses he had used whenever he had thought of dating her over the last two years, and now it seemed too late. For the first little while she had been engaged to a man whom many referred to as the "Shrimp."[2] David, meanwhile, had been dating many other girls. He'd had a feeling that once he started to date Emma Ray, he would not want to see anyone else. So instead of acting, he had kept putting it off until he graduated.

In the meantime, Emma Ray had become friends with David's sisters Jeanette and Annie. The girls had even invited Emma Ray home with them for visits to Huntsville. David's sister Jeanette had told him about an interesting conversation that took place during such a visit the summer before. Emma Ray had said to David McKay Sr., "You have been very successful in rearing a lovely family. Won't you tell me the secret?" David's father had replied, "Well, I think one thing has helped tremendously. All married couples have different opinions about various things, but Sister McKay and I make it a point never to disagree before our children. We go to our bedroom and talk things over, and when we come before our kiddies, we are of one mind."[3] David had always felt this was unique about his parents and had been impressed that Emma Ray had asked such a thoughtful question. Unfortunately, being impressed and taking action had not been synonymous. Now, right before graduation, just as he was going to start courting Emma Ray, that letter had come. He was no longer just thinking about a mission; now it was an official call from Box B, and he had to make a decision.

The few days before graduation were agonizing. Somehow he squeezed in a trip to Huntsville, hoping his father and mother would just make the decision for him. But his father's only comment was simply, "I think you should go, David O." Then his father removed one of the problems hindering David's decision by promising to somehow support him financially if he accepted the call.[4]

The other problem with going on a mission was the same one he had struggled with for years. How could the Lord expect him to serve a mission without really knowing the Church was true? Once again, he had pled aloud for the witness, and it had not come. He believed the Church was true with all his heart, but he did not know it was true from personal revelation. Instead, a couplet kept running through his head: "Do your duty, that is best, leave unto the Lord the rest."[5] When it came down to it, he made the same decision he had made previously as a young teen; once again he would rely on his father's testimony. No member of his family had ever refused a call in the Church, from his grandparents leaving their ancestral homes to his own father serving a mission when David was just eight years old. What he was being asked seemed minuscule when compared to what they had sacrificed. His heritage had taught him the ideal of obedience. So, after graduation, a few months away from his twenty-fourth birthday, he made a decision, which he formalized by writing a letter to Elder George Reynolds.

Since giving you a verbal answer about my mission, I received your communication requesting me to submit my answer in writing. I cheerfully do so by saying that I shall be ready to start on mission to Europe on the 7th of Aug.

Hoping to get a prompt reply stating what country I shall be assigned to, and praying for the blessings of God to attend all those promulgating the principles of truth,

I remain,
Your brother in the gospel
David O. McKay[6]

FAREWELL AND DEPARTURE

Having made the commitment to serve, David packed up his belongings in the Riggs cottage and headed for Huntsville to prepare to preach the gospel as a full-time missionary. Friends in Huntsville soon learned of his call and planned a going-away party for him on July 2. When David learned of the party, he did what he should have done long before. Deciding he was better late than never, he wrote and invited Emma Ray on a date—or a kind of a date. He wrote several drafts and finally settled on these words:

Dear Friend Ray:

A "Farewell Party" will be given in the second ward tomorrow (Fri.) night, at which, if you have no objection, I would be much pleased to have your company.

A committee meeting will prevent my being present before ten or
eleven o'clock; but if agreeable to you, I shall call for you about
7:30 and you can accompany Annie and Tommy to the party and
favor me with your company later in the evening. By doing this
you will not be deprived of half the evening's enjoyment.

I write this because it was too late to call to see you tonight after
Board meeting.

This invitation is late, I know,
but avoided it cannot be;
With tardy people, it's always so—
That's why it is so with me.
But late is better than never: they say—
I'm glad this saying was made
so please overlook my tardiness, Ray,
and accompany your true friend,

Dade[7]

David wondered about signing the invitation "Dade." He worried
it might be too personal, too familiar. He had told Emma Ray about
the nickname, though everyone else called him David O. to distinguish him from his father. "'Dade' was his own version of 'David'
when he was a toddler, and a name he encouraged from no one's lips
but [Emma Ray's]."[8]

What a relief it was when Emma Ray appeared in the foyer of the
Huntsville Second Ward chapel! There were so many people to talk
to, so many well-wishers, but David could not help but focus his
attention on Emma Ray. Throughout the night, they would catch
each other's eyes and then quickly avert them. At the end of the
evening David asked her if she would come back to Huntsville for his
farewell address in sacrament meeting, and she seemed eager to accept
the invitation.

Emma Ray Riggs as a teenager.

David's farewell was to be held on August 1, 1897. On July 28, David wrote a few lines to Emma Ray explaining the train schedules. The Oregon Short Line and Rio Grande both came through Ogden from Salt Lake City, but David hoped that Emma Ray would take the Oregon Short Line in the morning rather than the afternoon Rio Grande run, allowing them to ride through the Ogden Canyon in the daylight together. They would not be alone, however; Bell White, Emma Ray's cousin, was going along to chaperone. David closed the letter, "Hoping that nothing will prevent you from enjoying your visit here." This time he did not dare sign "Dade." Instead he wrote, "I remain very respectfully, Your sincere friend, David O. McKay."[9]

David picked up Emma Ray and Bell at the train depot a few days later, the night before his farewell. Just before sunset, he asked Emma Ray if she would like to take a ride. The sunset that night was more vibrant than most, and the mountains of Ogden Canyon seemed to be bathed in purple. As they rode, David found himself taking Emma Ray's hand and telling her things he had not told anyone else.[10] Thoughts of leaving in two weeks became even more poignant. That night he felt that he and Emma Ray had turned a corner in their feelings for each other. What timing! At least she had promised to write him. Maybe her letters would get him through the next two years of waiting and longing, but two years seemed forever.

The next week was filled with good-byes and a whirlwind of preparations. One of the saddest days of David's life was surely August 5, 1897, when he and twenty other elders destined for Great Britain left for Salt Lake together. As he sat on the train he recorded in his new missionary journal, "Saddest morning ever spent in Huntsville or anywhere else! At eleven o'clock, bid my home, dear ones, relatives, & friends 'good-bye.' Sobbed."[11] In the following days, David would experience a wide range of emotions, including excitement, anticipation, reverence, and comfort. On August 6, 1897, while in Salt Lake, David received his endowment in the Salt Lake Temple. Later that day, he also was set apart to be a missionary in the

British Mission by Seymour B. Young. Among other things, Elder Young promised David he would safely return home.[12]

David, along with the other elders, left Salt Lake and crossed the continent by train to Colorado, through Nebraska, to Chicago, and then to Washington, D.C. While in the nation's capital, David did some sightseeing but found a hollowness amidst the awe of seeing things he had only read about. He was not just missing home, but longing for someone in particular. While waiting to cross the ocean in Philadelphia, he divulged to Emma Ray,

> It gives me much pleasure tonight to write you a few lines that you may know where I am. Of course I think it will make but little difference to you. . . . I left Washington for N.Y. Thursday Aug. 12th at 3 p.m. Arrived in Jersey City about 8 p.m. and took the ferry boat across to N.Y. It was my first experience on the water. Oh, it was pleasant! The moon shone brightly, the air was cool and pleasant, and the river just billowy enough to make the ship rock a little. In the distance we could see the Brooklyn Bridge while underneath it as far as the eye could see up the river were illuminated ships and boats. Over to the right stood the Statue of Liberty, "majestic and grand." But I was alone, and don't you know, Miss Riggs that I cannot enjoy anything like that when I am by myself. I can appreciate it, but cannot enjoy it fully. "It is not good for man to be alone." I thought of you when I saw that beautiful sight and wished that you were by my side, showing your appreciation of the scene before you by that most expressive "mmm." Do you know what I mean?[13]

David included his future mailing address in Liverpool, hoping she would write soon and alleviate some of the loneliness he was feeling. On Saturday, August 14, the elders boarded the SS *Belgenland,* "a well-traveled old craft that had confronted and survived the storms and gales of the Atlantic for many years."[14] David was amazed that he was only seasick once during the twelve-day voyage, but he felt that the one bout made up for all the rest of the pleasant crossing. He was so "nauseated he feared he would part with his 'principal digestive organ . . . and all its appendages.'"[15]

When David finally arrived in Liverpool and first looked at the smoky city on August 25, 1897, he felt as sick as he had on the ship. All he could see on the dock were swarms of "little ragged urchins crying out."[16] Two days later, he was assigned to the "Scottish Conference," the area where he would spend most of his mission. After he arrived in Glasgow, he walked through the streets and was appalled by the slums. "Some of the women were bare-headed and bare-footed, ragged and dirty," he wrote, "and such women were rearing children." As he walked to the Conference House (mission home) at 130 Barrick Street, he also saw open drunkenness. He found Glasgow to be gloomy and said he was "a *gloomy-feeling* boy."[17] Adding to his depressed spirit was the fact that he still had not received a letter from Emma Ray.

"A THOUSAND SIGHS"

On August 30, David and three other elders were sent to Lanark.[18] David found Lanark even more discouraging than Glasgow. After the missionaries had been there a month, mission president Rulon S. Wells decided to close the town to missionary work. The four returned to Glasgow, and David was assigned to work at conference headquarters. There he would keep the mission accounts; track down information for emigrants; meet arriving members and missionaries; see off departing ones; receive, compile, and send out reports; handle mission correspondence; address and mail out copies of the Book of Mormon; and receive a thorough education in mission administration. One bright spot greeted David when he returned from Lanark: waiting for him was a letter from Emma Ray.

Unfortunately, her tone was one of worry. She wrote of a trip she had made with her mother to the doctors, and she was concerned about her mother's health. David wondered if that was the reason she had waited so long to write him. He wrote his reply, wishing he could be there to help her. He encouraged her not be discouraged and to remember that "behind the clouds there is always sunshine; and although the dark heavy mists of misfortune often seem to gather around us, yet we must not forget that the comforting rays of God's blessing can penetrate the gloomiest darkness." Then, in what would be a constant in his letters to Emma Ray, he complimented her:

> Your hesitancy in telling your trouble because you thought I had enough of my own showed another admirable trait in your character—one that would make you try to make others happy while your own heart might be heavy with care. Now, I haven't any troubles over here (save a little homesickness once in a while and the letters from home and friends tend to dispel this), so if you think I can say or do anything to help you, please don't hesitate a minute to tell me all. You know, sometimes, the mere confiding gives comfort. The reason I write this is because I fear the doctor's remark in connection with other things might make you feel sad; but don't worry, I am sure everything will be all right.[19]

David then told her of his day-to-day activities. He said that he liked to speak in halls, but speaking on street corners was not pleasurable. Worse than street meetings, however, was passing out pamphlets called tracts. Distributing tracts, he confided, is "unpleasant for me."

> When I first started, I could do nothing but heave sighs. I sighed as I knocked at the door, breathed heavily as I gave the tract, and sighed again as I walked away. This was repeated about seventy-five times in three hours. If I had continued I would have sighed myself away! As it is, my hair is falling out "thick and fast," and I know of nothing that would cause it save tracting and open-air preaching![20]

David's schedule of visiting members, holding open-air meetings, and distributing tracts was typical of most missionaries of the time. It was challenging work. After his first time distributing tracts, even though people generally treated him courteously and accepted the tracts, he said, "I never felt so gloomy in all my life. I have heaved a *thousand* sighs!"[21] In fact, he felt so "discouraged and downhearted" that he had to spend a lot of time on his knees to remove the feeling through "humble prayer."[22] Another time, he entered a close (an apartment house) and made his way through the building, leaving one tract at each door. At the entrance to the next close he was confronted by several angry housewives who were blocking his way. Although they parted to let him through, one woman called after him, "Ye can gan awa' hame; ye canna hae any o' oor lassies" (You can go on home; you can't have any of our lassies). David did not understand why the woman would make such an accusation, for he was sure his only motive was to preach the gospel.[23]

During this period of missionary work, "the number of tracts successfully distributed was seen as an index of the missionary's skill," and David worked hard to distribute as many as possible. During what he called his "first 'experience,'" he distributed 150 tracts. By the end of his mission, his highest record of achievement was 240 tracts in one day.[24] Still, tracting was never enjoyable for him, and a poem he composed in his diary expresses his feelings on the subject:

> Offering some people a gospel tract,
> Is like getting cold water poured down the back
> Such a look does one get
> As the door goes smack.[25]

TROUBLE AT HOME

In October, David received a letter from his brother Tommy, conveying the news that Emma Ray's mother, Emma Louisa Robbins Riggs, had passed away. David longed to be in Salt Lake to comfort Emma Ray, but all he could do was convey his feelings on paper the best he could:

In this your hour of sorrow, Ray, please accept my heartfelt sympathy and condolence. May He who comforts all give you that strength and peace of mind necessary to bear this heavy burden of grief. . . .

Ray, do not grieve. Remember you have friends who are praying for your comfort. . . .

Rely upon Him who alone can give comfort in such a dark hour. Your life is still before you; your mission yet to fulfill, and I assure you, Ray, nothing will give your friends more joy than to have the privilege of helping you to take your part cheerfully and well. I have often wished that I might be there with you so that I could do something to take your attention from that which grieves you; but of course such a wish is vain. I know that these few lines will fail in the purpose for which they are written; but if you can partake of the same feeling as that with which they are written, I am sure you will know that they come from the heart.[26]

A letter from Emma Ray crossed his in the mail. He found her attitude about her mother's death to be of a "resigned feeling." Such maturity surprised him and just added another gem to her already "sparkling character." On another subject, Emma Ray had declared that "babies and young men" did not like her, and David was amazed that she could have such a false notion. Then he wondered if Emma Ray no longer felt he was a young man—after all, he had complained to her that his hair was falling out. Carefully he replied,

I would give my own opinion in full of your little self to prove your assertion untrue if the loss of hair together with other marks of fading youth did not bar me from the happy privilege of calling myself young. Just think, already classing myself with bachelors—a most pitiful class of lonesome unfortunates!! I am living in hopes, however, that the completion of an honorable

mission and the possession of a welcome release will restore to a
certain extent some of the traces and spirit of youth; so that
when I meet my young friends again in Utah the old associations
and amusements will still be appreciated and enjoyed.[27]

David wondered if he had tipped his hand too much, revealed his
hopes too strongly in this letter, for nothing came in the return mail
until December from Emma Ray. Her tone in that letter had
changed, and he knew he had gone too far. At Christmas he wrote her
a short card and apologized: "I believe you took that 'hint' in the
'wrong way'—I shall not give another as long as I'm here."[28]

After Christmas, it was another three months before a letter from
Emma Ray crossed the Atlantic, and much to David's dismay, it
seemed all she could talk about was some "fine young man" she had
gone on a "pleasant sleigh ride with," who had "pleasing features and
charming attractions." On top of Emma Ray's letter, one had also
arrived from Tommy, telling him that Emma Ray had been at a
University of Utah dance, where she had been the "bell of the ball."[29]
As David wrote his reply, he knew the tone of his letter was wrong,
but he could not help himself. He was jealous, and it seemed he could
not do a thing about it. Emma Ray evidently did not miss his somewhat sarcastic tone. He would have to wait a full year for her to
answer his letter because of his impertinence. While he waited, he
decided he would focus more attention on his missionary work.

"ACT WELL THY PART"

The spring seems to have been a turning point for the missionary.
On March 23, 1898, a few days prior to writing Emma Ray, David
had left Glasgow for a new assignment in Stirling. Feelings of home-
sickness and discouragement, not unfamiliar to him at that point in
his mission, dominated David's mood. That afternoon he and his
companion, Peter G. Johnson, spent several hours visiting places in
and around historic Stirling, including Stirling Castle, and, as he said
later, "really not doing our duty." Even though such activities were

David O. McKay, missionary to the British Isles, December 1897. Photo taken in Scotland.

Emma Ray Riggs with the University of Utah graduating class of 1898. *Seated, left to right:* Ralph Varey Chamberlin, Mary Elizabeth Connelly (Kimball), and J. Reuben Clark Jr. *Standing, left to right:* Emma Ray Riggs (McKay), Herbert Thayer Hills, and Albert Johnston.

WHAT-E'ER·THOU·ART·
ACT·WELL·THY·PART·

JOHN·ALLAN·ARCHITECT·18

Stone inscribed with the inspiring words:
"What-E'er Thou Art, Act Well Thy Part," 1966.

not against the rules for missionaries in the late 1800s, David's attention was not focused on the work.

On their way back into the town, David saw a building under construction and noticed a large and unusual inscription chiseled on a stone arch above the door. David turned to Elder Johnson and said, "I want to go over and see what that is." He was just halfway up the path leading to it when the message carved on the lintel struck him: "What-e'er thou art, act well thy part."[30] Reading these words had an incredible effect on David. Here he was a missionary, and he wasn't acting the part at all; he was sightseeing. From that day forward, he sought to be a better missionary and to act well his part. His change in attitude prepared him for even greater responsibilities while he served in Stirling.

Several weeks later, on June 9, 1898, David was called to be a member of the presidency of the Scottish Conference. He wrote in his diary about his response to receiving the call: "I seemed to be seized with a feeling of gloom and fear, lest in accepting I should prove incompetent. I walked to a secret spot in the wood, just below [William] Wallace's monument, and there dedicated my services to the Lord and implored him for his divine assistance."[31] In David's letter of acceptance he wrote: "Realizing to some extent the responsibility thus placed upon me, I truly feel weak and unable to fill this position—and if I expressed my own desire, I would say, 'Choose another.' Yet I feel to say, 'Not my will, but Thine be done.' And since God, through His servants, has seen fit to place this duty upon me, I shall accept it, depending upon His unerring Spirit for guidance."[32]

As a leader in the mission, David had the opportunity to engage in some rather sobering experiences for a man of such a young age. He witnessed such difficult problems as spousal abuse, drunkenness, and immorality. He was called upon to perform baptisms and priesthood blessings for the sick. With a stewardship over the nine branches of Scotland, he consoled widows, counseled members, conducted funerals, and even performed a wedding, though he had never seen one before.[33]

David also had to nurse sick companions. On October 19, 1898, David received a letter from Elder John T. Edward telling him that Edward's companion, Elder David M. Muir, was seriously ill. The next day another letter came telling David that Elder Muir had passed away. To have one so young pass away under David's watch was a horrible ordeal.[34] That November, Elder Edward also became ill. Not wanting to repeat anything like what had happened to Elder Muir, David kept constant vigil at Elder Edward's bedside. The sick elder recorded in his diary that "no Prince could do any more for me than Bro. McKay. . . . He was up and down the whole night in my behalf, fixing the fire and giving me medicine and one thing and another."[35] Edward's health gradually improved. By the dawn of Thanksgiving Day, David and Elder Edward were discussing what they might be doing one year from that time, when they would be at home.[36] Thoughts of home flooded David's mind, and it must have been somewhat difficult to shove aside thoughts about one person he had not heard from for almost nine months. Christmas quickly came and went as David kept busy with the work.

It wasn't until February 28, 1899, that relief on the subject of Miss Riggs came. David had returned home that Saturday night "at the close of a busy and somewhat discouraging week" and looked at the mail.[37] As he saw the return address on the letter, he couldn't believe his eyes. The letter was from Cincinnati, Ohio. After her mother's death, Emma Ray had graduated from the University of Utah with a bachelor of arts degree and then moved to Cincinnati to live with her father and study piano at the Cincinnati College of Music.[38] There had been a twelve-month gap since Emma Ray and David had last corresponded. He could not believe the words he was reading. It was obvious from Emma Ray's letter that she had misunderstood him, but she had felt an "irresistible something" that had prompted her to write him.[39]

Surely David didn't feel discouraged or tired at all as he sat down and wrote her a reply:

Emma Ray Riggs at University of Utah graduation, 1898.

David O. McKay (front row, third from the right) and fellow missionaries in Great Britain. The picture was taken while David was president of the Scottish Conference.

> As the first spring flowers are refreshed and strengthened by the rays of sunshine immediately following a cold blighting storm, so I was strengthened and encouraged by your cheerful interesting letter. Its warm congenial rays seemed to dissipate the cold dismal clouds of discouragement, and I basked in the sunlight of Happy Memory! Could you have read my thoughts as I read your letter, you would have changed that opinion quickly, "that you for a long time have held that I cared not for further correspondence." Why you have been entertaining such an idea as that, I know not; unless the knowledge that I was corresponding with another young lady friend made you think that such an idea was exactly a correct one.
>
> No, Ray, you were wrong in your "opinion." Your letters, as your company, are appreciated and esteemed more highly than you evidently have thought; and it gives me pleasure to read in your letter that this esteem is mutual.[40]

From the moment he saw that Cincinnati address, his worries about Emma Ray Riggs dissipated, and during the closing months of his mission their letters back and forth across the Atlantic became "warmer and warmer."[41]

CONFIRMATION AT LAST

As the end of his mission neared, David was able to look back on his service with great satisfaction. Reports showed that, under his leadership, the past year had been one of the most successful in the Scottish Conference for many years.[42] There was only one regret. He had done his duty, he had held fast to his ideal of obedience, but his testimony was still one of belief rather than knowledge. He was beginning to wonder if that was all the testimony he would have in this life. He would just have to go on being obedient and hold on to others who had that sure knowledge. Then, only three months before he was to go home, it happened.

He was at a priesthood meeting held on May 29 in Glasgow for all the missionaries in the conference and the local priesthood brethren. The opening song, "O My Father," had been sung, the opening prayer had been said, and David, as the Scottish Conference president, had suggested that each elder make a few brief remarks. He also requested that they "all express themselves freely regarding the work of the Lord, and their feelings toward each other and the Priesthood of God."[43] When the last elder, John Young of Wyoming, finished speaking, an Elder Woolfenden arose, and, with his gaze fixed on Brother Young, he said: "There are two angels by your chair. One is your guardian angel. I do not know who the other one is." President James L. McMurrin, a member of the European Mission presidency, then assessed: "The other is the guardian angel of Elder Eckles. . . . Yes, there are angels in this room."[44] Though it had not occurred to David that there were divine beings present, he later recalled, "Strange as it might seem, the announcement was not startling; indeed, it seemed wholly proper. I only knew that I was overflowing with gratitude for the presence of the Holy Spirit." President McMurrin then turned to David and prophesied, "Let me say to you, Brother David, Satan has desired you, that he may sift you as wheat, but God is mindful of you. If you will keep the faith you will yet sit in the leading councils of the Church."[45] That was the same promise given in his patriarchal blessing; the words cut through him like a knife. For the first time, he knew the Church was true. He would never again have to just believe—he knew. His obedience had brought the testimony he had ached for all his life. Now he could go home without any regret.

HOMEWARD BOUND

On August 26, 1899, David set sail on the *City of Rome* toward his native land. Like most returning missionaries, David must have felt somewhat nervous as he began the voyage home. Several days at sea passed without incident. By the fifth day, the ship approached the icy waters off the coast of Newfoundland. After David had retired for the night, he was "rudely jarred out of the placidity of sleep by a loud crash that hurled loose furnishings against the bulkheads, unceremoniously dumped the slumberers on the deck, and created a scene of chaos and terror unlike anything [he] had ever experienced." The ship had rammed an iceberg. Fortunately, the vessel was not seriously harmed, and passengers and crew were able to continue on safely. However, "near this place, thirteen years later, another collision would not end so happily" when a cruise liner called the *Titanic* would "carry 1,513 passengers to an icy grave."[46]

David remembered the promise he had received when he was set apart, that he would return home safely. He felt it was divine providence that night that had saved him from a watery grave. David looked forward now to the opportunities awaiting him at home. Before he reached the United States, he had already received an appointment to teach at his alma mater, the Weber Stake Academy.[47] His future career seemed set. Besides that, there was a woman waiting to hear that "Dade" had arrived home.

NOTES TO CHAPTER 3

1. Conference Report, October 1912, 121.
2. Obadiah H. Riggs to Emma Ray Riggs, December 13, 1900, McKay Papers, box 1, folder 2, LDS Church Archives, Salt Lake City.
3. Emma Ray Riggs McKay, "The Art of Rearing Children Peacefully," *BYU Speeches of the Year* (Provo, UT: Brigham Young University, 1952), 9.
4. Keith Terry, *David O. McKay: Prophet of Love* (Santa Barbara, CA: Butterfly, 1980), 33.
5. Ibid.
6. David O. McKay to Elder George Reynolds, June 29, 1897, CR 1/68, box 12, folder 18, Church Archives.
7. Invitation, McKay Papers, box 3, folder 1, Church Archives.
8. David Lawrence McKay, *My Father, David O. McKay* (Salt Lake City: Deseret Book, 1989), 2.
9. Missionary Journal, July 30, 1897, "No. 1," McKay Papers, box 3, folder 1, Church Archives; see also David Lawrence McKay, *My Father,* 2.
10. See David Lawrence McKay, *My Father,* 2.

11. Missionary Journal, August 5, 1897, McKay Papers, box 3, folder 1, Church Archives.

12. Missionary Journal, August 6, 1897, McKay Papers, box 3, folder 1, Church Archives.

13. David O. McKay to Emma Ray Riggs, August 13, 1897, McKay Papers, box 3, folder 1, Church Archives.

14. Francis M. Gibbons, *David O. McKay: Apostle to the World, Prophet of God* (Salt Lake City: Deseret Book, 1986), 38; see also Stan Larson and Patricia Larson, eds., *What E'er Thou Art Act Well Thy Part: The Missionary Diaries of David O. McKay* (Salt Lake City: Blue Ribbon Books, 1999), 7.

15. Gibbons, *Apostle to the World,* 39; see David O. McKay to George Q. Morris, August 26, 1897, McKay Papers, box 3, folder 1, Church Archives.

16. Missionary Journal, McKay Papers, box 3, folder 1, Church Archives.

17. David Lawrence McKay, *My Father,* 18 (original emphasis); see Missionary Journal, August 27, 1897, McKay Papers, box 3, folder 1, Church Archives.

18. See David Lawrence McKay, *My Father,* 18.

19. David O. McKay to Emma Ray Riggs, September 9, 1897, McKay Papers, box 1, folder 1, Church Archives.

20. Ibid.; see also David Lawrence McKay, *My Father,* 18; and Missionary Journal, August 31, 1897, McKay Papers, box 3, folder 1, Church Archives.

21. Missionary Journal, August 31, 1897, McKay Papers, box 3, folder 1, Church Archives (original emphasis).

22. Minutes of meeting, August 7, 1899, Scottish Conference Records, British Mission, LR17716, ser. 11, Church Archives; cited in Larson and Larson, *What E'er Thou Art,* 13.

23. Terry, *Prophet of Love,* 37.

24. Larson and Larson, *What E'er Thou Art,* 13; see Missionary Journal, August 31, 1897, McKay Papers, box 3, folder 1, Church Archives.

25. Terry, *Prophet of Love,* 39.

26. David O. McKay to Emma Ray Riggs, October 5, 1897, McKay Papers, box 1, folder 1, Church Archives.

27. Ibid.

28. David O. McKay to Emma Ray Riggs, December 18, 1897, McKay Papers, box 1, folder 1, Church Archives.

29. David O. McKay to Emma Ray Riggs, March 25, 1898 letter, McKay Papers, box 1, folder 1, Church Archives.

30. Conference Report, October 1954, 83.

31. Jeanette McKay Morrell, "Life of President David O. McKay: A Few Highlights of a Busy Life," *The Relief Society Magazine,* November 1953, 730.

32. David O. McKay to Rulon S. Wells, Missionary Journal, June 9, 1898, McKay Papers, box 3, folder 1, Church Archives.

33. Larson and Larson, *What E'er Thou Art,* xxxi. See David O. McKay, October 3, 1898, McKay Microfilm, 1897–1970, reel 3:428, Church Archives.

34. John T. Edward Collection, October 18, 1898, accession 1710, Manuscripts Division, University of Utah Marriott Library, Salt Lake City; and Larson and Larson, *What E'er Thou Art,* 216.

35. John T. Edward Collection, November 7, 1898, accession 1710, Manuscripts Division, University of Utah Marriott Library; and Larson and Larson, *What E'er Thou Art,* 153.

36. Larson and Larson, *What E'er Thou Art,* 158; and John T. Edward Collection, November 24, 1898, accession 1710, Manuscripts Division, University of Utah Marriott Library.

37. David O. McKay to Emma Ray Riggs, March 4, 1899, McKay Papers, box 1, folder 1, Church Archives.

38. Emma Rae McKay Ashton, "Emma Ray Riggs McKay," *The Relief Society Magazine,* June 1960, 351.

39. David O. McKay to Emma Ray Riggs, June 15, 1900, McKay Papers, box 1, folder 2, Church Archives.

40. David O. McKay to Emma Ray Riggs, March 4, 1899, McKay Papers, box 1, folder 1, Church Archives.

41. Edward and Lottie McKay, interview by Mary Jane Woodger, July 30, 1995, Salt Lake City, McKay Research Project, College of Education, Brigham Young University, Provo, UT; transcript in author's possession.

42. David O. McKay to Emma Ray Riggs, March 4, 1899, McKay Papers, box 1, folder 1, Church Archives.

43. Larson and Larson, *What E'er Thou Art,* 239. See the Scottish Conference Records, the British Mission, LR17716, ser. 11, vol. 3, Church Archives.

44. Excerpts from Personal Diary of President James L. McMurrin of the European Mission, June 4, 1899, in which he give an account of an inspirational event which occurred at a priesthood meeting of the Leeds Conference on June 5, 1899, McKay Scrapbook, no. 188, MS 4640, Church Archives.

45. Preston Nibley, *The Presidents of the Church* (Salt Lake City: Deseret Book, 1971), 314–15.

46. Gibbons, *Apostle to the World,* 54.

47. The Utah State Historical Society, *Utah, a Centennial History: Personal and Family Records* (New York: Lewis Historical Publishing Company, 1949), 416; and Richard W. Sadler, *History of Weber State College: A Centennial History* (Salt Lake City: Publishers Press, 1988), 23.

CHAPTER 4

THREE GREAT EPOCHS

There are three great epochs in a man's earthly life, upon which his happiness here and in eternity may depend, viz., his birth, his marriage, and his choice of vocation. . . . Happy thought when I decided to become a teacher; for that decision was a factor in directing my footsteps to you. That third important epoch has been made fruitful and happy.

—David O. McKay to Emma Ray Riggs McKay[1]

Emma Ray returned from Cincinnati in the summer of 1899 and immediately started looking for a job. Though offered several positions in Salt Lake City, Emma Ray took a position in Ogden at Madison School. She would later be teased by her children about teaching in Ogden instead of in Salt Lake City, her hometown, to which she would reply, "Well, I believe Ogden paid more!"[2] The real reason for her teaching in Ogden came home in August 1899.

Emma Ray had wondered when David would arrive. His letters had been vague: no date, no time, no specific train. When Emma Ray received word that David was arriving, she found herself in a most inopportune location: on Antelope Island in the middle of the Great Salt Lake attending a family reunion. She convinced her cousin Bell to join her in rigging a sail to an old rowboat so that they could reach the station in time to meet David's train.[3]

"CLOUDS OF DOUBT"

After a two-year separation, the reunion was sweet, and the young man and woman discovered that through letters across the Atlantic their relationship had deepened and changed. David and Emma Ray could look forward to seeing each other frequently, as they were both teaching that fall in Ogden.

Throughout Emma Ray's youth, her plan was to become a schoolteacher for a while, then marry a good man and raise a large, intelligent, noble family. These desires began to be realized during the 1899–1900 school year. Emma Ray showed an exceptional depth of understanding as a teacher. On the first day of her career, her principal introduced her to the students and then pointed to one boy and informed her, "Miss Riggs, you will have trouble with that boy down there. He has been a disciplinary problem ever since he entered the class. Now, if you have any trouble with him, you just send him to me and we will see that he behaves himself."[4] Emma Ray noticed the little boy's face redden. After the principal left, Emma Ray wrote a note and secretly gave it to the boy: "Earl, I think the principal was mistaken about your being a bad boy. I trust you and know you are going to help me make this room the best in the school."[5] Later, Earl showed his mother the note and said, "Be sure to return it, Mother, because I want to wear it next to my heart." Because of Emma Ray's love and compassion, Earl became one of her top students.[6]

While Emma Ray taught at Madison, twenty-six-year-old David began his teaching career at Weber Stake Academy. David joined the faculty as school registrar and instructor of pedagogy and literature.[7] Earning a mere $850 for the year,[8] David also willingly took on extracurricular duties, such as directing the Thanksgiving program, supervising field days at a local amusement park, and overseeing sports games.

David and Emma began dating each other, continuing the relationship that had evolved with their correspondence during his mission.[9] The two were also seen together at social events, but at the end of the school year there was no engagement. Emma Ray left

Ogden in June with the intention of finding a teaching position in Salt Lake City.

Again, David would have to rely on written correspondence if the relationship was to continue. After the first of June, David wrote Emma Ray that a yearning had begun to come over him that he could not put off, knowing that the only person that could take that longing away was Emma Ray Riggs. In his correspondence, David often begged her for a response, and when her letters did not appear, he would write her again, expressing great disappointment. By mid-June, he accused Emma Ray of not keeping her word:

> Clouds of doubt occasionally cast a shadow over my hopes, and when driven away would hang angrily around. I did not know that they had gathered such force until the disappointment came. Then as I looked at the clouds and storm in nature I realized that there were also clouds over my thoughts and feelings, clouds of doubt—heralding the approach of a cruel storm by flashes of gloomy impressions. My happy anticipations of a kind letter were unrealized.[10]

David became worried that the "irresistible something" that had caused Emma Ray to write him on his mission had ceased to urge her so strongly. He was extremely concerned that the Salt Lake air and old associations had cooled her feelings and made her think of her associations in Ogden only as a dream. He begged her, "I shall only ask, that when you think of the dream—I was going to say 'just give a passing thought of Dade,' but I shall not say it; for if you remember it only as a dream, thoughts of Dade will give you the nightmare; so I shall save you this unpleasantness."[11]

A week or two later, David would have another chance to rekindle the dream. The couple spent an evening at the Saltair Pavilion, a dance hall located on the banks of the Great Salt Lake. After spending the evening together, David sent her a quick letter after they parted:

We were together at beautiful Saltair; tonight, there are forty miles between us; yet I feel that our thoughts and feelings cover the distance and still keep us in touch with each other. I wonder if, in so short a time, anything more obstructive than distance could ever come between us so as to sever the happy feeling now existing? I shall dismiss this thought, though, say "good night," and ask you to ever remember

Your loving Dade.[12]

It was in early August when Emma Ray finally showed her true feelings in returning David's ardor. There had been another dance at Saltair. David had decided to finish some work at the McKay's Dry Hollow farm in Huntsville rather than attend. Emma Ray had gone to the dance expecting to see David. Instead, a girl with coquettish eyes and her heart upon her sleeve informed Emma Ray she had written David a letter. Emma Ray became jealous and the very next day wrote a letter to David, expressing concern with the competition and finally telling David she had feelings for him. Upon reading Emma Ray's long-awaited disclosure of feelings, David quickly scribbled a letter of reassurance back, telling her that the other woman's letter had influenced him no more than "rippling waves affect the movement of a great vessel." Indeed, he confided, the letter from the other woman had made him only more determined than ever to continue on his "love course."[13]

By the end of August, David had gone to see the superintendent of Ogden City schools and requested that Emma Ray be allowed to come back to her position at Madison School.[14] During one of their lunch-hour dates that fall, under one of Lester Park's umbrella trees, David popped the question. Emma Ray asked, "Are you sure you want me?"

"Yes, I am very sure," he said.[15]

ENGAGEMENT AND MARRIAGE

When the term ended in December 1900, Emma Ray left for Salt Lake City to prepare for her upcoming marriage. David waited until she left to ask her father for her hand. Not being able to do it in person, David penned a letter to his future father-in-law, Dr. O. H. Riggs, in Cincinnati on December 9. Wanting to make a good impression, David wrote and rewrote the letter several times. Then, finally, in his finest penmanship, he sent the following:

> Dear Sir,—
>
> The purport of my letter suggests a more intimate form of address, and I wish the privilege were mine to adopt the suggestion; but as I am, comparatively speaking, a stranger to you I should not only use a conventional form of address, but proceed at once to introduce myself. This, however, I shall not do, trusting that the favorable mention of my name by your daughter Ray, will be sufficient introduction to at least warrant my proceeding, without further explanation, to the object of my writing.

David went on to compliment Riggs's daughter and explained how they met, the development of their friendship, and the ensuing courtship. Love, he wrote, "runs along the course of courtship until it finds contentment in mutual expression."

> This contentment is but temporary, for the stream of true love, whose source is Heaven itself, flows forever. From Mutual Expression it goes to the Engagement. Overflowing still, it pursues its course until it enters the sacred domain of Marriage, the only place that will contain in peace, purity, and honor, the ever lasting flow of Love.
>
> I have asked your daughter to be mine in marriage and now I ask you, Dr. Riggs, her father, if you will give your consent. She has

given hers, and by so doing, has conferred as great an honor upon me as was ever conferred upon a young man. In return for this I can give her nothing but a true love and a heart and mind whose one desire is to make her happy.

In eager anticipation of a favorable reply,
I remain,
Yours very respectfully,

David O. McKay
Weber Stake Academy[16]

Dr. Riggs was pleased with what David had written. He wrote to his daughter that he felt her engagement to the "Shrimp" was the work of others—that he really did not think her own heart's promptings were in it. But this time, Dr. Riggs knew the relationship with David was for keeps, though he accused her of being sly, keeping her love a secret for four years and not saying a word to him about it. However, he divulged that the last time his daughter had visited him, he had seen "which way her romantic needle pointed." Wanting to give advice, Dr. Riggs suggested to his bride daughter:

Now my darling daughter I want to impress upon you the fact that it is not any more difficult to get a man's love than it is to hold it after you have it. There are so many little things that a man appreciates in a woman, that some women never think of. A woman wants to study the likes and dislikes of her husband and try hard to do everything to accord with his likes. Some may say this is not possible. I think it is right and possible. It will pay a wife to do it all along the line. When a true man sees his wife doing every thing she can for his pleasure will he not do likewise for his wife? Surely he will, then that is mutual compensation and mutual happiness.[17]

Dr. Riggs reassured Emma Ray that he felt David was a very nice man of integrity, and his opinion after reading his letter was that she was to be congratulated. He assured her that he thought David was capable of making her happy and then gave one last bit of advice, "Now, my darling, never permit any one to interfere with your love for him—never allow any one to come in between you and him as some times meddlesome people do. Then is true happiness where there are two hearts that beat as one."[18]

As the Christmas holidays approached, being apart was especially difficult for David. During the last two weeks of December, David wrote Emma Ray almost every day. In one letter, just seven days before Christmas, David wrote, "I will be happy, I will be true, when I am married, Sweetheart, to you."[19]

Emma Ray was less constant with her letters, and when the letters did not come as quickly as David wanted, he became frustrated. Emma Ray had written a letter on Wednesday night and not posted it until Friday. David found her waiting two days troublesome, worrying that her feelings had turned from him and that she was not in the relationship wholeheartedly. He wrote asking for assurance:

Dearest Ray,

I would give almost anything if I had never felt that your feelings slightly turned from me; and the hour that gives me the assurance that only my approval and love will be all you ask, will be appreciated as the happiest and most sacred of my life.

To ask you to be satisfied with my love alone, is perhaps showing egotism—it is probably expecting too much. But, sweetheart, if you cannot do it, don't give me any of your love. Ever since I was old enough to appreciate the value of a true love, I have prized it above everything else. You manifested the true love I longed for, and I centered my love in perfect trust. Our souls united and you became part of my life. Ray, let not the trust I have in your love be shaken or perfect happiness will never be mine. I could outlive a rejection, I could endure disdain; but I cannot be happy with half a love.

Ray, the act that makes us one in the eyes of the world will soon be performed. Have you, forsaking all others, given me your confidence, perfect love, and trust? An assurance of this makes me the happiest man in the world![20]

Wishing to allay his fears, Emma Ray visited David the next Monday, and their relationship was once again solidified. That next Wednesday, the day after Christmas, David wrote, "Since your visit Monday, I have had the most contented feelings regarding your love for me, that I have enjoyed for several months. How sweet the feeling of perfect trust is!" David then told her how very difficult Christmas had been for him, that it had not been a happy one, and that he looked forward to their wedding: "One week from tonight, Ray! I am anticipating it as the happiest and most important hour of my life. Will it be your happiest? I hope it will be but the beginning of a perfectly happy life for both of us! I'm sure it will be, if your love is like mine, and I believe it is."[21]

Emma Ray's love would prove to be as strong and true as David's. The couple was sealed for time and all eternity on January 2, 1901, in the Salt Lake Temple by the Apostle John Henry Smith, the first couple married in that temple in the twentieth century. Little did they know that they would later be considered the first couple of the Church and that their marriage would be watched and emulated by Church members around the world. A reception followed at the home of David's Aunt Belle. After visiting his parents' home in Huntsville, the young couple settled into their own home on Monroe Avenue near the academy, and Emma Ray became a full-time home-maker.[22]

AN ADMIRABLE TEACHER

David was quickly becoming one of Weber's most popular teachers. He seems to have taught according to the advice he later shared with other teachers: "If you have thrilled them, or if unable to do that, if you have given them one thought which has appealed to them, you will find that their intention and desire to return will be manifest by their presence."[23] Often, David's very appearance and mannerisms improved students' behavior. In fact, he could usually govern a class without saying a word.[24] Once, he walked into a room where students were being rowdy. David simply walked to the window and stood there until the class quieted. He could control his class because he could control himself.[25]

At times, David found it necessary to mete out discipline. For instance, when one young man by the name of Greenwell stole a classmate's books and handkerchiefs, David asked him to apologize before the entire student body and make restitution. David then had the students vote on whether Greenwell should be forgiven.[26] Greenwell did as he was asked.

David's influence on some of his students lasted a lifetime. One student with whom he had a lifelong friendship was Aaron W. Tracy. Aaron was orphaned at a young age but worked for family and friends to support himself. He entered the academy in 1905 when he was eighteen years old but told David during the year he would have to drop out due to a lack of funds. David then invited Aaron to live in the McKay home, where he could do chores to earn money for his school expenses. After living with the McKays and graduating from Weber, Aaron went on to become a successful educator in his own right, and in 1922 he became president of Weber, where he served for thirteen years.[27] In a letter he later wrote to David, President Tracy expressed his gratitude for the hospitality David and Emma Ray had shown him during his years at Weber Stake Academy:

> I was going to leave the dear Old Academy and work for a wage
> of $20 per month, but you would not permit me. You took me

in the library and made me accept the opportunity of my life by
sharing your home with me. At this time you did not even know
me, yet you served me an unending blessing . . . I often look
back upon those days and count the blessings which have come
to me through you and the training I received at the Academy.[28]

For the rest of his life, Aaron Tracy said that whenever he read
something very good, he always saw David O. McKay in it.[29]

A FRUITFUL FAMILY AND VOCATION

As David commenced the "great epochs" of marriage and vocation, he was blessed with great success. In 1901, the Weber Stake
Academy announced that Professor Louis F. Moench was resigning as
school president and David would become the new principal.
Accepting the salary of $1,500 a year, David took on the added
responsibilities of running the academy. Under his leadership, new
departments were added, including the Domestic Science and
Domestic Arts Departments and a women's basketball team.[30]

As a principal, David believed that education was for everyone. In
an era when very few women received a secondary education, he set
out to change this at Weber. During his tenure, female student enrollment greatly increased.[31] David once said that "if he had to choose
between educating his sons and educating his daughters, he would
choose his daughters" because of "their important influence on children."[32] David's reward for his seven years of unstinting effort was the
academy's phenomenal growth. When he left at the end of the school
year in 1908, Weber's overall enrollment had increased 55 percent.[33]

Along with Weber growing, the McKay family also began to grow.
Soon after they were married, Emma Ray was expecting their first
child. By April 1901, she was so sick that David insisted she go to
Huntsville for a week. (All his life David had an unwavering faith in
the therapeutic effects of his hometown.) She had been gone just one
day when he wrote: "I want my comforting Ray. This isn't home
without you. When I came from school tonight, I missed you; as I

David O. McKay and Emma Ray Riggs McKay when David was president of Weber Academy (1902–1908).

David O. McKay and Emma Ray Riggs McKay with their eldest son, David Lawrence McKay, two years old.

walked to meeting, I wanted you by my side; and since coming home, I have longed for you."[34]

Though Emma Ray was sick, they gladly anticipated the birth of their first child and were filled with joy at the safe arrival of David Lawrence McKay on September 30, 1901.[35] David and Emma Ray were delighted to be parents.

These new responsibilities, however, gave rise to the young couple's first major quarrel. Within weeks of their marriage, David had been called as the second assistant to Thomas B. Evans, the Weber Stake Sunday School's superintendent. Fully committed to his calling, the new father apparently underestimated the requirements of his little family.

> They had engaged a nurse, but the first night the nurse left them alone, David had to go to a meeting. As he started to put on his hat and coat, Ray had thought, "Surely you aren't going to a meeting tonight." As if reading her thoughts, David turned and looked at her for a moment, and said, "Have you forgotten that it is Sunday School Board Meeting tonight?" There was no warmth in her kiss as she bade him good-bye. The closing door wakened the baby. Still weak, she sat and rocked the crying baby while tears of weakness, frustrations, and hurt welled down her cheeks.[36]

Emma Ray decided that scene would not be repeated, and the McKays learned to balance family and busy schedules. David's calling required him to travel often, and since he always wanted Emma Ray to go with him, she would bundle up the baby in a heavy shawl and ride in the buggy through the heat, mud, rain, or snow, to country towns like Hooper, Plain City, and North Ogden. Once there, David would show Sunday School teachers how to outline their lessons. As Emma Ray watched her husband in such leadership roles, she became convinced he was "inspired of God in everything he did." Many times in the mornings, he would tell Emma Ray what would happen down

David O. McKay bringing flowers to Emma Ray.

at the office or in his Sunday School work before he would leave. When he would come back at night, Emma Ray would ask, "Well, did it happen as you said it would, David?" And David would reply, "Just exactly."[37]

David's spiritual development corresponded with continued growth both at home and in his career. Another son, Llewelyn Riggs McKay, joined the family on June 5, 1904.

Meanwhile, enrollment at Weber Stake Academy continued to rise. With the increasing size of the student body, space at the academy was tight. David had to move his office into "the vestibule between the inner and outer doors because the Moench Building, then the only building on campus, was so overcrowded."[38] On July 6, 1904, the day after his son was born, David submitted a request to the Weber Stake Board of Education that a new building be constructed. Board members were leery about beginning construction at that time, but principal McKay promised he would personally be responsible for collecting the necessary funds. Hence, he organized the faculty, and they went to work raising funds. Their efforts were met with success. With the money they raised and with the matching funds from the Church, they were able to add a west wing to the Moench Building.[39]

Though David's professional endeavors were certainly noteworthy, it was not his great success at Weber Stake Academy that gained the attention of General Authorities of the Church. Instead, it was the great success of the Weber Stake Sunday School. Serving as the second assistant to Superintendent Thomas B. Evans, David was given the responsibility of directing class work. At this time, there was little direction for the Sunday School organization from Church headquarters. David developed a plan for grading students, creating more uniform and focused courses of study, calling a sufficient number of teachers in each ward, and implementing stake supervisors who could show Sunday School teachers how to implement his program.[40] As a result of David's developments, the teaching in Weber Stake Sunday Schools improved.

David "acted well his part" in a calling which is hardly ever noticed. But it was through this work that the Lord was able to bring David to the prophet's attention.[41] In 1905, David organized and directed a parents' convention in the Ogden Tabernacle. It was a great surprise when President Joseph F. Smith arrived to attend the convention. President Smith was pleased with David's ideas and investigated his other innovations. However, David probably could not have imagined what would come as a result of the prophet's visit. He and Emma Ray were happy and content to live out their days in Ogden, with David acting as Weber Stake Academy's principal. David loved Weber. Later he would reminisce, "Oh, those were the days, when I used to teach. My heart will always be there."[42] Indeed, he felt, "When I cease to be interested in youth, when my confidence in youth begins to wane; then . . . my work is done."[43] Though David's work as a secular teacher and principal would end soon, true to his declaration, his interest in youth would never wane throughout the next sixty-two years of his life.

NOTES TO CHAPTER 4

1. David O. McKay to Emma Ray Riggs McKay, January 2, 1921, McKay Papers, box 1, folder 4, LDS Church Archives, Salt Lake City.
2. David Lawrence McKay, *My Father, David O. McKay* (Salt Lake City: Deseret Book, 1989), 4–5.
3. Susan Arrington Madsen, *The Lord Needed a Prophet* (Salt Lake City: Deseret Book, 1990), 139.
4. "Tribute to Emma Ray McKay" (Salt Lake City: International Society of the Daughters of Utah Pioneers).
5. "She Has Gift of Understanding," *Church News,* 24 January 1970.
6. "Tribute to Emma Ray McKay."
7. Clarisse H. Hall, *The Development of the Curricula at Weber State College: 1889–1933* (Ogden, UT: Weber State College, 1969), 42.
8. Minutes, Weber Stake Academy, Board of Education, July 29, 1900, Archives, Weber State University Stewart Library, Ogden, UT, typescript.
9. "Tribute to Emma Ray McKay."
10. David O. McKay to Emma Ray Riggs, June 15, 1900, McKay Papers, box 1, folder 2, Church Archives.

11. Ibid.

12. David O. McKay to Emma Ray Riggs, June 24, 1900, McKay Papers, box 1, folder 2, Church Archives.

13. David O. McKay to Emma Ray Riggs McKay, September 15, 1921, McKay Papers, box 1, folder 6, Church Archives.

14. William Allison to David O. McKay, August 31, 1900, McKay Papers, box 1, folder 2, Church Archives. Another note to Emma Ray Riggs, dated August 31, 1900, reads, "I saw Mr. McKay yesterday. We are holding your old place at the Madison school for you. I am glad to know that you have decided to be with us." McKay Papers, box 1, folder 2, Church Archives; cited in David Lawrence McKay, *My Father*, 6.

15. "Tribute to Emma Ray McKay."

16. David O. McKay to Obediah H. Riggs, December 9, 1900, McKay Papers, box 1, folder 2, Church Archives.

17. Obediah H. Riggs to Emma Ray Riggs, December 13, 1900, McKay Papers, box 1, folder 2, Church Archives.

18. Obediah H. Riggs to Emma Ray Riggs, December 17, 1900, McKay Papers, box 1, folder 2, Church Archives.

19. David O. McKay to Emma Ray Riggs, December 18, 1900, McKay Papers, box 1, folder 2, Church Archives.

20. David O. McKay to Emma Ray Riggs, December 22, 1900, McKay Papers, box 1, folder 2, Church Archives.

21. David O. McKay to Emma Ray Riggs, December 26, 1900, McKay Papers, box 1, folder 2, Church Archives.

22. Keith Terry, *David O. McKay: Prophet of Love* (Santa Barbara, CA: Butterfly, 1980), 46.

23. David O. McKay, "Youth and a Better Future," baccalaureate sermon, University of Utah, June 3, 1945 (Salt Lake City: University of Utah Press), 8.

24. Gunn McKay, interview by Mary Jane Woodger, June 28, 1995, Huntsville, UT, McKay Research Project, College of Education, Brigham Young University, Provo, UT; transcript in author's possession.

25. Minutes, Weber Stake Academy, Faculty Meeting, February 1, 1900, Centennial History Project, Archives, Weber State University Stewart Library, Ogden, UT, holograph, WA38 /12/ vol. 3, 51–52.

26. Richard C. Roberts and Richard W. Sadler, *A History of Weber County* (Salt Lake City: Weber County Commission, Utah State Historical Society, 1997), 412.

27. Aaron Tracy to David O. McKay, February 22, 1913, McKay Papers, box 1, folder 9, Church Archives.

28. Ibid.

29. Jeanette McKay Morrell, *Highlights in the Life of David O. McKay* (Salt Lake City: Deseret Book, 1966), 52.

30. "Weber Stake Academy," *[Ogden] Standard,* September 10, 1904, 5.

31. Edward McKay, as quoted by Leslie Moore, interview by Melissa Randall, 1996, McKay Research Project; transcript in author's possession.

32. Hall, *The Development of the Curricula,* 153.

33. David O. McKay to Emma Ray Riggs McKay, April 23, 1901, McKay Papers, box 1, folder 2, Church Archives; see David Lawrence McKay, *My Father,* 10.

34. Zella Farr Smith, "A Romantic Story from the Life of President and Sister McKay," McKay Scrapbook, no. 131, MS 4640, Church Archives.

35. Ibid.

36. Emma Ray Riggs McKay, Wells Stake Conference, Granite Stake Tabernacle, Salt Lake City, September 8, 1957, McKay Scrapbook, no. 39.

37. David Lawrence McKay, *My Father,* 37.

38. William Z. Terry, "Weber College Items of Early History" (Ogden, UT: Weber College, 1952), typescript, 5–7, Archives, Weber State University Stewart Library; see also David Lawrence McKay, *My Father,* 37.

39. Jeanette McKay Morrell, "Life of President David O. McKay: A Few Highlights of a Busy Life," *The Relief Society Magazine,* November 1953, 732–33.

40. Francis M. Gibbons, interview by Mary Jane Woodger, August 19, 1996, McKay Research Project; transcript in author's possession.

41. Robert L. Simpson, interview by Mary Jane Woodger, December 30, 1996, Salt Lake City, McKay Research Project; transcript in author's possession.

42. David O. McKay, Commencement Address for Graduates, Centennial History Project Archives, Stewart Library, Weber State University, typescript, May 29, 1929, WA38, series 10, 1–2.

David O. McKay at the time of his call to the apostleship, April 1906.

CHAPTER 5

AN APOSTLE'S FAITH

To know one's duty, to learn the truth, is the duty of every Latter-day
Saint. . . . The man who knows what his duty is and fails to perform
it, is not true to himself; he is not true to his brethren; he is not
living in the light which God and conscience provides. . . . It is not
enough to feel; *we must* act.

—*David O. McKay*[1]

David, Emma Ray, and their two boys, David Lawrence and
Llewelyn, attended general conference in April 1906,
coming down from Ogden to Salt Lake on the Bamberger
express. It was the family's tradition to attend conference and get
together in between sessions with family and friends. Everything was
routine until the afternoon of April 8, when events occurred that
must have forever stood vibrant in David's mind. The family was
having an enjoyable meal when a knock came at the door. The
messenger had a rather cryptic note for David from Francis M.
Lyman, President of the Quorum of the Twelve. He requested that
David come immediately to the Guarder House, a facility used as a
Church office building at the time. David excused himself from
dinner, told Emma Ray he would be right back, and quickly left.[2]
David did not know why the summons had come, although there had
been some Church leadership interest in his Weber Stake Sunday
School work and David had recently been invited to prepare an

article that was published in the April 1905 issue of the *Juvenile Instructor.* The only thing he could think of was that he might be asked to join the Deseret Union Sunday School or the General Church Board of Education.[3] As these possibilities entered his mind, he must have chided himself; he might have thought such high honors were certainly beyond his grasp of experience.

The year of 1905 had been a turbulent one for Church leadership. In October of that year, John W. Taylor and Matthias F. Cowley had resigned from the Quorum of the Twelve. Both men, just forty-seven years old, had continued to preach and practice polygamy in Canada and Mexico, respectively, even though the Second Manifesto had made it clear that polygamy was to be discontinued everywhere. The two Apostles could not reconcile themselves and stepped down from the Quorum, leaving two vacancies. Then, in February 1906, seventy-four-year-old Apostle Marriner W. Merrill had passed away, leaving another. As the April conference approached with three vacancies in the Twelve, Church members were knee-deep in speculation. David had overheard many conversations on the subject, and he and Emma Ray had probably discussed the possibilities of replacements themselves. They must have been especially interested when the *Deseret News* unofficially suggested Orson F. Whitney as a possible replacement for the late Elder Merrill.[4] David had always loved Elder Whitney, who had visited the McKay home in Huntsville. As a boy, David had often listened to him entertain the McKay family by reading his own poems and those by his favorite authors. Elder Whitney had even composed one of his longest and most famous poems, "Elias," at the McKay home. Even if Whitney was not the choice, the *Deseret News* was certain that any man chosen would not be a polygamist.[5] However, if David had thought of Elder Whitney, it is doubtful his own name entered his mind as a possibility. As he and Emma Ray had had attended the Friday and Saturday sessions of conference, and even that Sunday morning, nothing had been said about filling the vacancies. Like most Church members, the McKays probably assumed that the vacancies would not be filled at this conference.

David entered Temple Square Sunday afternoon and was greeted by Apostle George Albert Smith, who led him to the office of President Francis M. Lyman. Elder Lyman began:

"So you're David O. McKay."

"Yes, sir."

"Well, David O. McKay, the Lord wants you to be a member of the Quorum of Twelve Apostles."

[David] was speechless.

"Well," continued Elder Lyman, "haven't you anything to say?"

[David] was able to respond, "I am neither worthy nor able to receive such a call."

"Not worthy! Not worthy!" exclaimed Elder Lyman. "What have you been doing?"

[David] explained, "I have never done anything in my life of which I am ashamed."

"Well, then," pursued a calmer Elder Lyman, "don't you have faith the Lord can make you able?"

"Yes sir," responded [David] humbly. "I have that faith."

"Very well, then," said Elder Lyman briskly. "Don't say anything to anyone about this until your name is presented in conference this afternoon."

[David], somewhat dazed, returned to the Whites' apartment.

On his way, he encountered his father, who asked if he had been called to the Board of Education. "I've been asked not to say anything about this until it's announced," [he] explained.

[His father] replied, "Then don't say anything."[6]

Not telling Emma Ray about what had happened was very hard for him to do. Much to her credit, Emma Ray passed the equally hard test of not asking, although she could probably tell by his demeanor that something of great importance had happened. After just a few minutes, the McKays left David Lawrence and Llewelyn with their cousins and went to the last session of general conference.[7]

The conference continued with a business-as-usual tone until President Joseph F. Smith called upon President Lyman to give the concluding address. President Lyman spoke on the subjects of education and developing Utah's natural resources and then noted the circumstances of the three vacancies in the Quorum of the Twelve.[8] President Lyman then presented the General Authorities and officers of the Church for a sustaining vote. As he presented the Quorum of the Twelve Apostles, he read the names of the three new members: George F. Richards, Orson F. Whitney, and David O. McKay. As Emma Ray heard David's name come across the microphone, she burst into tears. "Now he will never be home," she thought.[9] She heard someone behind her say, "There's the wife of one of them. See, she's crying."[10]

One can only wonder what David was thinking. Perhaps he compared his lack of experience with that of the two men filling the other vacancies. David had never served as a bishop, a high councilor, or a stake president. He was not even ordained a high priest.[11] He had been home only seven years from his mission and was only thirty-two years old.[12] The other two new Apostles were well known in the Church. Forty-five-year-old George F. Richards was the second counselor in the Tooele Stake presidency and an ordained patriarch. Fifty-one-year-old Orson F. Whitney had served as the bishop of the

Elder McKay of the Quorum of the Twelve wore a reserved handlebar mustache.

Eighteenth Ward in Salt Lake City, the ward that geographically encompassed Church headquarters.

For the rest of that Sunday, he perhaps thought he was sleep-walking, that someone else was talking and walking and he was just a sideline observer. And yet, when he was set apart, he must have experienced feelings that were so potent and intense he could not doubt that something significant was happening to him. That Monday at the meeting of the First Presidency and the Twelve, hands were laid upon David's head, and President Joseph F. Smith ordained him a high priest and an Apostle and promised some miraculous things:

> God our Heavenly Father . . . will enable you by the light of His Spirit to see with your eyes, to hear with your ears, and to understand with your whole heart the great and glorious truths of salvation and exaltation, and that they may be impressed upon your soul, that they may inspire you to the fulfillment of every duty devolving upon you in this high and holy calling; and that there may not be one shadow of doubt in your mind with regard to the divinity of these things, but on the contrary that your understanding may be enlarged, and that you [may] comprehend these things and see them as God our Father sees them, and that fear and doubt of any kind may not find place in your heart.[13]

NEW RESPONSIBILITIES

And so David's duties as an Apostle were added to his other day-to-day responsibilities. Previously, he had asked Elder Lyman that he be allowed to stay at Weber to see the completion of the building through. He felt personal responsibility for the construction. David received permission to remain principal until the building was completed, which was in 1908.[14]

David was young and strong and was somehow capable of handling both responsibilities, but the schedule he started to keep must have been over and above anything he had ever experienced. David would put in a full day at the academy and then another full day after four-thirty in the afternoon at the Church offices. Each Thursday he attended the General Authority meeting in the Salt Lake Temple, where he accompanied the Quorum on the organ. Wearing the two hats of Apostle and Weber's board president was not easy, but David's faith kept him going. The following schedule David recorded one day in his journal was typical:

> 7:45—Rhetoric class
>
> 8:40—Faculty prayer meeting
>
> 8:45—Devotional
>
> 9:15—Theology class
>
> 10:30—English class
>
> 11:20—Gen. school work
>
> 12:10—Dinner
>
> 1:15 p.m.—Boarded train for Salt Lake City
>
> 2:30 p.m.—Committee meeting
>
> 3:30 p.m.—Special S.S. [Sunday School] work
>
> 5:30 p.m.—Committee arrangements
>
> 7:00 p.m.—Gen. S.S. Board meeting
>
> 11:45 p.m.—in company with Bro. Evans, boarded train for Ogden
>
> 1:30 a.m.—Retired, tired[15]

Each day ended only to have another packed schedule start the next morning, and the work that David was involved in became increasingly critical to those it affected. Although the Church's population in 1906 was "comparatively small, . . . approximately 330,000 members divided into fifty-five stakes and twenty-one missions, [he] was surprised at the scope and volume of matters brought before the council for discussion and decision."[16] Weekends offered no respite as David visited various stakes along the Mormon corridor. Authorities traveled in pairs, and when they made long trips to distant cities and towns such as Panguitch, Kanab, St. Johns, Snowflake, Parowan, St. George, or even farther to places in Canada, it wasn't uncommon for them to be away from their families two weeks or more. In the winter, traveling to and from conferences, David was so cold that he placed hot bricks wrapped in blankets around his legs to prevent frozen toes.[17]

TWO MILESTONES

After six months of being a General Authority, David passed two important milestones in his life. The first was his maiden talk in October 1906 general conference. Though David had six months to prepare for the tabernacle pulpit, he was probably nervous and anxious. Emma was there for that talk, as she would be for many others, and she provided silent support and encouragement. David often said to her, "It helps to look down and see you sitting there."[18]

Addressing the Saints for the first time as an Apostle of the Lord Jesus Christ, David felt deep apprehension and tried to convey the weight of the burden. "Along with the enjoyment of the spirit of this conference," he said, "my soul has had a struggle with a feeling of dread of this moment, and if I am not able to make you hear, . . . it is because a great deal of my energy has been expended in suspense." He then made a plea to the audience that he would repeat many times in many places over the years: "I pray for your sympathy, and for your faith and prayers, that the words which I utter may conform to the Spirit."[19] As David began his address, the Saints became aware that the new Apostle was going to be different in his speaking style from other general conference speakers. David freely quoted from memory secular poets, philosophers, and writers, finding gospel principles in secular places not previously mined by other brethren to elaborate and illustrate ideas.[20] He also introduced to the Saints the wonderful world of Scottish dialect and humor and often quoted lines from his favorite poet, Robert Burns.[21]

The other milestone of October 1906 was the laying of the cornerstone for the new building on Weber campus on the nineteenth. Unfortunately, though, by the time the roof and walls were up, contributions trailed off, with most of the interior construction still undone. For the next two years, David spent much time trying to get funds for the new building; when construction was completed, much to David's dismay, money was still owing on the building. Tired to the point of exhaustion, he wrote the following in his journal on May 1, 1908: "There is yet due on the new Building $5,500.00 or more, and the funds for current expenses are not sufficient to meet the bills due, and to pay salaries. My being away so much makes my labors here in school a burden. They used to be a pleasure. Thirty more days and, I hope, I shall be relieved."[22] The new building was used for the first time at the end of May for graduation. David was pleased with how things had gone, recording in his journal: "My dream of two years ago was this night realized. The building was not yet finished but it is near enough completed to serve our purposes for commencement week. It was truly a pleasing sight to see the graduates and their many friends in the new hall."[23]

Paying tribute to David's dedication to the academy, the members of the Weber Stake Academy board gave David a surprise dinner on May 26, 1908. Four hundred people attended, including President Joseph F. Smith. The climax of the event was the announcement that, in David's honor, the faculty, bishops in Ogden, and the First Presidency were contributing a total of $6,050 that would enable the academy to pay every penny of its former and current debts.[24] That night David wrote in his journal that he "tried to respond [to this generosity] but made a poor failure of it." It was "a great deal more than [he] expected."[25] Four days later he simply wrote in his journal, "The chapter of my school life is closed."[26]

EDUCATION IN THE CHURCH

That summer, Elder McKay was sent on tour to southern Utah to hold as many as three meetings per town in ten towns. He visited about thirty-five stakes a year. By 1910, with only sixty-six stakes in the Church, he had visited all the stakes in just two years. The frequency of these visits increased his sphere of friends among the Church membership and left just one Sunday a month for David to be home. On those Sundays, he was usually involved with local requests for speaking in his own or surrounding wards.[27]

Along with speaking assignments, David devoted his energy to furthering the efforts of the Deseret Sunday School Union. On October 6, 1906, David was called to be the second assistant to President Joseph F. Smith in the general superintendency of the union. Three years later, on April 4, 1909, David became President Smith's first assistant, and in 1918, he became the general superintendent himself.[28] David's appointment established a new precedent. For the first time, a member of the Quorum of the Twelve rather than a member of the First Presidency was called as president of the auxiliary organization. As president of the Deseret Sunday School Union, David chose Stephen L Richards and George D. Pyper as assistants. Richards had become an Apostle in 1917 at the age of thirty-seven and became one of David's greatest friends and best advocates of his ideas. Richards was known for his humility, tact, and superior intelligence, and David relied heavily on his support. During this time, David also wrote *Ancient Apostles,* which was used as one of the first official manuals for the Sunday School. As Sunday School superintendent, he introduced ideas that became standard procedures throughout the Church. David took the innovations he had instituted in Weber Stake and revolutionized Sunday School teaching. If David wondered what the response to his work in the Sunday School was, he was pleasantly surprised when, several months after the new superintendency was sustained, Edward P. Kimball paid the following tribute to him as superintendent in the *Juvenile Instructor:*

> David O. McKay is signally honored by his call to preside over the Sunday Schools of the Church in all the world. . . . His appointment comes as a merited recognition for the faithfulness and zeal which he has displayed during his long association with the Sunday Schools, and that confidence in his training for the great responsibility of his new calling, and in his capabilities in and fidelity to the great Sunday School cause, exhibited by his brethren in placing him at the head of the wonderful work, will

David O. McKay (back seat, closest to viewer)
as an Apostle during the 1920s.

General superintendency of the Deseret Sunday School Union, 1916. *Left to right:*
Stephen L Richards, first assistant; David O. McKay, superintendent; George D.
Pyper, second assistant.

find an echo in the heart of every Sunday School worker throughout the Church.[29]

David envisioned the Sunday School as an organization that could guide and build character in children and further educate adults. As a step toward his dream, Church leaders declared "that beginning in 1928 formal theological study would be shifted from the weekly priesthood meetings into the Church Sunday School, which was to be lengthened to a full two hours. Lessons for adults were to be prepared under the direction of the Council of the Twelve."[30] The name of the adult Sunday School class was changed from "Parents' Class" to "Gospel Doctrine Class." This small change emphasized the importance of studying the gospel. Sunday School superintendent McKay thought these developments a "distinct epoch" in the history of Sunday School.[31] He also published a plan that defined every aspect of the Sunday School organization, including enrollment, curriculum, schedule, organization, atmosphere, teacher training, student responsibility, and stake board directives. Furthermore, in the words of his nephew, George R. Hill, David was an excellent leader: "He would counsel with those who worked under him, but also relied on [their] creativity. . . . He would talk through problems and then was willing to change his mind. He believed that people were entitled to get their own revelation for the callings they had."[32]

Along with the Sunday School, Elder McKay's responsibilities increasingly affected the Church's educational programs. As early as 1911, his efforts as a junior Apostle and member of the executive committee of the Church Board of Education helped to save Brigham Young University (BYU). A special committee had been formed to curtail spending in education, and they considered abandoning the teachers' college at BYU.[33] Some suggested discontinuing the whole institution, but David was emphatic that the Provo school remain open; he even envisioned it one day becoming a full-scale university.[34] After hearing David's plea, the First Presidency not only decided to support the educational programs at BYU but also promoted the university's expansion.[35]

With such influence, it was not surprising that in 1919, under the leadership of President Heber J. Grant, a new Church Commission of Education was created to assume the responsibility of administering Church education, an area that the First Presidency had previously directed. On April 3, David was appointed as the first Church commissioner of education, with fellow Apostles Stephen L Richards and Richard R. Lyman serving as assistant commissioners. It was under David's leadership that the face of Church education changed dramatically. Under his watch, the Church changed direction from supplying schools for LDS children to training LDS teachers for public schools. At a meeting of the board of education in 1920, David declared, "Now is the time to step right in and get teachers into these public high schools and eliminate the spirit which dominates the schools now."[36] David's timing was perfect. The Church was shutting down many of its academies because of financial concerns and because Church leaders thought it expedient to accommodate the state's educational system. Furthermore, the state legislature of Utah passed a law in 1921 forbidding sectarian control of any public schools.

FAMILY OF AN APOSTLE

And so David went on in a busy, almost frantic pace during the third decade of his life. He had so many varied duties to attend to that he was unable to devote enough time, effort, or energy to any one thing. Perhaps more than any other activity, David wished for more time with Emma Ray. Constant responsibilities must have strained David and Emma Ray's home life. In his journal he would record such statements as "Returned home at midnight and met Ray for the first time in two days."[37]

Although the life of Elder McKay was busy, he tried to make enough time for his family. With two children ages three and five, Emma Ray was expecting at the time of David's call to the apostleship. At that time babies were born at home rather than in the hospital. As Emma Ray went into labor with her third child, the little

The McKay family in Liverpool, England, 1922. Children, left to right: Emma Rae, Robert, Lou Jean, and Edward.

boys could hear their mother crying. Thinking it was the baby, they came downstairs to ask their dad if it was a boy or girl. David told them to return to their room upstairs. When the baby finally came, David ran upstairs to his little sons and, beaming from ear to ear, announced, "It's a girl!"[38] Named after Emma Ray's and David's mothers, Emma Louisa Robbins and Jennette McKay, Louise Jeanette quickly became the apple of her daddy's eye. The family immediately began to call her Lou Jean. During David's tenure as a junior Apostle, he and Emma Ray would welcome four more children to their home.

Their fourth child, Royle, was sweet and endearing. He was a bright, blond-haired boy that always greeted David with a hug and kiss when David returned home. In 1912, David experienced a great test of his faith when Royle took ill at two-and-a-half years old. David recorded the child's sickness in his journal:

> O what a night of suffering for our darling boy! Every breath he drew seemed agony to him! The doctors examined him this morning, and discovered that his pain was due to Pleurisy on both sides. At this we almost lost hope; but later when [the doctor] told us that by an examination . . . he knew what germ had caused the infection and that he had the anti-toxin, we again took courage.[39]

David and Emma Ray kept close watch over him while the nurses administered the stimulant to help him fight off the disease, and David gave Royle a blessing. A hopeful Emma Ray took a break from her vigil and lay down next to her little boy. As the night fell, Royle became weak, and they knew that they were losing him. David's grief-stricken words at the passing of his son show him to be a tender and loving parent: "'Mama' was the last word on his precious lips. Just before the end came, he stretched out his little hands, and as I stooped to caress him, he encircled my neck, and gave me the last of many of the most loving caresses ever a father received from a darling child."[40] Years later, in 1949, David and Emma Ray moved to Salt

Lake City and bought a family plot in the Salt Lake Cemetery, where they had Royle's coffin moved. As Emma Ray watched the little coffin descend a second time, unearthing painful memories from forty years back, she turned to her daughter-in-law and exclaimed, "Oh, Mildred, I hope you never know such grief."[41]

While dealing with their grief, David and Emma Ray tried to concentrate on their other children. Not long after Royle's death came two more boys: Edward, known as Ned; and Robert, known as Bobby. When Emma Ray gave birth to their second daughter, they decided to name her Margaret Verl. However, as David gave the baby a blessing, he named her Emma Rae instead, after her mother, but with a slight alteration in the spelling.[42]

As his family and responsibilities grew, David found it difficult to juggle family time with his busy Church schedule. He did make time on many occasions to play baseball with his boys. He also read to his little children. He had a big library chair that was given to him by his students at Weber. On each side of the chair was a board, and inside those boards was a secret place where the children loved to put toys. David would let them do this because he was never one to correct unnecessary things.[43] He loved to sit in the chair with the children on his lap and read to them *The Lady of the Lake, Ivanhoe,* or *The Bluebird.* The children were especially delighted when he spoke in Scottish dialect.[44] The McKays were "well read in the great stories of authors. The children grew up conversant with the Shakespeare plays. Quotations and stories flowed through the family."[45]

David and Emma Ray had a unique parenting style that allowed their children independence within boundaries. Early on, David and Emma Ray decided to set high expectations for their children based on principle. Honesty was one of the foremost values taught in the McKay home. When Lou Jean was a little tot of the age of three or four, David and Emma Ray warned her never to charge something at the store or cross the street alone. One day, Lou Jean walked across the street, went into the store, and charged a penny's worth of Indian head chocolates and went home. The store's owner telephoned Emma

Ray and told her what had happened. When Lou Jean got home, Emma Ray turned her around to go back to the store and apologize to the owner. Lou Jean obeyed, went back, and returned the candy. Her mother said nothing else. Lou Jean knew that what she had done was wrong and later went into her room, where she sobbed and sobbed. Her mother came in later and asked if she wanted any dinner. Lou Jean answered, "No!" Emma Ray then came in and rocked her and told her that she loved her. Lou Jean had learned her lesson. Honesty was exemplified by David and Emma Ray, and later Lou Jean remarked, "I knew all my life, what my father and mother told me was true. I could trust them. I knew they loved me and love was the secret of the family. . . . If mother had spanked me or told me I was naughty, I wouldn't remember it."[46]

Once, Llewellyn went to the store, and when he got his items he took them to the cash register and paid for them with a five-dollar bill. The young man running the cash register was flirting with a girl and not paying attention. He gave Llewellyn a ten-dollar bill back as change. Llewellyn came home elated and told his mother of his good fortune. His mother told him to go and tell the story to his father. After telling his father what had happened, Llewellyn remarked that no one would ever know that he had received more change. His father replied: "There will always be one person who will know." Llewellyn questioned: "Who's that?" His father replied: "You!" and walked away. There was no chastisement or discussion. Llewellyn returned the money and apologized.[47]

Another principle the McKays followed in raising their children was: "Never give a child . . . a command that you cannot immediately see is carried out."[48] With David gone so much of the time, it was likely Emma Ray who bore the brunt of the responsibility for following through. However, one day David gave this principle more than just lip service. One summer evening, the family was returning from Huntsville to Ogden. One of the boys was fighting and teasing in the buggy's back seat. Emma Ray had told him twice that if he did not calm down, he would walk home. The boy persisted, and she warned him a third time. He ignored her and continued teasing, so David stopped and asked him to get out of the buggy. The boy climbed out and the family drove on. A few moments later David gently chastised Emma, "Woman, when you say a thing, mean it."[49] David's son later spoke of this experience. "Father let me walk just far enough to contemplate the lesson, . . . then stopped and waited for me. I was a much-chastened boy when I climbed back into the surrey. There was no more teasing or quarreling."[50] This same son observed, "Our parents' expectations provided the path for us to follow, and our love for them provided an irresistible motivation for us to walk that path. We learned to love them because they first dearly loved each other and us."[51]

Along the same lines, David insisted on a firm rule: "Never repeat a clear command. If you repeat it, the child will always wait for the repetition." In one of his letters home to Emma Ray on May 22, 1929, while he was riding the train to a conference assignment, he recorded:

> There is a lively two-year-old boy here in the car, and a mother who is constantly, constantly, constantly saying, "Donald! . . . Donald, don't do that! . . . Donald, dear, come here!" etc., etc. And Donald does "that," and Donald doesn't come here, and so another future American citizen gets his first lessons in disregard for law and order.
>
> I am so glad I have a loving wife who is also a wise mother, and I love her because she is both and more.[52]

Though he admired Emma Ray's wisdom, there were times when David sometimes held firmly to principles against Emma Ray's wishes. One time, when the boys were playing baseball, a ball inadvertently went through a basement window. Llewelyn found his father and admitted the mistake: "It was an accident and I am very sorry."

David replied, "I am sorry, too, but just being sorry will not repair the damage."

Llewelyn asked, "How much will a new window cost?"

"I do not know," replied David, "but we shall have a repairman come up and he can tell us the exact amount."

Llewelyn said, "I haven't much money, but I am willing to pay what I have." So Llewelyn paid what he had. When Emma Ray remonstrated, "How could you take his money when he has such a small allowance?" David replied, "He has received a valuable lesson in the cost of keeping up a home, and now he has a monetary interest in this home which he will protect." David was right; Llewelyn never broke another window.[53]

On occasion, Emma Ray could put her foot down as well. David Lawrence gives us an example:

> I was in my early teens and saw an advertisement for a combined subscription to the *Literary Digest* and the *Youth's Companion.* I asked Mother whether we could take advantage of this offer.
>
> "I think we can," she answered, "but ask your father."
>
> When I asked Father, he said, "No."
>
> I knew we were on a very strict budget and thought no more about it, but Mother gave me a look I couldn't interpret. A few days later, Father said, "You were asking about a subscription to the *Literary Digest* and the *Youth's Companion.* That will be all right."[54]

Obviously, something had taken place between his parents behind the scenes.

The children, though, generally saw their father and mother in agreement as they worked together to rear them.[55] Though the McKay home was one of order and obedience, the children were not given any definite rules, and neither Emma nor David believed in scolding.[56] One Sunday, Emma Rae asked her father, "Do I have to go to Sunday School?" David answered back, "You don't have to go! Just hurry and get your coat on so we won't be late."[57] As a father, David just "looked" and the children knew they were out of line. Occasionally, a child would receive the "finger treatment" when misbehaving: David would tap one of his progeny gently on the temple and say, "Think about it, boy."[58]

Although there was discipline in the McKay household, David had a sense of humor with his children. David thoroughly enjoyed a clabber, a tangy cream which is less firm than traditional sour cream. One time he told his son Bobby, "I'll give you a quarter for every bowl of clabber that you will eat." David tried hard not to laugh as Bobby's face scrunched up in disgust "while he was downing that stuff—full of dislike and yet determination to get through with it." David just wanted "somebody in this family to enjoy clabber with him." Bob lasted three bowls.[59]

Courtesy and manners were also valued. The children were taught to be polite, to say "please" and "thank you," to rise when an adult came into the room. Whenever the block (home) teachers came, the family was asked to gather around in the front room for them. One lesson on courtesy came during dinner when Emma Rae was asked to replenish a bread plate. As she returned to the table, she took a piece of bread first before placing it on the table. David corrected her, "You never help yourself first. Pass the plate to others, and then serve yourself last."[60]

At the same time, David believed in personal agency and tried to give his children as much latitude as possible. David Lawrence told the following story:

> Father was a firm believer in free agency. I don't know that there
> was any proscription against face cards, but we never had any in
> our home. Llewelyn got a streak of independence when we were
> in high school and bought . . . a deck of cards that he kept in his

top drawer. . . . Father once came in to look for something and found the deck of cards.

"Whose are these?" he asked.

"Mine," answered Llewelyn.

Father looked at him, put them back in the top drawer, and walked out. He never referred to them or mentioned them again to Llewelyn; but as I recall, they didn't stay in the top drawer very long.[61]

The McKay household participated in music, art, and literature, and the children took music lessons at some financial sacrifice. David and Emma Ray both played the piano, and Emma Ray could play by ear. The McKays would sing hymns and popular songs to their children.[62]

LEARNING TO LIVE BY THE SPIRIT

As a father, David tried to let the Spirit direct his efforts, just as he did in his Church responsibilities. He tried to set a good example for his children by having the faith to act on the promptings he received. It was on one of these occasions that David recognized and acted on a premonition that might have saved his son's life. David Lawrence was hauling a load of beet pulp west of Ogden over a viaduct while David was at home reading. Suddenly, David closed his book and stood up. Surprised by the abrupt movement, Emma Ray asked David, "Where are you going?" David answered, "To save Lawrence's life."[63] David Lawrence continues the story:

[Father] met me at the top of the viaduct, just as I was about to start the descent. He reminded me that I was driving a team of four horses abreast, . . . that they were pulling four tons of beet pulp, and that the wagon had no brakes. While I held the reins, he got out of the car to block a wheel. . . . Unfortunately, we were holding up traffic and a car honked behind me. I moved the team to get out of the way, but we had started the descent. The team could not stop. By the time we reached the bottom, the horses were racing out of control on the left side of the road. We hit a car that emerged from behind the candy factory, smashing the motor but sparing the driver. . . . If Father had not stopped us and if that car had not come out at that moment, we would have careened onto busy Washington Avenue, . . . and probably knocked over pedestrians.[64]

However, on a Thursday morning early in March 1916, David did not listen to such promptings and paid for it dearly. That fateful day, the furnace was acting up, and David had been tinkering with it when he looked at his watch and found it was past 6:30 A.M. Earlier, David had agreed to take his brother Thomas up the canyon to Huntsville that morning before David caught the train to Salt Lake for a council meeting. Just as David was thinking about his busy morning, a distinct thought came into his mind. "Go up to the bridge and back." The Ogden River had overflowed that spring, and the day before he had taken his children up to see the flood. While there, David had been warned that the bridge might be washed out. It was there he was supposed to stop. They started the Model T, driving through rain up Twenty-First Street. On the way to the bridge, his brother suggested, "I think you had better not attempt to cross the bridge." As he got to the place he had taken the children the day before, he ignored the prompting he had received earlier and decided, "Oh, well, I can take Thomas E. a little bit further."[65] So he did, and a cable he had not seen hanging across the bridge hit him squarely under his chin.[66]

The next few minutes were always a blur in David's mind when he tried to remember them. He could remember the initial shock of something hitting him in the face and the blood, but he could remember little else. Thomas E. was untouched and managed to get into the driver's seat. When David got to the hospital, he was immediately prepared for surgery. They stitched up his face and bandaged his jaw and head so that only his eyes peered out under bandages.[67] The first three visitors who came to the hospital after the operation were Thomas B. Evans, David's stake president; Bishop Olsen, his bishop; and Heber Scowcroft, a close friend.[68] His stake president and bishop promised him in a blessing that he would have no pain and a quick recovery.[69]

As comforting as the bishop and stake president's blessing must have been, another blessing given that next Saturday likely strengthened David even more. Early that morning, the door to David's room opened and in stepped two of David's brethren in the Quorum of the Twelve, Heber J. Grant and Orson F. Whitney. Elder Grant went to the bed and patted David's shoulder, saying, "David, don't try to speak. I'm here to give you a blessing." Elder Grant repeated what David's bishop had said—that he would feel no pain—but then added a remarkable promise. He told David he would have no scars and be able to talk as easily and beautifully as before. Elder Grant patted his shoulder again when he was done and exited the room. Then he leaned against the wall and said to himself, "What have I done? I've promised something that is not possible."[70]

On Sunday morning, Emma Ray called her three oldest children, David Lawrence, Llewellyn, and Lou Jean, into the living room. They had been fasting. Emma Ray told them to break their fast, eat some breakfast, and then they would go to Sunday School instead of the hospital. She told her children that they had been praying for David at the temple and that he would be made well. Llewellyn, who was ten at the time, wouldn't eat. Emma Ray coaxed him, "Come on Llewellyn, Don't worry any longer; Daddy will be all right." Llewelyn went out the front door and walked to the hospital. On the way he picked his father a bouquet of bluebells and buttercups. Llewelyn asked a nurse to give them to his "Papa." Instead, the nurse offered to let Llewelyn into the room, and David's son put the flowers in his hand. The nurse and Llewelyn were both crying.[71]

That Sunday in the hospital, the head surgeon, who was not a member of the Church, came into David's room. As he began to change the dressing on David's face, the surgeon was amazed at what he saw. David's face was practically healed. The doctor said, "I'm not going to put any dressings back on your face." On the way out he proclaimed, "Mr. McKay, it pays to lead a good life."[72] Though bruised, lacerated, and with a fractured jaw and missing teeth, David felt no pain. He returned home on Wednesday.[73]

Thursday found David in the dentist's office. David's remaining teeth were pushed up into his gums so that the roots were hanging out. The dentist said, "David, you must have endured great pain." David replied, "I've had no pain." The dentist fixed his mouth the best he could, and David went home.[74] Few knew that David wore false teeth for the rest of his life; he was never bothered by them, nor did they affect his speech. A few days later, David wrote to President Francis M. Lyman:

> Never before in my life have I felt nearer to the Lord than today. Never before have I been so grateful to Him for blessings He has given me. . . . I have been practically free from pain. I acknowledge this as a direct blessing from the Lord.
>
> My face is almost entirely healed, and it looks as though I shall be practically free from scars. It will take some time, of course, to get my mouth in shape; but the fracture is healing rapidly. I am more willing than ever to devote my life to the Cause we love.[75]

Six months later, during October conference, the Twelve and First Presidency were sitting at a long, narrow table for dinner. David was seated opposite Heber J. Grant. During the entire meal, Elder Grant stared at David's face; then Elder Grant got up, went around the table and put his hand on David's shoulder and said, "I have been studying your face and searching it. I can find no scar." David replied, "There are no scars, your blessing was realized completely."[76] Faith in a priesthood blessing had healed David completely.

The accident seemed to have a remarkable impact on the young Apostle, and afterwards he remarked: "Things which before seemed troublesome and burdensome, now seem to be almost real pleasures." David was happy and grateful to be alive.[77] Subsequently, David would apply what had happened to him as a pattern for what happened to others. In 1944, President John Q. Adams of the Samoa Mission wrote David of a terrible tragedy that took place in Pago Pago. A faithful leader, his wife, and his daughter-in-law, who had been expecting a baby in a few weeks, had died in a huge landslide that had dropped from a high mountain in back of an LDS chapel. The congregations in Samoa were stunned and grief-stricken. President Adams told David the tragic event was "the first and only event of its kind in all [the Samoan] annals."[78] David wrote back an interesting observation:

> Not infrequently shocking incidents occur in which friends and loved ones are maimed or lose their lives, which are wholly inexplicable to our circumscribed minds. The tragedy at Pago Pago is one of those incomprehensible occurrences to which we must humbly, though sometimes blindly, submit. And just to what extent the Lord tried to warn the faithful members who lost their lives we shall never know. Perhaps he gave an impression which was not heeded, or at least not understood. We do not know of such incidents whereof the Lord warned of impending danger, but the warning was unheeded with the resultant accident. If, in such cases, the accident had resulted in death, no one in this life would ever have known that the Lord tried to intervene for the victim's safety. . . . No matter how inexplicable the catastrophe, of this we may be sure that the Lord will overrule all things for the good of those who remain faithful and true to His laws, and we also have the assurance that Death whether he come slow or fast is to the righteous but an entrance into another room of our Father's kingdom which is far more peaceful and glorious than that which we have lived in this mortal sphere.[79]

After David's accident, it would seem he never ignored a prompting. Such faith in promptings would be necessary for what would proceed in the near future, where listening to the Spirit would have to guide David's every move as he traveled further than ever before in difficult and dangerous circumstances.

NOTES TO CHAPTER 5

1. Conference Report, October 1906, 112–13 (original emphasis).
2. Keith Terry, *David O. McKay: Prophet of Love* (Santa Barbara, CA: Butterfly, 1980), 47–48.
3. Terry, *Prophet of Love,* 47–49; David Lawrence McKay, *My Father, David O. McKay* (Salt Lake City: Deseret Book, 1989), 39.
4. Terry, *Prophet of Love,* 47–49.
5. Ibid., 49.
6. David Lawrence McKay, *My Father,* 39.
7. Ibid., 39.
8. Francis Lyman, Conference Report, April 1906, 93–94.
9. Zella Farr Smith, "A Romantic Story from the Life of President and Sister McKay," McKay Scrapbook, no. 131, MS 4640, LDS Church Archives, Salt Lake City; David Lawrence McKay, *My Father,* 40.
10. David Lawrence McKay, *My Father,* 40.
11. Francis M. Gibbons, *David O. McKay: Apostle to the World, Prophet of God* (Salt Lake City: Deseret Book, 1986), 68.
12. Richard N. Armstrong, *The Rhetoric of David O. McKay, Mormon Prophet* (New York: Peter Lang, 1993), 5.
13. Joseph Fielding Smith, Ordination of David O. McKay to the Apostleship, April 9, 1906, McKay Scrapbook, no. 188.
14. Jeanette McKay Morrell, *Highlights in the Life of David O. McKay* (Salt Lake City: Deseret Book, 1966), 54–55.
15. McKay Microfilm, March 19, 1907, reel 3: 429, Church Archives.
16. Gibbons, *Apostle to the World,* 71–72.
17. Llewelyn R. McKay, *Home Memories of President David O. McKay* (Salt Lake City: Deseret Book, 1956), 30.
18. Smith, "A Romantic Story."
19. Conference Report, October 1906, 111.
20. Gibbons, *Apostle to the World,* 88; Notes from Remarks by Clare Middlemiss at

the U.S. Circuit Conference, Hotel Utah, McKay Scrapbook, no. 77. Middlemiss was the concluding speaker for a secretary conference about President McKay.

21. Notes from Remarks by Claire Middlemiss at the U.S. Circuit Conference.

22. McKay Microfilm, May 1, 1908, reel 3: 430; and David Lawrence McKay, *My Father,* 52.

23. David Lawrence McKay, *My Father,* 46.

24. Richard W. Sadler, *History of Weber State College: A Centennial History* (Salt Lake City: Publishers Press, 1988), 27–28.

25. McKay Microfilm, May 26, 1908, reel 3:430, 56.

26. Ibid., May 30, 1908, reel 3:430, 62.

27. David Lawrence McKay, *My Father,* 91.

28. David O. McKay file, 1955, International Society of the Daughters of Utah Pioneers, reading room, Salt Lake City.

29. Edward P. Kimball, "The General Sunday School Superintendency Reorganized," *Juvenile Instructor,* February 1919, 59.

30. Richard O. Cowan, *The Church in the Twentieth Century: The Impressive Story of the Advancing Kingdom* (Salt Lake City: Bookcraft, 1985), 156.

31. Ibid., 156.

32. George R. Hill, interview by Mary Jane Woodger, October 28, 1995, Salt Lake City, McKay Research Project, College of Education, Brigham Young University, Provo, UT; transcript in author's possession.

33. Thomas G. Alexander, *Mormons in Transition: A History of the Latter-day Saints, 1890–1930* (Urbana: University of Illinois Press, 1986), 167–68.

34. Francis M. Gibbons, interview by Mary Jane Woodger, August 19, 1996, McKay Research Project; transcript in author's possession.

35. Alexander, *Mormons in Transition,* 168.

36. Minutes from the General Church Board of Education, March 3, 1920, Church Archives, CR102 26:1:28; cited in James R. Clark, "Church and State Relationships in Education in Utah" (Ph.D. dissertation, Utah State University, 1958), 269.

37. Gibbons, *Apostle to the World,* 75.

38. David Lawrence McKay, *My Father,* 45.

39. McKay Microfilm, April 8, 1912, reel 4:433.

40. David Lawrence McKay, *My Father,* 84–85.

41. Ibid., 84–86.

42. Emma Rae Ashton interview by Mary Jane Woodger, June 20, 1995, Salt Lake City, McKay Research Project; transcript in author's possession.

43. Lou Jean McKay Blood, interview by Mary Jane Woodger, August 8, 1995, Salt Lake City, McKay Research Project; transcript in author's possession.

44. David Lawrence McKay, *My Father,* 89.

45. Lavina Fielding Anderson, interview by Mary Jane Woodger, October 24, 1995, McKay Research Project; transcript in author's possession.

46. Blood interview.

47. Richard McKay, interview by Mary Jane Woodger, 1995, Salt Lake City, McKay Research Project; transcript in author's possession.

48. David Lawrence McKay, *My Father,* 99.

49. Terry, *Prophet of Love,* 194.

50. David Lawrence McKay, *My Father,* 100.

51. Ibid., 99.

52. David O. McKay to Emma Ray McKay, May 22, 1929, McKay Papers, box 1, folder 7, Church Archives.

53. Morrell, *Highlights,* 44, 47. Llewelyn was not identified as the child involved in the retelling of this story, but because he was the source of the incident, his name was inserted.

54. David Lawrence McKay, *My Father,* 103.

55. Ashton interview.

56. Edward and Lottie McKay interview.

57. Ashton interview.

58. David Lawrence McKay, *My Father,* 100.

59. Ibid., 184.

60. Ashton interview.

61. David Lawrence McKay, *My Father,* 102–103.

62. Ibid., 89.

63. Ibid., 94.

64. Ibid.

65. David O. McKay, "Privilege and Blessing of a Man Who Holds the Melchizedek Priesthood to Receive Warnings Through the Holy Ghost," McKay Scrapbook, no. 188.

66. Emma Ray Riggs McKay, Remarks, Quarterly Conference, Salt Lake City, September 8, 1957, McKay Scrapbook, no. 131.

67. Blood interview.

68. David O. McKay, "Priesthood Quorums as Effective Aids to an Individual in a Job-Finding Program," April 5, 1949, McKay Scrapbook, no. 14.

69. Blood interview.

70. Ibid.

71. Ibid.

72. Ibid.

73. David O. McKay to Francis M. Lyman, April 2, 1916, Ogden, UT, McKay Scrapbook, no. 188.

74. Blood interview.
75. David O. McKay to Francis M. Lyman, April 2, 1916, Ogden, UT, McKay Scrapbook, no. 188.
76. Blood interview.
77. David O. McKay to Francis M. Lyman, April 2, 1916, Ogden, UT, McKay Scrapbook, no. 188.
78. John Q. Adams to David O. McKay, June 4, 1944, McKay Scrapbook, no. 127.
79. David O. McKay to John Q. Adams, August 2, 1944, McKay Scrapbook, no. 127.

Elder David O. McKay (right) with his traveling companion, Hugh J. Cannon, leaving San Francisco for a world tour, March 29, 1921.

Hugh J. Cannon and David O. McKay in Egypt, in front of the Sphinx, October 26, 1921.

CHAPTER 6

CULTURE AND TRAVEL

The essence of true culture is consideration for others.
—David O. McKay[1]

Parting from those we love is never an easy task," Elder McKay once wrote, but on December 4, 1920, parting seemed "more difficult than ever." In the preceding days, small tasks around the house seemed to say to him, "This is the last time for a while." "Even the fire in the furnace," he wrote, "looked gloomy when I threw in the last shovel full of coal. However, I kept my feelings pretty well under control until I began to say good-bye to the children. Baby [Robert], thinking I was going to coo to him, looked up and gave me his sweetest smile."[2]

David choked back tears as he realized that the "beautiful innocent radiance of his baby face" was going to have to last in his memory for more than a year. When Ned, who had slept by David's side the night before, snuggled up to David's cheek, it was too much, and he let the tears fall. Worst of all was the moment of bidding farewell to Emma Ray. His feelings at leaving her for such a long period of time were indescribable. Though he had often traveled to stake conferences and various other assignments, he had never been gone for more than a few weeks. This was going to be a parting of long months.[3]

When Elder McKay was called to be Church commissioner of education, President Grant had told him that part of his responsibility would include a worldwide tour of all the Church missions and schools, with the objective being "to obtain firsthand information regarding Latter-day Saints in all parts of the world."[4]

When President Grant had first mentioned the tour, David had thought it could be completed in three months. At the time, three months had seemed like a long journey, but then it was decided the tour would perhaps take an entire year. As a parting gift, members of his ward had given him "a watch chain charm containing a miniature photograph" of Emma Ray.[5] Now, as he sat at the Union Station waiting for the train to pull out, he opened his watch and looked at Emma Ray's picture, realizing that the only connections they would have for the next year would be that picture and letters.

On December 2, 1920, two days before David left, he had received a wonderful blessing in the Salt Lake Temple. Members of the First Presidency and Quorum of the Twelve laid their hands upon his head, and comforting promises were made. The memory of what was said gave him some strength. President Grant had told David that this mission had been given "under the inspiration of the Spirit of the Lord." David was promised he would have "every gift and grace and every qualification necessary for you to possess in order to fully magnify this calling." He was blessed with "power over disease, not only in your own person, but with power so that when you lay your hands upon the sick and the afflicted . . . where you are requested to administer to the sick, the healing power of the Almighty God shall follow your administration." In addition, he was blessed "with great wisdom, with a retentive memory, with capacity and ability to comprehend and understand the needs of the various missions that you shall visit, so that from time to time as you meet . . . with the brethren of this council you shall be able to give them valuable information that shall be of great benefit in shaping the affairs of the missions throughout the world." He was comforted that he would be "warned of danger . . . and be given wisdom and inspiration from God to avoid all the snares and pitfalls that may be laid for your feet by wicked and designing men." As David looked at Emma Ray's picture again, he remembered that the blessing also promised "every righteous desire of your heart" and bade him to "go forth in peace, and pleasure [and] happiness."[6] What he was feeling was anything but pleasure or happiness. The only desire he had was to get off the train at the next stop and go back home. But, as in everything, David's first commitment was to the gospel and his apostolic duties. He opened the locket one more time to look at Emma Ray's photo, closed it, and resigned himself to his duty.

Hugh J. Cannon, editor for Church publications and son of George Q. Cannon, a counselor in the First Presidency, had been set apart to be David's missionary companion. As the first few minutes clicked away on the train, David experienced a myriad of emotions. He was glad for Brother Cannon's companionship, but he also wished to be left alone with his melancholy feelings. The plan was to go by train to Vancouver to board the RMS *Empress of Japan* on December 7 and to visit Japan first. Soon they were on board, and just five hours later he wrote to Emma Ray, and his heart seemed even more tender than it had been at their parting. He had promised to send her copies of his journal pages. Calling her "the dearest and sweetest of sweethearts," he regretted not being able to send her his diary because he had not written a word in it yet. Trying to reassure himself as much as her, he comforted, "Though thousands of miles of ocean separate us, we shall be closer together than ever before in our lives; for never were you dearer to me than you are now."[7]

David discovered firsthand that "a winter crossing of the northern Pacific is a tempestuous and gloomy affair."[8] Accordingly, he spent most of the time below deck. He wrote Emma Ray of the following attempt to come above:

> I reached only the top of the stairs, when that intense yearning to be alone drove me back to my cabin. Good-bye last night's dinner! Good-bye yesterday's Rotary luncheon! And during the next sixty hours, good-bye everything I had ever eaten since I was

a babe on mother's knee. I'm not sure I didn't even cross the threshold into the pre-existent state.[9]

In between battles with nausea, David's thoughts turned to Japan.

JAPAN

When David arrived in Japan, twenty years after President Grant had opened the Japanese Mission at the turn of the century, there were just 125 converts to the Church in the nation.[10] As David spent time with the Japanese people, they won his "admiration and . . . esteem." Japanese refinement, courtesy, and manners touched a heart-chord in David because he highly valued such qualities. "Manifest at nearly every turn, the taste in dress, and the beauty of . . . [their] women, . . . the graceful, well-preserved trees in the groves and forests that abound everywhere, the . . . gorges and waterfalls . . . all combine to attune a man's sense of appreciation to the highest pitch."[11] However, David was quite surprised to observe "that no man (in Japan) ever gave up his seat in a street car to a woman, unless it be an older woman, or a woman with a baby on her back or carrying bundles." That's why it quite surprised him that he and Hugh were often given seats, and at first he could not decide why men were giving up their seats for them. One day, the light dawned; David turned to Hugh and said, "Do you know, I believe I understand why these men give us their seats in the car?" Smiling, Hugh said, "Has it just dawned on you?" Then he chuckled and added, "And I've noticed that you've always been the first to be given consideration."[12] David's white hair belied his age. The Japanese people looked at the color of his hair and naturally assumed that he was aged.

While in Japan, David was able to see the emperor's palace. As he visited the building, an accompanying Japanese Church member, an ivory carver by trade, "stood at the gates, . . . very hesitant about approaching. . . . At that time, [the Japanese people] worshiped the Emperor, and [this Church member] felt unworthy to approach even the entrance of the palace." Turning to him, David spoke.

"You have something which the Emperor has not, and it is more precious than all of his palaces, gold, and precious stones."

The man looked at him and queried, "What is it?"

"You hold the priesthood of the Almighty, given to you by direct authority by the servants of the Lord who received it themselves." The humble carver of ivory stood with a look of awe on his face, realizing for the first time that his possession of the priesthood was greater than being the emperor of Japan.[13]

David was in Tokyo when he celebrated his twentieth wedding anniversary. Writing to Emma Ray, he reminisced,

> You were my sweetheart twenty years ago this day; you are twenty times twenty times my sweetheart now!
>
> It doesn't seem possible that a score of years have passed since you and I covenanted to walk side by side and heart in heart along the Pathway of life through Eternity; yet the reckoning of Old Father Time says such is the fact!
>
> . . . It is generally conceded that American men and women, unlike the Japanese, have the right to make their own marriages, the right or privilege of each one's choosing a mate being almost inviolate. With this thought in mind, I pride myself in having manifested for once in my life perfect wisdom. But when I analyze the conditions I find that very little credit is due to me, for it required no superior or discriminating judgment on my part to choose any life's partner when once I had met her. No other girl—and you know my girl acquaintances were not a few—possessed every virtue with which I thought a sweetheart and wife should be endowed. All these you seemed to have. I thought so, even when I met you for the first time, in the doorway of your old home. . . . So, after all, it was not any judgment, but your superior endowment to which I am indebted for my first interest and choice.

But I give credit this Twentieth anniversary to even a higher source. When I think of the varied circumstances that brought us together; of the nearness with which we both came several times of making a mistake; of the hundred and one little experiences that combined to draw us together rather than to separate us, I am willing to acknowledge the guiding influence of a Divine Power.[14]

DEDICATING CHINA

From Japan, David and Hugh departed for the Chinese realm. Before they had left Salt Lake City, President Grant had suggested to David that, "if [he] felt so impressed," he should dedicate China for the preaching of the gospel.[15] David and Hugh arrived in Peking (now Beijing) on the evening of Saturday, January 8, 1921. As David prayed, he felt impressed that "on the following day, as that was the only Sabbath" they would be in China's principal city, he should dedicate the land for the preaching of the gospel. The next step was to find "a suitable spot." Peking was built "on a level, barren plain" with no forests or groves for privacy. According to Hugh, "January 9 dawned clear and cold. With no definite goal in mind, we left the hotel and walked . . . into what is known as 'The Forbidden City.'"[16] President McKay later recalled, "[As we] walked by the famous old buildings formerly used as temples, . . . we came to a small grove of cypress trees on the edge of what appeared to have been an old moat. . . . We passed a tree with a large branch shooting out on the north side, and I distinctly received a prompting."[17]

"This is the spot," he said to Hugh.

Remarkably, "in the heart of a city with a million inhabitants," David and Hugh were almost entirely alone. There and then, by "the authority of the holy apostleship," David turned the key to unlock the door for the entrance of "four hundred and fifty millions of people now living, and of millions and perhaps billions yet unborn," to receive the true and restored gospel of Jesus Christ.[18]

MANIFESTATIONS IN HAWAII

From China, Hugh and David set sail for the Hawaiian Islands, arriving in Maui. Hugh had expressed his great desire to tread the same ground his father had walked as a missionary. George Q. Cannon, his father, had been a missionary on the island of Maui in the 1850s where, on one occasion, he had conducted a meeting following which 129 people had been baptized. Hugh had been excited to go to that same spot where this had taken place. Upon visiting that spot, David was moved by the surroundings and the thought of what had taken place there so many years before. Being prompted, he said, "I think we should have a word of prayer." They moved into the shade of a pepper tree, out of the heat of the sun. Besides Hugh Cannon, Wesley Smith (president of the Hawaiian Mission and the son of Joseph F. Smith) and Brother Keola Kailimai (president of the Maui District) were also present. As David closed his eyes and began to pray, the Spirit began to work on his heart. As soon as he said amen and opened his eyes, Brother Kailimai rushed to Wesley Smith and spoke rapidly in his native tongue. Wesley Smith then turned to Elder McKay and said, "Brother McKay, do you know what Brother Kailimai has told me?"

"No," David said.

"Brother Kailimai said that while you were praying, . . . he saw two men who he thought were Hugh J. Cannon and E. Wesley Smith step out of line in front of us and shake hands with someone, and he wondered why Brother Cannon and Brother Smith were shaking hands while we were praying. He opened his eyes, and there stood those two men still in line, with their eyes closed just as they had been. He quickly closed his eyes because he knew he had seen a vision."

At once, David thought of Hugh's father, George Q. Cannon, and Joseph F. Smith, Wesley Smith's father, who had both passed on. David declared, "Brother Kailimai, I do not understand the significance of your vision, but I do know that the veil between us and those former missionaries was very thin."

Hugh's eyes were now filled with tears as he disclosed, "Brother McKay, there was no veil."[19]

From Maui, Hugh and David set sail for Hilo, Hawaii. In Hilo, one night they visited the Kilauea volcano, where David and his company stood on the edge of the active volcanic crater, while a cold wind swept down from the peak of Mauna Loa.

> Tiring of the cold, one of the elders discovered a volcanic balcony about four feet down inside the crater where observers could watch the display without being chilled by the wind. It seemed perfectly sound, and the "railing" on the open side of it formed a fine protection from the intense heat [of the volcano]. . . .
>
> After first testing its safety, Brother McKay and three of the elders climbed down into the hanging balcony. As they stood there warm and comfortable, they teased the others . . . to take advantage of the protection they had found. For quite some time . . . all watched the ever-changing sight as [the group's members] alternately chilled and roasted.
>
> After being down there in their protected spot for some time, suddenly Brother McKay said to those with him, "Brethren, I feel impressed that we should get out of here."
>
> With that he assisted the elders to climb out, and then they in turn helped him up to the wind-swept rim. . . . Almost immediately the whole balcony crumbled and fell with a roar into the molten lava a hundred feet or so below.

Nothing was said as the elders walked down the slope. They all knew they had been saved by inspiration from a fiery death.[20]

A DETOUR, THEN ON TO THE SOUTH PACIFIC

After the Hawaiian Islands, the next stop was to be the South Pacific. However, upon inquiry, David and Hugh discovered they could not get a ship for the South Pacific from Honolulu and decided to return to San Francisco and reembark. On February 20, Emma Ray learned that David and Hugh were sailing to San Francisco. She wistfully wrote to her son, David Lawrence, who was serving a mission in Lausanne, Switzerland:

> Wouldn't it be great if he could drop in and say Halloo! before starting out again? But of course he could not, using Church money and being known so well he would be besieged with questions. Oh, it makes me feel so lonesome to think of his being "so near and yet so far." But it's a comfort to know that two of the places to be visited are through with.[21]

Then Emma Ray got a surprise; unbeknownst to David and Hugh, President Grant arranged for her and Sister Cannon to accompany him to San Francisco to see their husbands. The interlude was lengthened when word arrived that President Anthon H. Lund had died and the entire party returned to Utah to attend the funeral. David's two-week stay quickly filled up with meetings, but the limited time at home with Emma Ray and the children was precious to him. Still, his longing for them seemed to intensify as he left for San Francisco again. Absence certainly was making his heart grow fonder. To make matters worse, letters would be few and far between on the next leg of his trip. Leaving San Francisco seemed even more melancholy than leaving Vancouver had been. Thankfully, the long trip from San Francisco to Tahiti was enlivened by an agreeable captain and passengers, an occasional unusual sight off the deck, the ceremonious "initiation" of those who had never before crossed the equator, and a total respite from seasickness. "He thoroughly enjoyed" the voyage this time.[22]

When David and Hugh landed in Papeete, Tahiti, David was surprised with "the slow-paced life-style" of the people. He was disappointed in the circumstances he found in Tahiti but reminded himself that the prophet had asked him "to appraise conditions worldwide as a basis for action . . . to improve or expedite the work," and that meant appraising the negative as well as the positive. After Tahiti, they made a quick trip to Raratonga in the Cook Islands and then headed for New Zealand.[23]

David and Hugh landed at Wellington, New Zealand, in February 1921. Whereas David was disappointed in Tahiti with the lack of progress in the work of the Lord, in New Zealand he was delighted at the many dedicated Maori Latter-day Saints who had embraced the gospel. These Saints' warmth and charm was far from what he had been taught about the Maori people. He concluded that "the further I travel and the more I see of other peoples, the more convinced I become that the European . . . has no monopoly on the fundamental truths that contribute to real manhood and true womanhood." He reported, "I cannot say the natives have interested me—they have fascinated me! Their contentment, the cheerfulness, their hospitality, generosity, . . . have all combined to add a charm" that turned the islands into "a veritable Garden of Eden." David found that "most of the ills and evils" that were produced on these islands came from "so-called civilization," not from the so-called "savagery."[24]

As David observed the Maori Saints in New Zealand, in "feat after feat," he was sure that he had never seen such "manly strength, true intelligence, and an aptitude and adoption of new habits and constitutions unexcelled by their self-styled superior critics." It was true that many of them lived in huts, ate with their fingers, and did not dress like people influenced by European culture. However, these primitive conditions did not create a people who were "lacking in tender sympathy and loving service." His eyes were being opened in the South Pacific as he discovered that European living standards and fashions were not a gauge for other nations. David began to know that Christ's teaching, "Judge not, that ye be not judged," was "preg-nant with the philosophy of peace and good will" that he, as an

Apostle of the Lord Jesus Christ, was now to share with Latter-day Saints across the world.[25]

In Huntly, New Zealand, David first attended a *hui tau,* "the annual Conference of members of The Church of Jesus Christ of Latter-day Saints in New Zealand."[26] Nearly "a thousand people . . . sitting, reclining, and standing—assembled" to hear an Apostle of the Lord "with curiosity and high expectations."[27] The *hui tau* lasted several days as David spoke on many subjects. He testified of the Prophet Joseph Smith and held the Book of Mormon up in his hand while witnessing to them that it was "the writing, the history, of your ancestors."[28] He reminded them, "Your boys, your parents, your grandparents, back to Lehi, who came from Jerusalem—that is where you trace your ancestry, and the world, the skeptics of the world, are recognizing your relationship to Judea."[29]

It was during one of his discourses on the Book of Mormon that David ran into opposition. On April 24, David felt ill, too hoarse to speak. Before he began, he offered a silent prayer for divine assistance. As he arose, his "voice was tight and husky." He recalled, "Five minutes after I began, someone shouted from the group standing on my right, 'Joseph Smith didn't receive the revelation on polygamy!'"[30] Two Josephites had entered the tent to heckle David; "Josephite" was a common name for a member of the Reorganized Church of Jesus Christ of Latter Day Saints.[31] David recounts, "I hesitated a moment, turned my head in his direction, saw some men scuffling, and the crowd beginning to sway towards them. Motioning to the audience to remain quiet, I said with as much good nature as I could muster, 'When the sons of God met, the devil came also.' Many in the audience grasped the application and broke into laughter; some began to clap, but I motioned for order, and continued with my discourse."[32]

What my friend says about polygamy is merely the repetition which the enemy tries to defy the work of God. They have seized upon one condition about which they know nothing, and like the raven that feeds upon the carcass, they like to feed upon slander. I want to tell you that when you find a man that is attacking [an]other, that likes to live upon slander, on vilifications, you will find a man that is not prompted by the Spirit of Christ.

And since there are some others here who do not understand, the Church does not sanction polygamy, and I will say that the history is published for the people. If they want to look into it and test it, we will be willing to abide by their decision.[33]

David returned to his theme of the Book of Mormon and Joseph Smith once again "with all the earnestness and vehemence I could command and spoke as loud as possible." He felt his "voice getting clearer and more resonant" as he spoke. Soon he forgot about his illness "and thought only of the truth I wanted my hearers to understand and accept. For forty minutes I continued with my address, and when I concluded, my voice was as resonant and clear as it ever was!"[34] One of the Josephites then approached David with an upraised hand, ready to strike him. David "raised his right hand, and instantly the Josephite cowered down in a kneeling position, whimpering and mourning before the Apostle, who, without stopping his discourse or showing any facial expressions or signs of fear, continued. . . . [When] he finished speaking," David turned and "raised up the Josephite."[35]

After the meeting, the second Josephite approached the Apostle

and in a sarcastic manner said to him, "I would like to shake hands with an Apostle of the Church of Jesus Christ of Latter-day Saints, for I have never seen one before." He then extended his hand, and as soon as it came in contact with the Apostle's he shivered with an ague and collapsed at the Apostle's feet, and sobbed. The Apostle thereupon lifted him up by the hand and said, "Brother, let me give you some advice: never tear another man's house down. If you wish to use a hammer, use it in building a house of your own." The other Josephite then came and took his friend away.[36]

This miraculous experience with the Josephites was followed by another manifestation in the final meeting of *hui tau.* David had used an interpreter during the entire conference, but during the last session, as David stood to speak, he "yearned, most earnestly, for the gift of tongues that I might be able to speak to them in their native language. Until that moment, I had not given much serious thought to the gift of tongues, but on that occasion I wished with all my heart that I might be worthy of that divine power." He turned to the audience and confided:

> I wish I had the power to speak to you in your own tongue, that I might tell you what is in my heart; but since I have not the gift, I pray, and I ask you to pray, that you might have the spirit of interpretation, of discernment, that you may understand at least the spirit, and then you will get the words and the thought when Brother Meha interprets.

David's sermon continued without interruption for forty minutes. He had "never addressed a more attentive, more respectful audience. My listeners were in perfect rapport—this I knew when I saw tears in their eyes. Some of them at least, perhaps most of them, who did not understand English, had the gift of interpretation." When Brother Meha, the interpreter, gave a synopsis of the speech in Maori, "during the translation, some of the Maoris corrected him on some points, showing that they had a clear conception of what had been said in English."[37] David's heartfelt desire of speaking in tongues had become a reality.

While traveling in New Zealand, David related to Church leaders an experience he had had while in Hawaii:

> Recently I was in Hawaii, and there found a school run entirely under the auspices and expenses of the Church, patronized not

only by the Americans and Hawaiians, but by Japanese, Filipinos, Koreans, [and] Chinese . . . [in] a little town called Laie, in the midst of which was an amusement hall for the young, and libraries and a plantation school. . . . I mention these things because in the little town of Laie you have a graphic presentation of the work of Mormonism in all the world. I hope in the future that they may have the same. . . . Industrial, temporal, social, intellectual and spiritual salvation of man, that is Mormonism. Let the world see what it means.[38]

David envisioned the same scene he described above being duplicated on a large scale, with the community of Laie as the Pacific's intellectual center. Ever after, David felt a great need to supply education to Latter-day Saints in the Pacific. David also promised that there would someday be a temple in New Zealand when the Saints were prepared to keep it busy.[39]

While David was in New Zealand, Emma Ray's letters from the previous four months finally caught up with him. As he read the letters, some of them several months old, large tears "dropped on the Maori mat covering the floor" of his bedroom. He read the letters over and over again, realizing they might be the only messages he would receive for at least another month.[40]

From New Zealand, David headed for Samoa, where he was lavished with the wonderful hospitality of the South Pacific. He recorded in his journal, "In kindness and thoughtful and attentive courtesy, Samoa is unexcelled!" David was treated royally by the Samoan Saints with feasts, which he called "a most sumptuous affair." One menu included "one hundred and five . . . pigs, 1 beef, . . . 25 chickens, 153 parcels of fish, . . . 4 cases of salmon," plus many more dessert and fruit dishes.[41]

Amidst such hospitality in Samoa, David had the opportunity to give many healing blessings. He administered to a young woman by the name of Puipui who was completely blind and "promised her that if she would serve the Lord devotedly that her sight would come

David O. McKay Monument at Sauniatu, Samoa. Dedicated May 31, 1922.
Erected in commemoration of the apostolic blessing of David O. McKay.

back. . . . The healing blessing came and she had a complete restoration of her sight."[42] In Sauniatu, Samoa, David also blessed several mothers with babies for their faith and love. As he was leaving, the Latter-day Saints formed two rows and the women sang a farewell song as David passed. The women began to cry and kiss David's hand, and as "their sobs interrupted the song, I began to feel the tears spring in my own eyes." As David and his party neared the end of the crowd, it began to rain. They raised their umbrellas, waved farewell, and began to wind their way down the road. David had no sooner turned a corner and crossed a bridge when the rain ceased, and the people, led by the band, came hurrying toward them, and as many as could crowded around again to shake his hand amidst sobs that were no longer controlled. As David mounted his horse again, he moved a quarter of a mile ahead but, feeling moved to return and pray with them one last time, he turned his horse around and made his way back to the people. When David told the Saints why he had returned, their sobs almost drowned his shaking voice as he again invoked God's blessing upon this wonderful group of Latter-day Saints.[43]

> He prayed for their health, prosperity, and for the righteousness of their leaders. He prayed for peace and harmony in the village, that above all, "Our Father, may they have clear understanding of the truth and make rapid progress in gaining a knowledge of Thee and Thy divine work. . . .

> Before the day was over the Saints of Sauniatu erected a lava-rock marker on the spot where Elder McKay gave the blessings. A year later they constructed a monument . . . in commemoration of the apostolic visit. Each year for many years thereafter a special service was held at Sauniatu on May 31, "McKay Day."[44]

Leaving Samoa on his way to Australia, David marked in his diary the twenty-fourth anniversary of telling Emma Ray that he loved her, having first told her on August 7, 1897. As he reminisced, he realized that the three possessions he prized most dearly were his family, friends, and Church membership. He wrote to Emma Ray:

> The great joy of my life is the fact that my Sweetheart of a quarter of a century ago has made this earth a heaven—much more so for me than I have made it for her. But, we are true to each other, we love each other, we have children of whom we may be justly proud, so why shouldn't we be happy! And happiness is only heaven![45]

He also told Emma Ray they would not be visiting South Africa, for to do so would require another six months. He was glad President Grant had eliminated that leg of the journey from his tour. David wrote that he hoped there would be no "unnecessary delays between now and the happy hour" when he would hold Emma Ray in his arms.[46]

David's letters had been brief while he was in the South Pacific, but one evening as he approached Australia's Darwin port, he found more time to write. David sat at "a writing desk in a nook that form[ed] part of the Music room" on the ship *Marella* and spent two hours communing with Emma Ray, telling her that even though it was by letter, when she was by his side, he was at peace with himself and with the world, and happy.[47]

Mentioning the pianist at a baby grand, he delighted to tell Emma Ray of an incident that had happened the evening before. David had listened to the man play for over an hour, when a lady came in and sang "Believe Me, If All Those Endearing Young Charms" as the man accompanied her. David told Emma Ray he had previously hoped the pianist would play that very song because it had special meaning for him and Emma Ray. As the evening progressed, David asked the piano player once again to play "Believe Me, If All Those Endearing Young Charms." However, the young woman did not come in to sing because she and her companions had a falling out. David thought, "Well, whether she joins them tonight or not, he will play 'Believe Me' as written by Tom Moore; and when he does, I shall repeat the words and say them with all my heart to you."[48]

As the clock stuck ten o'clock, David closed his letter by repeating for Emma Ray the words to the song he had heard the pianist in the lounge on the ship perform earlier.

> Believe me, if all those endearing young charms,
> Which I gaze on so fondly today,
> Were to fade by tomorrow, and fleet in my arms,
> Like fairy-gifts fading away,
> Thou wouldst still be adored, as this moment thou art,
> Let thy loveliness fade as it will;
> And around the dear ruin each thought of my heart
> Would entwine itself verdantly still.
>
> It is not while Beauty and Youth are thine own,
> And thy cheeks unprofaned by a tear,
> That the fervor and faith of a soul can be known,
> To which Time will but make thee more dear.
> No, the heart that has truly loved never forgets,
> But as truly loves on to the close;
> As the sunflower turns on her god when he sets
> The same look which she gave when he rose.[49]

TRAVELS IN ASIA AND THE NEAR EAST

After holding conferences in Australia, David and Hugh went from Java to Singapore and then on to Calcutta, India. It was in Calcutta on October 6 that David first experienced bedbugs. "When I entered the bathroom this morning, I noticed some little black things around my right ankle, which I thought to be cinders, but as I started to brush them off, they began hopping and crawling! I stripped and found my clothes alive [with them]. The things seemed smaller than fleas, and yet related to them." Hugh also had undressed and caught 120. That afternoon they reserved a room in a different hotel in hopes that they would "be free from bedfellows."[50]

From Calcutta, Elder McKay and his companions sailed on the SS *Egypt*. As on other vessels, while on board, David participated in church services, usually conducted by the captain. This captain, who seemed "to be a fine Christian Gentleman," invited David "to join with him and others in this hour of Sabbath observance." David wrote, "But as I listened to the dead letter, to vain repetitions, to spiritless prayers, interspersing readings, I could not refrain from saying in my mind, 'They have a form of Godliness, but deny the power thereof. They teach the doctrine and commandments of men. They draw near me with their lips, but their hearts are far from me.'" For ten months, David continued, "we have been traveling among 'heathen' nations among so-called 'Christian' people and 'Mormon' communities. We have seen the fruits of the religion of each group as exemplified in the daily lives of men and women." In his mind, as he compared Mormons with others, he decided that Latter-day Saints had "no reason to hang their heads." He declared that "the poverty, squalling, superstitions, and wickedness in India . . . is a direct result of false, adulterous worship." He also felt "that the so-called Christian Sects are about as far from the divine spiritual doctrine of the Redeemer" as they could be. He had found "much adultery among the various sects in India and elsewhere" and, on every point, "inconsistencies between doctrine and practice of the professors of the Christian Creeds." David had become more and more "persuaded that the simple, sublime gospel of Christ has likewise become prostituted" and that the Christian "churches no longer have the power to influence men and women to live better and pure lives." David knew that it was the Church of Jesus Christ that made "men and women honest, temperate, kind to one another and to all living things, virtuous, charitable, and desirous of working for the eradication of . . . suffering in the world and for the establishing on earth of the universal brotherhood of man."[51]

On deck, David exhibited these Christian principles by helping a mother who was

> exhausted from jostling her little boy. . . . David smiled at her, got up, and asked, . . . "May I hold the little boy for a while? You go rest."
>
> "Thank you, but no. He would not be good," came her reply.
>
> "May I try? You know I have a houseful at home. I might be able to get him to sleep, who knows?"
>
> "Okay, I'm nearly dead from trying—I'll be so glad to get off this hot ship."
>
> She handed the squirming tot to David. He beamed at the little lad . . . and began walking the deck . . . , humming a faint tune, patting, lulling [him to sleep]. . . . Against strong shoulders, the child fell into a slumber.[52]

David wished to have the same opportunity with his little ones who were at home.

On October 24, the boat moved "noiselessly and unquiveringly through the Suez Canal." Trenches and piles of sandbags were a "grim reminder" to him of World War I's destruction. After arriving in port safely, David and Hugh took a six-hour train ride to Cairo, where they visited the pyramids. Though the trip had been hot, burdensome, and tiring, David could still only say of his tour that it was "Wonderful! Wonderful! and still more Wonderful!!" While in the Orient, David had met globetrotters who made him feel that his few thousand miles of travel were really insignificant; but by the time David landed in Israel, he found fewer and fewer who had visited more lands and people than he.[53]

More than any other destination, David was thrilled to visit the Holy Land. It was on November 2 in the Holy City that David witnessed significant world events. Michael, their tour guide in Jerusalem, unexpectedly changed their plans to go to the Mount of Olives that morning. When David asked Michael the reason for this change and for his visible nervousness, Michael replied, "This is a day of mourning; today the Mohammedans and the Christians throughout Palestine unite in protesting against Lord Balfour's declaration that Palestine shall be set apart as a gathering place for the Jews."[54] David then witnessed the immediate response of the mixed population of Jerusalem to the Balfour Declaration. He wrote,

> I shall never forget that scene in that Jewish street of Jerusalem—frightened women and children on balconies or peering out of windows—men moving about in groups expecting something, or consulting in lowered tones in ominous groups! I seemed to see not many years hence, those doorways and stone steps covered with blood in the great struggle that is impending, of which the spirit of this day is but the rumbling as of a great volcano! I was glad to see the British "Tommies" around with helmets on their heads and bayonets fixed. . . . They had a subduing influence upon the rising spirit of what soon could be a frenzied mob.[55]

David's feelings were justified. Their guide, who had not accompanied them to that sector of Jerusalem, later reported to them that the very street David and his party had visited had been the scene of a bombing soon after they had left it. One man had been killed instantly, another two fatally injured, and several others critically wounded. "Later in the day, near the Damascus Gate, three Jews were killed—clubbed and stoned to death in . . . vengeance! Wild rumors were afloat, and the tension was high." Because of a five o'clock emergency curfew, by six that evening "the streets of Jerusalem were as deserted as a cemetery. Only the soldiers on guard and an occasional warning shot" proved that anyone inhabited the city. As David considered the events of the day, he felt overwhelmed as he realized that a prophecy from the Book of Mormon had been fulfilled that "the Gentiles shall be the means of restoring Israel to the Promised Land."[56] David then had the distinct impression that the time of the Gentiles was about to be fulfilled.[57]

Because of these feelings, David wrote a letter to Herbert Samuel, governor general of Palestine, as follows:

> I have been somewhat disappointed to find such a strong, and I say *bitter* sentiment against Lord Balfour's declaration to make Palestine a Jewish state.
>
> May I, a stranger to you, kindly ask you to give me briefly the present status of the Zionist movement, and whether you look upon the opposition from both Mohammedans and local Christians as a serious menace to the peaceful return of the Jews to their promised land.[58]

While in Israel, David and Hugh visited the Garden of Gethsemane but decided that, "as at every other sacred spot in Jerusalem, there are too many modern things . . . to realize at first that this is the garden to which Jesus and his disciples repaired so frequently for prayer." But he did find a huge rock and gratefully thought, "Thank heaven they can't change that." He thought that maybe it could have been on this rock that "the three disciples sat and 'watched.'" And he could, in his mind's eye, sufficiently conjure the scene of "the fatal night when Judas betrayed his Lord!"[59]

The next stop on David's tour was to be Armenia. Relief funds for Latter-day Saints in Armenia who had survived World War I and the Turks had been sent with J. Wilford Booth, former mission president of the Turkish Mission. David was to visit the country and report to the First Presidency about the condition of the Armenian Saints. David had received a cable that Booth was on his way but had no idea exactly where he was. In Jerusalem, David and Hugh had ascended the Mount of Olives, and, choosing a secluded spot . . . we knelt in humble supplication and thanksgiving, [and] prayed that we should be led by inspiration on our trip to the Armenian Mission.

Upon returning to the hotel, I felt strongly impressed that we should go by train and not by auto to Haifa [as they had planned]. When I said as much to President Cannon, he replied, "If you feel that way, we had better take the train."

They hoped the Lord and the train would lead them to Booth. If they did not meet him, their trip would be futile, since they could not speak the language nor find scattered Church members by themselves.[60]

On November 3, they left Jerusalem for Haifa, en route to Aleppo, Armenia. As they arrived at the door of their hotel in Haifa, another traveler reached it at the same time. The stranger tapped David on the shoulder and said, "Isn't this Brother McKay?" To his astonishment, David turned around and recognized Elder Booth, "the one man above all others whom we were most desirous of meeting. We had met, too, at the most opportune time and place." It could not have been more perfect planning. As Elder McKay and Elder Booth exchanged accounts of their experiences, "we had no doubt that our coming together was the result of divine interposition. . . . Indeed, had it not been for our having met at Haifa, our trip to the Armenian Mission would have been . . . a total failure. As it was, . . . we organized the Armenian Mission to take the place of the Turkish mission."[61]

EUROPE AND RETURN

Leaving the Middle East from Port Said, they headed for Naples on November 17 and arrived in Rome seven days later. From Rome, they visited Lausanne, Switzerland, where David was able to visit his missionary son, David Lawrence. After Lausanne, they traveled through the rest of the European Mission, ending up in the British Isles and leaving Liverpool on December 10, homeward bound on the SS *Cedric*.

Traveling more than 62,000 miles, David and Hugh had visited all the Latter-day Saint missions and schools except for the mission in South Africa. As David's train entered Union Depot in Salt Lake City, "Emma Ray and the whole family—sons and daughters, sisters, brothers, and cousins—along with friends," and all the General Authorities, including President Heber J. Grant, were there to welcome the two missionaries home.[62]

David was so glad to be back. As he sat in his home on 2071 Madison Avenue in Ogden on that December 24, he reminisced on all that had happened on his world tour. David had found that each culture possessed unique characteristics. In Japan he had found courtesy and consideration; in China, wonder and inspiration; and among the Polynesians, a depth of love he had not before experienced.[63] David was sure the Lord had been with him on every leg of the trip. He had been with him "when we stood beneath that tree in old China when we dedicated that land to the preaching of the gospel. . . . Again, the veil was thin between us and departed [Church leaders] in Haleakala. . . . I knew of His protecting care in the Tongan Islands . . . when the vessel was submerged by a mountainous wave." He had "felt His presence on several occasions, especially in that memorable farewell at Sauniatu." And he had felt "God's guiding hand when we met Joseph Wilford Booth at the very time and place . . . to make our mission to the Armenians successful."[64]

Elder McKay returned with a deeper sense of his apostolic calling to witness of Christ. Central to this testimony was an event that had taken place on May 10, 1921, in the harbor of Apia, Samoa. That night he had fallen asleep and then "beheld in vision something infinitely sublime." David remembered his experience:

> In the distance I beheld a beautiful white city. Though far away, yet I seemed to realize that trees with luscious fruit, shrubbery

with gorgeously-tinted leaves, and flowers in perfect bloom abounded everywhere. The clear sky above seemed to reflect these beautiful shades of color. I then saw a great concourse of people approaching the city. Each one wore a white flowing robe, and a white headdress. Instantly my attention seemed centered upon their Leader, and though I could see only the profile of His features and His body, I recognized Him at once as my Savior! The tint and radiance of His countenance were glorious to behold! There was a peace about Him which seemed sublime—it was divine!

The city, I understood, was His. It was the City Eternal; and the people following Him were to abide there in peace and eternal happiness.

But who were they?

As if the Savior read my thoughts, He answered by pointing to a semicircle that then appeared above them, and on which were written in gold the words:

"These Are They Who Have Overcome The World—Who Have Truly Been Born Again!"[65]

When David had awakened, dawn was breaking over the harbor.

After receiving this vision, David was dedicated more than ever to serve as an Apostle of the Lord Jesus Christ to the best of his abilities. He had seen the final experience of mortality and would ever after desire to be numbered among those who had truly been born again and overcome the world.

NOTES TO CHAPTER 6

1. David O. McKay, "Ideals for Courtship and Marriage," *Improvement Era,* February 1960, 110.

2. Notes written by David O. McKay, December 4, 1920, McKay Scrapbook, no. 126, MS 4640, LDS Church Archives, Salt Lake City.

3. Ibid.

4. W. Dee Halverson, *Stephen L Richards, 1879–1959* (Salt Lake City: Heritage, 1994), 127.

5. "Apostle M'Kay Begins World Circling Tour," *[Ogden] Standard-Examiner,* December 5, 1920.

6. David O. McKay, Notes, December 2, 1920, McKay Scrapbook, no. 188.

7. David O. McKay to Emma Ray McKay, 7 December 1920, McKay Papers, MS 668, box 1, folder 4, Manuscripts Division, University of Utah Marriott Library, Salt Lake City.

8. Francis M. Gibbons, *David O. McKay: Apostle to the World, Prophet of God* (Salt Lake City: Deseret Book, 1986), 103.

9. Quoted in Keith Terry, *David O. McKay: Prophet of Love* (Santa Barbara, CA: Butterfly, 1980), 65.

10. Gibbons, *Apostle to the World,* 104.

11. Quoted in Llewelyn R. McKay, *Home Memories of President David O. McKay* (Salt Lake City: Deseret Book, 1956), 51.

12. Ibid., 51, 45.

13. David O. McKay, Address, January 15, 1955, Apia, Samoa, McKay Scrapbook, no. 143.

14. David O. McKay to Emma Ray McKay, McKay Papers, MS 668, box 1, folder 4, Manuscripts Division, University of Utah Marriott Library.

15. Quoted in David O. McKay, *Cherished Experiences from the Writings of President David O. McKay,* comp. Clare Middlemiss (Salt Lake City: Deseret Book, 1955), 87.

16. Hugh J. Cannon; quoted in David O. McKay, *Cherished Experiences,* 87. Located in the heart of Beijing, the Forbidden City is the imperial palace complex of the Ming and Qing dynasties, who ruled China from 1420 to 1924. It includes 9,999 buildings and gardens.

17. David O. McKay; quoted in David Lawrence McKay, *My Father, David O. McKay* (Salt Lake City: Deseret Book, 1989), 122.

18. Hugh J. Cannon; quoted in David O. McKay, *Cherished Experiences,* 89–90.

19. Ibid., 50–52.

20. Virginia Budd; quoted in ibid., 55–56.

21. Emma Ray McKay to David L. McKay, February 20, 1921, McKay Papers, MS 668, box 2, folder 2, Manuscripts Division, University of Utah Marriott Library.

22. David Lawrence McKay, *My Father,* 124.

23. Gibbons, *Apostle to the World,* 114.

24. David O. McKay, To "Squire," July 18, 1921, McKay Scrapbook, no. 127.

25. Ibid.

26. David O. McKay, "Hui Tau," *Improvement Era,* July 1921, 769.

27. Ibid.; and World Tour Diary, April 24, 1921; quoted in David O. McKay, *Cherished Experiences,* 85.

28. David O. McKay in New Zealand, April 24, 1921, McKay Scrapbook, no. 127.

29. David O. McKay in New Zealand, April 25, 1921, McKay Scrapbook, no. 127.

30. Quoted in David O. McKay, *Cherished Experiences,* 85.

31. The Reorganized Church of Jesus Christ of Latter Day Saints is now called the Community of Christ, and much of the open hostility of earlier relations between that group and the Church has been abated.

32. World Tour Diary, April 24, 1921; cited in David O. McKay, *Cherished Experiences,* 86; see David O. McKay in New Zealand, April 24, 1921, McKay Scrapbook, no. 127.

33. David O. McKay in New Zealand, April 24, 1921, McKay Scrapbook, no. 127.

34. World Tour Diary, April 24, 1921; quoted in David O. McKay, *Cherished Experiences,* 86.

35. Testimony of W. Smith, February 1, 1935, McKay Scrapbook, no. 127.

36. Testimony of Sydney Christie, February 1, 1935, McKay Scrapbook, no. 127.

37. Testimony of President McKay during an Illustrated Lecture on his World Tour of the Missions, December 25, 1934, McKay Scrapbook, no. 107; "President McKay Received Manifestation of Gift of Interpretation of Tongues while Serving in Puketabu, Waikato, New Zealand," *Church News,* May 3, 1969.

38. Graham Doxey, A Report of the Sermons of Elder David O. McKay, in *Annual Conference of the New Zealand Mission of The Church of Jesus Christ of Latter-day Saints,* Huntley, New Zealand, notes of sermon attached to New Zealand Mission Manuscript History, April 23, 1921, LR6048, Church Archives.

39. President McKay in New Zealand, April 25, 1921, McKay Scrapbook, no. 127.

40. David O. McKay to Emma Ray Riggs McKay, McKay Papers, MS 668, box 1, folder 4, Manuscripts Division, University of Utah Marriott Library.

41. Llewelyn R. McKay, *Home Memories,* 77, 66.

42. President McKay later received a letter from Apostle Mark E. Petersen in 1962 telling him what had happened to this woman after David's blessing: "She married a man named Aumua and for a time was active in the Church. Then she fell into inactivity and after some years of inactivity, her blindness returned. Today she is over seventy years of age and still blind. However, she has returned to faithfulness in the Church and asked through her branch president if I would leave word with you that she prays for you daily and that she knows that you are a man of God. The woman lives in one of the outer villages so I was

not able to visit her, but her branch president brings this message." Mark E. Petersen to David O. McKay, April 9, 1962, McKay Scrapbook, no. 127.

43. David O. McKay to Emma Ray McKay, June 2, 1921, McKay Papers, box 1, folder 5, Church Archives.

44. R. Lanier Britsch, *Unto the Islands of the Sea: A History of the Latter-day Saints in the Pacific* (Salt Lake City: Deseret Book, 1986), 390–91.

45. David O. McKay to Emma Ray Riggs McKay, August 8, 1921, McKay Papers, MS 668, box 1, folder 5, Manuscripts Division, University of Utah Marriott Library.

46. David O. McKay to Emma Ray Riggs McKay, September 13, 1921, McKay Papers, MS 668, box 1, folder 6, Manuscripts Division, University of Utah Marriott Library.

47. David O. McKay to Emma Riggs Ray McKay, September 15, 1921, McKay Papers, MS 668 box 1, folder 6, Manuscripts Division, University of Utah Marriott Library.

48. Ibid.

49. Thomas Moore wrote the lyrics for "Believe Me, If All Those Endearing Young Charms," an Irish song, in 1808.

50. Quoted in Llewelyn R. McKay, *Home Memories,* 93.

51. David O. McKay to Alma Peterson, October 16, 1921, McKay Scrapbook, no. 127.

52. Terry, *Apostle of Love,* 83–84.

53. David O. McKay to Emma Ray Riggs McKay, 24 October 1921, McKay Papers, MS 668, box 1, folder 6, Manuscripts Division, University of Utah Marriott Library.

54. World Tour Diary; quoted in David O. McKay, *Cherished Experiences,* 123.

55. Quoted in David O. McKay, *Cherished Experiences,* 128–29.

56. Quoted in ibid., 129–30; see also 1 Nephi 13.

57. David O. McKay to John Q. Adams, July 30, 1923, McKay Scrapbook, no. 127.

58. David O. McKay to the Honorable Herbert Samuel, Governor General of Palestine in Jerusalem, November 18, 1921, McKay Scrapbook, no. 127.

59. Quoted in David O. McKay, *Cherished Experiences,* 120.

60. Ibid., 79–81.

61. Ibid., 82–83.

62. Terry, *Prophet of Love,* 88.

63. Doxey, A Report of the Sermons of Elder David O. McKay.

64. Quoted in David O. McKay, *Cherished Experiences,* 134–35.

65. World Tour Diary, May 10, 1921; quoted in David O. McKay, *Cherished Experiences,* 102; see also David Lawrence McKay, *My Father,* 132.

David and Emma Ray in the park at Zurich Lake, Switzerland, 1922, while he was presiding over the European Mission.

CHAPTER 7

If our hearts are truly anchored in a firm testimony of the divinity of the restored gospel of Jesus Christ, all difficulties will be overcome.

—David O. McKay[1]

When David arrived home from his world tour in December 1922, Emma Ray was delighted and felt her home life could now settle down to some kind of routine and normalcy. Just nine months later, in the summer of 1923, anything but normalcy was introduced into Emma Ray's life. She was "putting up fruit" when David walked into the kitchen, put his arm around her, "and told her that the First Presidency had called him to preside over the European Mission."[2] Suddenly, Emma Ray had no energy to finish bottling the fruit. The announcement sank in her stomach like an unripe apple. She wanted to say, "But you've only been home less than a year," but she held her tongue. Instead, she simply asked,

"When?"

"November."

"November?" she gasped. That gave them less than three months to get ready. At least, this time, David would not be going alone. She and the children would accompany him. Her mind began to race with the many things she would need to get ready for a mission presidency.

The months of September and October flew by as she prepared to accompany her husband to Europe. Later, Emma Ray would say that being a mission president's wife was the hardest experience she had ever gone through up to that point in her life—interesting, but the hardest.[3]

A few days before leaving, on November 3, 1922, David was set apart to preside over the European Mission. Emma Ray was also given a blessing. She was promised by President Heber J. Grant that she would know "when to speak and what to say, when to act and what to do," that she would never be left "barren [or] forsaken" during the mission experience. Knowing how hard accepting this call had been, President Grant reassured Emma Ray that the Lord was pleased with her devotion to her husband and family. Because of that devotion, she was promised that the Lord would "magnify you and make you strong wherein you may be weak." She was assured that if she would "depend on Him, [the Lord] will give [her] the necessary strength to discharge every responsibility" given her.[4]

David had been set apart right before Emma Ray, and his blessing was equally comforting. He was promised "vigor of body as well as of mind, with inspiration . . . to warn you of dangers seen and unseen" and enable him to avoid them. He was also blessed that he would have "great influence with the elders and gain their love and . . . confidence and . . . respect," that he would "have joy in writing for the *Millennial Star* and in delivering messages through the columns of that paper to the people." Through his writing, he was promised he would "have influence with those not of our Church, influential people, those that are honorable and . . . willing, through your friendship with them and their confidence that you shall gain, to defend the Latter-day Saints and to assist you in allaying the prejudice of the press and in stemming the opposition to the spread of the gospel . . . in that land."[5] The statements about the press were a precursor of what was to become David's most daunting task while serving as president of the European Mission. But as David and Emma Ray departed from Salt Lake City, both felt great solace from their blessings.

TO ENGLAND BY SEA

For the most part, the trip across the Atlantic was a delightful experience for the McKays. The ship, the SS *Montcalm,* was literally "a palace on water" with excellent meals. The McKay family found every possible comfort supplied: little Emma Rae, Ned, and Bobby enjoyed an onboard playroom; seventeen-year-old Lou Jean was ecstatic to find twelve fine young elders aboard on their way to the mission field; and Llewelyn had everyone playing Rook.

The group was jovial until the third day. That morning, almost all of the passengers succumbed to seasickness. The waters seemed smooth, but there was a "three quarter sea" that gave the boat a "peculiar rolling, quivering motion," which resulted in "seven elders and every McKay" getting "a peculiar, rolling, quivering stomach" to match. Even amidst the sickness, the circumstances in the McKay cabin at noon were so comical that David almost "overcame seasickness by laughing." Emma Ray and Bobby were lying on the lower berths, David on the upper one. For about two hours, David and Emma Ray "had practiced as a duet, keeping very good time and rhythm, and obeying in a very expressive manner the rules of crescendo and diminuendo until [Bobby] decided it should be a trio." Bobby's little face went pale, and just as he was vomiting, "Ned opened the door and said in his matter-of-fact way, 'I've just had a vomiting spell.' . . . Following upon his heels came daughter Emma Rae, with one hand on her limpy head and one on her stomach, crying, 'Oh-h, Mamma, I'm so sick! I don't want to go to England! I want to go home!'" Emma Ray felt so sick herself that she was able to give little sympathy to her son or her daughter. Meanwhile, Lou Jean was in her own room throwing up. Llewelyn, on the other hand, was on the deck, exclaiming that that was where everyone else should be too. He wasn't going to miss a meal over seasickness! However, Llewelyn's demeanor changed as he entered the room to retrieve some music. "With a dash of ease, he drew a suitcase from under the divan." Envying Llewelyn's ability to stoop over, David lifted up his head to watch. "Suddenly, [Llewelyn] sprang to his feet, gave a hasty gulp, grasped his stomach with both hands, looked up somewhat appealingly to [David] and said, 'Touch of seasickness!' The pale green streak that ran across his face showed . . . it was more than a 'touch.'" Llewelyn dropped the music and presently lost his "lunch, breakfast, dinner, lunch, and then breakfast" back to the first day of the trip. As soon as he composed himself, Llewelyn opened the door and called out to his friends, "Excuse me a minute, fellows. I am detained." David could not help laughing to the point of tears. As soon as he caught his breath he thought, "I have said that there is no cure for seasickness but the shade of a tree, but . . . a good hearty laugh comes next to it." The next day all of the McKays but Emma Ray were found in the dining hall. She had to wait two days until she felt well enough to eat.[6]

IN THE FACE OF OPPOSITION

Landing on Saturday, November 25, the McKays headed for Edge Lane in Liverpool to the mission home. After getting settled in their new home, the McKays went to Liverpool College to register Lou Jean (age seventeen) and Emma Rae (age ten) but found that Mormons were not accepted. Lou Jean was also refused at the Anglican school and at a Catholic school, where a Catholic nun had held both Lou Jean's and Emma Rae's hands for fifteen minutes while she told them that although the school did accept people of other denominations, "people just shudder when a Mormon is mentioned and we must consider our people."[7] Emma Ray reported that David thought the ignorance and bigotry they encountered were even worse than they had been a quarter of a century earlier.[8] He felt the English prejudice was "quite in keeping with the dense fog that hangs like a pall over Liverpool."[9] Eventually, Emma Ray was able to register Lou Jean at Queen Mary's public school and enroll the younger children at another school.[10]

As Lou Jean went to the school, she became acquainted with the other girls attending and became friendly with one of the leaders of the class, a girl named Jessie, and two other girls.

Emma Ray and youngest son, Robert R., at Durham House in Liverpool, England, while President McKay presided over the European Mission, 1922–1924.

Everything went fine for the first week because religion was never brought up. . . . In English class the next week the teacher was describing a man who [dressed in] a robe, tall hat, and beard. The teacher then commented, "Just like a Mormon."

Lou Jean was furious. . . . She bravely told the teacher that she was wrong. "Mormons do not dress that way."

The teacher replied, "Oh really? How do you know that?"

Lou Jean answered, "Because I'm a Mormon myself." There was then complete silence in the room. One girl on the back row blurted out, "Oh, how awful!" The teacher then came to her senses and said, "Millie, you shouldn't talk that way about something you know nothing about." . . .

Lou Jean went home and sat on the sofa and told her father and mother what had happened. She commented, "I dread going tomorrow. I don't know what will happen."

Her father told her, "You were brave to get up, and I'm proud of you."

The next day Lou Jean returned to school; class was conducted as usual, and nothing more was said. During a break that day, the three girls who had previously befriended Lou Jean came to her, and Jessie invited her to a picnic. At that point Lou Jean knew that she had passed the test. As the girls got to know Lou Jean better, they asked her questions about religion, and when the McKays left England the girls came to the ship to see Lou Jean off. In time one of them joined the Church and mentioned that it had a lot to do with Lou Jean standing up that day and saying, "I am a Mormon girl."[11]

Though Lou Jean had overcome opposition with her classmates, resistance followed David constantly while he served as European

Mission president. For instance, in Cardiff, South Wales, during a mission conference, David found opposition to the Church so intense that it was not possible to rent a hall suitable for the meetings.[12]

When David entered the mission office on the first day, he found that the previous mission president, Orson F. Whitney, as if to prepare him, had left a stack of newspaper clippings with headlines such as "Mormon Missionaries Assaulted by Students in Edinburgh, Scotland," "Latter-day Saints Wild Hyde Park Scene," "Assassins Who Carry Out Orders of Utah Saints," and "Women in Chains of Slavery." Included in the pile were Elder Whitney's editorials that had been printed in the eighty-year-old *Millennial Star,* the Church's official serial publication in Great Britain. Reading Elder Whitney's replies, David could see that his predecessor was an outstanding writer. He, on the other hand, had little writing experience under his belt. As he walked out of the mission office that first day, he knew that his writing would be as important as leading the five hundred missionaries in Europe at the time.[13]

From the beginning, David's approach to the press was simple. "Whenever he read . . . a vile newspaper or magazine article [concerning the Church], he sat down and personally wrote the editor a letter asking why the printing of such a story had been allowed. David's letters employed a tone that would both clarify the Mormon stand and show the falsity of the reporting." He tried to write patiently, "in kindness and gentility," as "he pleaded with editors to be fair and honest." His style eventually won over his readers.[14]

The first such letter David wrote was to *John Bull,* "one of the oldest and best weekly newspapers in Great Britain. His long letter appealed to English sportsmanship and love of fair play, and requested that only the truth be told about the Latter-day Saints. To the amazement of all [including David], the next issue of the newspaper contained a large headline which read 'A DANIEL COME TO JUDGMENT,' and under this caption appeared the complete text of President McKay's letter."[15] Before his arrival in Great Britain, newspapers had refused to print rebuttals written by missionaries or other Latter-day Saints. David's approach had found success.

One of the most virulent opponents of the Church was a woman by the name of Winifred Graham. At one point David wrote to the First Presidency, saying that Winifred Graham was "deluging England with the vilest slander that impure minds can imagine." David wished that "the Lord would take her in hand" because he disliked the idea of fighting a woman.[16] At no other time was David called upon to be so patient. He had to delve into the wellsprings of his soul to keep from railing against those who were reviling him, his children, or the Church.

Prejudice was so intense at the time that people sincerely believed Latter-day Saints to be "unchaste and lawless."[17] Even with such great opposition, David refused to become discouraged. In writing to one friend in Samoa, he confided:

> Difficulties may come, and clouds of discouragement may often hover over us; misunderstandings may sometimes spring up, and enemies of the truth may heap upon us scorn and ridicule; but if our hearts are truly anchored in a firm testimony of the divinity of the restored gospel of Jesus Christ, all difficulties will be overcome, clouds of discouragement will be dissipated by the sunshine of the Holy Spirit, misunderstandings will be supplanted by confidence and love, and enemies who scoff will be led to pray.[18]

Through David's efforts, the tide begin to turn; and when Emma Ray and David called on the U.S. consul, Horace Lee Washington, in January 1923, Washington remarked to David that "no member of your association has ever given the Dep't one moment's trouble or concern." Washington wished he "could say the same of other organizations."[19]

MOTIVATING THE MISSIONARIES

David's efforts also bore fruit with the missionaries of Europe. To stay in touch with missionaries and local Church members, David

McKinley Oswald and David O. McKay playing horseshoes, London, April 1924.

scheduled conferences almost every weekend. "In January [1923], he was in Holland. In February, he and [Emma Ray] went through Paris, Zurich, Basel, Dresden, and Berlin, holding meetings as they went. In March, they held meetings in Wales and Grimsby, near Hull." Just before Christmas of 1923, David recorded in his journal that he had held "a five-session conference in London—the last of fourteen successful conferences in as many weeks."[20]

President McKay put emphasis on retaining a close relationship with the district leaders and missionaries in order to keep them motivated and obedient. The *Millennial Star* proclaimed David "'a genius at leadership' when he reorganized the elders into groups" and appointed several "traveling elders to spread better teaching methods." During his two-year stay, he knew over five hundred missionaries in Europe by name.[21] One other situation requiring great patience was "deal[ing] with elders who forgot the purpose of their mission, especially when their indiscretions brought the Church into disrepute."[22] David tried to teach the missionaries to be strict in their obedience, even in small things. For instance, at one conference David "asked the missionaries to speak for only three minutes each. During the meeting several elders took longer than three minutes. David . . . didn't say anything and just let them go [on]. As he got up as the last speaker, he just announced the last song and sat down. He didn't give a talk [as they expected him to]. After the meeting he said to the missionaries, 'When I say to talk three minutes, I mean to talk three minutes.'"[23]

To improve the missionaries' effectiveness, David would assign specific topics in advance to be discussed at the area conferences for the missionaries. At one conference in the British Mission, he assigned talks on "Time Wasting Tendencies among Elders," "How Best to Use Auxiliary Associations as Missionary Factors," "Difficulties of Conference Presidents and How to Overcome Them," and "The Conference President as an Exemplar."[24]

MEMBERS AND MISSIONARY WORK

David knew that his and the missionaries' efforts would succeed only if local members adopted the idea of "Every member a missionary," a phrase he began using at the inception of his tenure as mission president. As early as February 5, 1923, in a letter to President Rudger Clawson of the Quorum of the Twelve, David noted that he was using "the local priesthood and the Church membership as a means of influencing nonmembers to investigate the truth. Our aim is to have every member a missionary, not in the sense of leaving their homes or work, but in the sense of opening the way for elders to get in the presence of men and women who honestly desire to know the truth."[25] As the European Mission president, David appealed to the Saints of Europe to pledge themselves "to bring one new member into the Church each year. He suggested that the new convert might be a relative, friend, working companion, or even a casual acquaintance or stranger. The result was a great increase in membership in the mission during 1923, exceeding that of previous years by a large margin."[26]

The year 1924 was equally successful and busy for David. During one twelve-day period, he "traveled 2,000 miles, held 15 meetings each ranging in length from 2 to 10 hours, met 228 Elders . . . , addressed [almost] 7,000 people . . . , spent 64 hours in meetings and 68 hours on trains." During this time, he was also writing weekly editorials for the *Millennial Star* and tackling huge stacks of correspondence whenever he went to the office.[27]

RETURNING TO A NEW HOME

As the busy year drew to a close, so did President McKay's tenure in Europe. On December 5, 1924, David, Emma Ray, and the children headed back to Utah, hoping that life would settle down. When the family returned, they "decided to purchase a large home in a residential neighborhood" in Salt Lake City, "a two-story red brick home with a basement and an attic, located at 1037 East South Temple Street."[28] On January 12, 1925, David resumed his responsibilities as a member of the Quorum of the Twelve after experiencing two years away from Church headquarters and seeing the lives of the Latter-day Saints in Europe firsthand.

David O. McKay home at 1037 East South Temple Street,
Salt Lake City, 1939–1960.

NOTES TO CHAPTER 7

1. David O. McKay to John Q. Adams, July 30, 1923, McKay Scrapbook, no. 127, MS 4640, LDS Church Archives, Salt Lake City.
2. David Lawrence McKay, *My Father, David O. McKay* (Salt Lake City: Deseret Book, 1989), 216.
3. Undated notebook in which Emma Ray Riggs McKay made pencil drafts of personal letters, this one to a Sister Sorensen; quoted in David Lawrence McKay, *My Father*, 159–60.
4. Blessing given to Emma Ray Riggs McKay prior to her departure to Europe to accompany her husband, who had been set apart to preside over the European Mission, McKay Scrapbook, no. 188.
5. Blessing given to David O. McKay, by President Heber J. Grant, setting him apart as president of the European Mission, November 3, 1922, McKay Scrapbook, no. 130.
6. David O. McKay to Thomas E. McKay, November 24, 1922, McKay Scrapbook, no. 130.
7. Emma Ray McKay to David Lawrence McKay, January 21, 1923, McKay Papers, MS 668, box 1, folder 7, Manuscripts Division, University of Utah Marriott Library; quoted in David Lawrence McKay, *My Father*, 160.
8. David Lawrence McKay, *My Father*, 160.
9. Quoted in Francis M. Gibbons, *David O. McKay: Apostle to the World, Prophet of God* (Salt Lake City: Deseret Book, 1986), 125.
10. David Lawrence McKay, *My Father*, 161.
11. Lou Jean McKay Blood, interview by Mary Jane Woodger, August 8, 1995, Provo, UT, McKay Research Project, College of Education, Brigham Young University, Provo, UT; transcript in possession of author; see also David Lawrence McKay, *My Father*, 161–62.
12. David Lawrence McKay, *My Father*, 162.
13. Gibbons, *Apostle to the World*, 124–25.
14. Keith Terry, *David O. McKay: Prophet of Love* (Santa Barbara, CA: Butterfly, 1980), 91.
15. Jeanette McKay Morrell, *Highlights in the Life of President David O. McKay* (Salt Lake City: Deseret Book, 1966), 74–75.
16. Gibbons, *Apostle to the World*, 124.
17. David Lawrence McKay, *My Father*, 162.
18. David O. McKay to John Q. Adams, July 30, 1923, McKay Scrapbook, no. 127.
19. Quoted in David Lawrence McKay, *My Father*, 162.
20. Ibid.

21. Terry, *Prophet of Love,* 93.
22. David Lawrence McKay, *My Father,* 162.
23. Gunn McKay, interview by Mary Jane Woodger, July 28, 1995, Provo, UT, McKay Research Project, College of Education, Brigham Young University; transcript in author's possession.
24. Gibbons, *Apostle to the World,* 126.
25. Ibid.
26. Morrell, *Highlights,* 75.
27. David Lawrence McKay, *My Father,* 169.
28. Gibbons, *Apostle to the World,* 188.

CHAPTER 8

THE IDEAL OF SUPPORT

The hardest battles of life are fought within the chambers of the soul. A victory on the inside of a man's heart is of far more worth in character building than a dozen conquests in the everyday battle of business, political, and social life.

—David O. McKay[1]

On December 11, 1931, Charles W. Nibley, a member of the First Presidency, passed away. Though President Grant announced to the Twelve who his new counselor would be on February 18, 1932, the vacancy would remain open for more than a year. After President Nibley's passing, President Grant had sent a letter to J. Reuben Clark Jr., then United States ambassador to Mexico, calling him to be the second counselor in the First Presidency. Clark had not answered the letter until after Christmas. Though he was willing to accept the calling, Clark was concerned about resigning from the ambassadorial post at that time and explained in detail the responsibilities he had assumed and the detriment that would occur to the government, the Church, and himself if he were to leave immediately. Clark suggested that President Grant might want to select someone else because of the delay he would cause. President Grant declined reissuing the call.[2] He waited until April 1933 to fill the position, sixteen months after he had invited J. Reuben Clark to become a counselor in the First Presidency.

NEW COUNSELORS TO PRESIDENT GRANT

Although President Grant's decision to select a counselor outside the Twelve and other General Authorities was unusual, it was not unprecedented.[3] Also unusual was Clark's lack of Church experience when compared to other current Apostles. Prior to his call, he had not even been ordained a high priest. Clark's inexperience put members of the Twelve in a somewhat awkward position, since there was a great disparity between the Church leadership experience of the current Twelve and the man who was to become second counselor in the First Presidency. As President Clark accepted the calling, he seemed to be aware of that disparity and the awkwardness it caused.[4] In his first conference address as a member of the First Presidency in April 1933, he disclosed, "If any of you have misgivings, I can only say that your misgivings can hardly be greater than my own."[5]

Elder David O. McKay accepted the calling of President Clark wholeheartedly, and his public reaction to Clark's inexperience seems to have been one of indifference. Without addressing the organizational changes, Elder McKay made this significant statement after the announcement of Clark's new call: "I think this conference will take its place among the most impressive conferences ever held in the Church, in its timely teaching, in its spiritual uplift, in the awakening of a desire to live better, and in its confirmation of the truth of the gospel of Jesus Christ."[6] Elder McKay was far more concerned with the proposed repeal of the Eighteenth Amendment (which prohibited alcohol) than he was with any controversy over callings.[7] In the next general conference, Elder McKay expressed his confidence in President Clark, referring to his early acquaintance with him at the University of Utah: "I admired him then. I considered him one of the choicest young men I had ever seen or had ever known. . . . I love him as a friend, and to be associated with him now . . . makes me feel very happy and thankful, but also very humble."[8]

Part of David's total acceptance of the choice of counselor had to do with his great respect for the prophet. President Grant had been the prophet who sent David on his world tour, placed him in the presidency of the European Mission, and gave David the confidence to fulfill his assignments. President Grant would soon extend to Elder McKay another important calling.

When the first counselor in the First Presidency, Anthony W. Ivins, passed away peacefully in his sleep on September 23, 1934, President Grant asked Elder McKay to fill the vacancy by becoming second counselor. When President Grant told J. Reuben Clark of his choice, President Clark replied, "I am very glad; he is the man that I had thought of and would like."[9] At the time, David was sixty-one years old and the fourth senior member of the Quorum of the Twelve. He was sustained as a member of the First Presidency on October 6, 1934. In David's first conference address as second counselor in the First Presidency, given the following day, he shared his humble feelings of inadequacy in his new calling:

> If it were possible, I would have you interpret my feelings this morning by looking into the depths of my soul, and thus save me the seeming impossibility of describing them to you. Needless to say, I am overwhelmed. During the past few days I have had difficulty in keeping my thoughts and feelings under control. The light heart, the buoyancy of spirit that should accompany the high appointment that has come to me has been somewhat counter-balanced by a heaviness incident to the realization of the great responsibility that comes with the call to the First Presidency. . . . I appreciate the trust you, my brethren and sisters, have manifested in me. . . . I agree with him who says that to be trusted is a greater compliment than to be loved. Love is the sweetest thing in the world, but to be trusted throws upon him who receives that trust an obligation that he must not fail to discharge. And so I pledge you here, my fellow workers in the First Presidency, you, my brethren of the priesthood, in whose company I have spent so many happy hours in priesthood and auxiliary work, I pledge you, my brethren and sisters, to give my best in the service of God.[10]

David O. McKay and J. Reuben Clark then began a service in the First Presidency that would last nearly twenty-seven years, until J. Reuben Clark's death in 1961, serving together longer than any other two First Presidency members in Latter-day Saint history.

COUNSELORS IN CONTRAST

Although they shared similarities in upbringing and interests, these two counselors' personalities, philosophies, and Church backgrounds were very different.[11] No one came into the First Presidency with a stronger background in Church administration than did President McKay, whereas, with his government assignments, President Clark was new to Church administration procedures. President McKay was an unflappable optimist who was always ready to believe that things would improve and that human nature basically wanted good. President Clark, on the other hand, was seen as being more cautious. President McKay was the "gentle poet-philosopher"; President Clark was the "determined administrator-legalist."[12] President McKay's professional background was with inexperienced young people. President Clark's colleagues had included corporate lawyers, business executives, and government employees.[13] President McKay was flexible in changing previous decisions; President Clark arrived at conclusions slowly and maintained them with little variance.[14]

Especially in the area of education, President Clark and President McKay may have agreed to disagree. President McKay "believed that if people had good information they would make good choices." He had always viewed "education as a form of spiritual and temporal salvation. He had [an appreciation] for the liberal educational tradition."[15] In contrast, President Clark seemed to be wary of highly educated people.[16] It was paradoxical that J. Reuben Clark "was a living exemplary of higher education but preferred limited education in Church colleges."[17]

Some overexaggerated the differences between the two leaders during their years together and began to call people either a "Clark man" or a "McKay man,"[18] but David and J. Reuben seemed to get along in spite of their differences. They became a pair of counselors who counterbalanced each other's philosophies in the First Presidency,[19] and they were able to iron things out as they served.[20] They had a great deal of admiration and respect for each another and "were great friends and complemented each other tremendously"; even though they had differing opinions, they were not enemies. "They spoke highly of each other, and they worked well together."[21] Whatever their differences were, the First Presidency was united. The fact that these two very different men with very different ideas were able to come to a consensus on policy is an important indicator of the solidarity of the First Presidency of the Church.

THE ADMINISTRATION MOVES FORWARD

Right after David's call to the First Presidency, J. Reuben Clark was hired by the Mexican Eagle Oil Company to direct negotiations in Mexico. He was also elected to the Foreign Bondholders' Protective Council, the Commission of Experts on the Codification of International Law of the Pan-American Union, and the American Journal of International Law board of editors. President Clark was also actively involved in Republican candidate Alfred M. Landon's campaign for president in 1936. President Grant had approved of and encouraged each of these obligations. David often, "at the Prophet's request, stepped into the breach to give administrative direction."[22]

For his secular labors President Clark "received what would be today's [1996] equivalent of a five-million-dollar settlement." President Clark had appreciated the way his fellow counselor had carried the workload of the First Presidency while he was absent, and he "gave a cash gift to David . . . to help him get out of debt. . . . That gift from [President] Clark provided the first financial stability that [David] had ever had in his life."[23]

Another fringe benefit David received as a member of the First Presidency was that his travels were cut dramatically, leaving him more time to be home with Emma Ray and his family. However, other duties took up vast amounts of time. David spent entire days in consultations, and "as the marriage season approached, he was inundated with requests to perform temple marriages."[24] In the sealing ceremonies David gave three bits of advice: never to "say or do anything which might embarrass the other" spouse; never to "go to sleep in anger"; and, finally, "that marriage is a never-ending courtship, an everlasting courtship where kindness and love and appreciation need to be constantly cultivated and used."[25]

He also participated in training classes held in the "Mission Home" (precursor to the Missionary Training Center) on State Street in Salt Lake City, where he gave counsel to young missionaries preparing to leave for the field. One of the missionaries who came under David's tutelage was a young man by the name of Gordon B. Hinckley. As Elder Hinckley was preparing to go on his mission to Great Britain, President McKay, as one of the instructors, asked each new elder to write a paper. Elder Hinckley wrote his paper and handed it in. A few days later, President McKay called Elder Hinckley to his office to compliment him on the paper. Two years later, when Elder Hinckley returned from his mission, it was David O. McKay who invited him "to come and begin the public relations work of the Church."[26] David also met with mission presidents in special seminars. Among other things, he always told the missionaries to teach by the Spirit and to preach the Book of Mormon.[27]

TRIALS AT HOME AND ABROAD

More than any other subject during this time, the Great Depression weighed heavily on everyone's mind. It was under David's leadership that the welfare program of the Church, then known as the Church Security Plan, emerged. In the mid-1930s, as the welfare program began to take shape, David told the General Authorities and the leading brethren that "the organization necessary to accomplish the goal" would be the priesthood, "already in place." He reminded Church leaders at the time that the priesthood "had been established by divine revelation and that all that was necessary for success was 'to turn on the power and to start the wheels in motion.'"[28] For months,

David prepared an outline of the welfare program before it was introduced in the October 1936 general conference. Reminding the congregation that welfare was not just about temporal needs, he explained,

> It is something to supply clothing to the scantily clad, to furnish ample food to those whose table is thinly spread, to give activity to those who are fighting desperately the despair that comes from enforced idleness, but after all is said and done, the greatest blessings that will accrue from the Church Security Plan are spiritual. Outwardly, every act seems to be directed toward the physical: remaking of dresses and suits of clothes, canning fruits and vegetables, storing foodstuffs . . . , but permeating all these acts, inspiring and sanctifying them, is the element of spirituality.[29]

Only a year and a half later, David became seriously ill for the first time in his life. During general conference of April 1938, while sitting on the stand, he was struck with such intense pain that it became difficult for him to draw a breath. As he shifted in his chair, trying to find a position that would ease the agony, Emma Ray noticed the look on her husband's face and realized that he was in pain. Quietly, she left her seat and phoned the family physician. During a break in the meetings, David was taken to the hospital, where the doctor identified his pain as a kidney infection and ordered hospitalization.[30]

A year later, David was ill again. On December 1, 1939, he underwent surgery to repair a double hernia. As he was trying to recover from that, a pulmonary embolism brought about severe congestion in his lungs. His hospital stay went on for six weeks, through both Christmas and New Year's Day.[31] During the rest of the winter of 1940, David spent a month in California and another month in Arizona trying to recover, returning to Salt Lake just before April conference.[32]

David O. McKay, 1942.

Emma Ray Riggs McKay.

In the last few months of 1940 David began to regain some of his original health and vigor. Part of that health and vigor, David believed, was restored as he would visit Huntsville, Utah. Often he would gather up his sons, Lawrence, Llewelyn, and Robert, and take a work party up to the Dry Hollow Farm. There David, along with his boys, would repair fences, clear dead trees, dredge clogged ditches, and attend to the horses. But illness continued to plague him as, in August 1941, he began to suffer from Ménière's disease (hemorrhaging in the canals of the inner ear) that made him constantly dizzy.[33]

While President McKay struggled with ill health, another worry began to manifest itself, not just for him, but for the world, as Hitler's regime lifted its vicious head. England and France became more embroiled in war fever, and it became necessary to evacuate all American Latter-day Saint missionaries from Europe. As a member of the First Presidency, David was involved in the evacuation of 697 missionaries in August 1939. Also, "pressures exerted by the war in Europe erupted in South America when Argentina suddenly balked at issuing visas to Mormon missionaries."[34] Along with the rest of America, David was shocked on December 7, 1941, when Pearl Harbor was bombed. Six days after that "date which will live in infamy," the First Presidency signed a message encouraging Latter-day Saint servicemen to serve in the armed forces of their countries.[35]

During the war, President McKay became a voice of comfort and reason, and in 1940, the First Presidency gave servicemen this incredible promise:

> To our young men who go into the service, no matter whom they serve or where, we say, live clean, keep the commandments of the Lord, pray to Him constantly to preserve you in truth and righteousness, live as you pray. . . . Then, when the conflict is over and you return to your homes, having lived the righteous life, how great will be your happiness—whether you be of the victors or of the vanquished—that you have lived as the Lord

commanded. You will return so disciplined in righteousness that thereafter all Satan's wiles and stratagems will leave you untouched.[36]

A NEW ERA IN CHURCH ADMINISTRATION AND THE WORLD

During the closing months of World War II, after Germany had surrendered and before Japan's defeat, on May 14, 1945, President Heber J. Grant passed away. When President George Albert Smith was sustained as the prophet on May 21, 1945, he also chose President McKay and President Clark to serve as his counselors.

With the war over, the servicemen coming home, and a new First Presidency in place, the Church turned to a more positive event: the centennial celebration of the pioneers entering the Salt Lake Valley in 1847. David was named chairman of the Utah Centennial Commission. At the April 1946 general conference, David delivered an address that outlined his plans for the Centennial Commission. Excitedly he announced: "Besides the best that home talent can produce, it is proposed to bring to the state outstanding educational and entertainment features which normally could not be presented in communities of our state—symphony orchestras, stars of stage and screen, Metropolitan Opera singers, sports events of the type our state normally could not finance."[37]

David was thrilled with what took place that July, among which was the dedication of This Is the Place Monument, a reenactment of the trek from Nauvoo to Salt Lake City commemorating the original wagon train of 1847, and a new and highly successful musical called *Promised Valley.* During its run, "two performances had been rained out, and the play was scheduled to close after two weeks on a Saturday night. The pressure to extend the performance raised the question of holding a final performance on Sunday night." Ultimately, "after a day's deliberation, [President McKay] authorized . . . a final performance on Sunday at 8:30 P.M., after sacrament meetings in the valley wards would be over."[38] No sooner was the announcement made than critical calls began to flood in to the directing manager of the play, Lorin F. Wheelwright. When one high-ranking Church official questioned Wheelwright about breaking the Sabbath and running the show, Wheelwright responded by thanking the caller and then observed, "You flatter me to think that I possess the authority to make this decision alone. The fact is, it was made by our chairman, David O. McKay. His office is not far from yours. I suggest that you discuss the decision with him." When David became aware of the criticism, he simply replied, "I have given this matter full consideration, and I am willing to face my Maker on this decision."[39] Such actions only endeared David to the public more.

As the 1950s dawned, David found himself becoming better known among Latter-day Saints and non–Latter-day Saints alike. It was becoming almost impossible for him to walk down the streets of Salt Lake City and not be mauled by well-wishers. For instance, on July 19, 1950, David tried to "buy a gift for Emma Ray at a store only a block from his office. 'I was forty-five minutes getting back to the office . . . [because] so many people stopped me on the street to ask questions, to extend greetings.'" It became so difficult for him to navigate the city streets that he almost decided to quit.[40] One reason for this problem was that he was a good listener; as Francis Gibbons states:

> One talking with David O. McKay never felt he was intruding or that the Apostle would rather be somewhere else or talking with another person, or, perhaps even worse, that he was a mere blip in the great man's consciousness, flitting there among matters and personalities of more monumental importance. . . . [David] would never interrupt his conversation with someone to nod or wave to another, or to shake hands with a passerby, or to pardon himself while he spoke just a word to someone else who had approached. Instead he focused only on the person with whom he was speaking.[41]

For David it was paradoxical that, as his influence widened as a member of the First Presidency, "the scope of his private life" narrowed. David's "activities in Salt Lake City" began to consist only of "his work at Church headquarters, his private life at home, his public appearances, and his social contacts with family and a close circle of friends." His private life became even more restricted in 1951 when President George Albert Smith passed away.[42]

NOTES TO CHAPTER 8

1. David O. McKay, "Sylvester Q. Cannon," *Improvement Era,* August 1943, 465.
2. D. Michael Quinn, *J. Reuben Clark: The Church Years* (Provo, UT: Brigham Young University Press, 1983), 37–41.
3. Francis M. Gibbons, *David O. McKay: Apostle to the World, Prophet of God* (Salt Lake City: Deseret Book, 1986), 147.
4. Ibid., 148–49.
5. Conference Report, April 1933, 102.
6. Ibid., 89–90; Gibbons, *Apostle to the World,* 150.
7. Gibbons, *Apostle to the World,* 150.
8. Conference Report, October 1934, 90.
9. Heber J. Grant Journal, 1934; quoted in Quinn, *J. Reuben Clark,* 113.
10. Conference Report, October 7, 1934, 90.
11. Quinn, *J. Reuben Clark,* 114.
12. Marion G. Romney, interview by D. Michael Quinn, 1977; cited in Quinn, *J. Reuben Clark,* 115.
13. Quinn, *J. Reuben Clark,* 47; and D. Michael Quinn, interview by Mary Jane Woodger, February 20, 1996, Provo, UT, McKay Research Project, College of Education, Brigham Young University, Provo, UT; transcript in author's possession.
14. Quinn, *J. Reuben Clark,* 46; Quinn interview.
15. Lavina Fielding Anderson, interview by Mary Jane Woodger, October 1995, Provo, UT, McKay Research Project; transcript in author's possession.
16. See Quinn, *J. Reuben Clark,* 164.
17. Ibid., 161.
18. Quinn interview.
19. Romney interview; cited in Quinn, *J. Reuben Clark,* 114.
20. J. Reuben Clark, Office Diary, 1944; Spencer W. Kimball, Journal, 1960; both cited in Quinn, *J. Reuben Clark,* 119.

21. Glen L. Rudd, interview by Mary Jane Woodger, February 8, 1996, Salt Lake City, McKay Research Project; transcript in author's possession.

22. Gibbons, *Apostle to the World,* 159–60.

23. Quinn interview.

24. Gibbons, *Apostle to the World,* 163.

25. Richard L. McKay, David O. McKay Honor Day Celebration at Ogden LDS Tabernacle, September 29, 1968, McKay Scrapbook, no. 99, MS 4640, LDS Church Archives, Salt Lake City.

26. Gordon B. Hinckley, interview for David O. McKay School of Education, October 7, 1996, Salt Lake City; video in author's possession.

27. Robert L. Simpson, interview by Mary Jane Woodger, December 30, 1996, St. George, UT, McKay Research Project; transcript in author's possession.

28. Gibbons, *Apostle to the World,* 160, 162.

29. Conference Report, October 1936, 103.

30. Gibbons, *Apostle to the World,* 179.

31. Ibid., 190.

32. David Lawrence McKay, *My Father, David O. McKay* (Salt Lake City: Deseret Book, 1989), 207.

33. Emma Ray Riggs McKay to Lou Jean McKay, August 23, 1941; cited in David Lawrence McKay, *My Father,* 209.

34. Gibbons, *Apostle to the World,* 264, 184–85, 204–205.

35. Ibid., 204–5; "Message to Men in Service," 1940, *Messages of the First Presidency of The Church of Jesus Christ of Latter-day Saints,* ed. James R. Clark (Salt Lake City: Bookcraft, 1965), 6:156–63.

36. Messages of the First Presidency, "Message to Men in Service," 6:161.

37. Jeanette McKay Morrell, *Highlights in the Life of David O. McKay* (Salt Lake City: Deseret Book, 1966), 84.

38. David Lawrence McKay, *My Father,* 215.

39. Ibid.; Lorin F. Wheelwright, "Adventures of the Spirit: From Personal Experiences with President David O. McKay," *The Instructor,* January 1963, center spread.

40. Quoted in Gibbons, *Apostle to the World,* 263.

41. Ibid., 194–95.

42. Ibid., 263–64.

CHAPTER 9

PROPHET, SEER, AND REVELATOR

No one can preside over this Church without first being in tune with the head of the Church, our Lord and Savior, Jesus Christ. He is our head. This is His Church. Without His divine guidance and constant inspiration, we cannot succeed. With His guidance, with His inspiration, we cannot fail.

—*David O. McKay*[1]

By the October 1950 general conference, President McKay had served for five years as President George Albert Smith's second counselor. During that conference, President Smith had seemed to be in relatively good health, but by February, his condition had worsened considerably. President McKay took him to the hospital for a checkup because President Smith had been running a temperature, but the doctors could not pinpoint what was wrong with the prophet.[2]

David and Emma Ray began a trip to California for a rest in March of the next year. They got as far as St. George when a "distinct impression" came to David that he needed to return to Salt Lake City. Having learned long ago to follow such impressions, David turned the car around and went home. A few days later, on March 21, 1951, President Smith suffered a small stroke that affected his entire right side and rendered his speech "pretty thick." On March 22, David and

Emma Ray found that President Smith "seemed to brighten up during [their] visit" and that "his mind seemed as clear as a bell." David felt sure that the prophet would recover. But just a few days later, when David visited on April 2, President Smith did not recognize his counselor, and David was "shocked" at the prophet's diminished appearance.[3]

The next night, on April 3, David entered President Smith's room, and this time President Smith recognized him, smiled at him, and, as David left, simply said, "Good night." David knew that would be President Smith's last words to him.[4] A deep heaviness settled on him as he wrote in his journal that night and realized the "possibility that the end was not far off." To David "it came as quite a shock" as he finally began to feel the full impact of what President Smith's passing would mean. On April 4, shortly before noon, David administered to President Smith. Unable to suppress his emotions, he broke down several times during the blessing. That evening he stood at President Smith's side while the prophet quietly passed away and felt the heavy responsibility of leading the Church shift to his own shoulders.[5]

A PROPHET CALLED OF GOD

The timing of President Smith's passing was remarkable, since general conference began only two days later. During the first session, David eulogized the deceased prophet by reading various tributes received from those around the nation.[6] David then repeated what he had said so many times before at other funerals:

> [Funeral services are] to bring solace and comfort to sorrowing hearts. This is done by three principal means.

> First, in contemplation of the fact that he, whose departure strains the heart strings, has lived a useful, noble life. What consolation that will bring to any bereaved father, mother, or child. Second, comfort in the consciousness that loved ones were true and loyal as his children and kinsfolk, and that particularly

during illness they did everything humanly possible to administer to his needs, to alleviate his pain, and to give him comfort. And third, comfort in the assurance of the immortality of the human soul; the assurance that their father is just away.[7]

Though saying good-bye to President Smith during the opening session was difficult, it was not the hardest part of that April general conference; rather, it was when David stood in the solemn assembly and was sustained by Church members as prophet, seer, and revelator. Never before had a leader of the Latter-day Saints served so long as an Apostle—more than forty-five years. Standing at the pulpit, David reassured Church members that it would not be he that would guide the Church during his administration.

No one can preside over this Church without first being in tune with the head of the Church, our Lord and Savior, Jesus Christ. He is our head. This is His Church. Without His divine guidance and constant inspiration, we cannot succeed. With His guidance, with His inspiration, we cannot fail. Next to that as a sustaining potent power, comes the confidence, faith, prayers, and united support of the Church. I pledge to you that I shall do my best so to live as to merit the companionship of the Holy Spirit, and pray here in your presence that my counselors and I may indeed be "partakers of the divine spirit."[8]

David's remarks were without doubt intended to address the rippling effect that he had both anticipated and observed in the congregation when his counselors had been presented for the sustaining vote of the Church. At that time, he had reminded the Saints that when a president was chosen and sustained, it was the practice of the Church to let the president name his counselors:

Anticipating that the Council of the Twelve would grant to me that same privilege, I thoughtfully and prayerfully considered what two men would be most helpful and most contributive to the advancement of the Church. The impression came, I am sure, directly from Him whose Church this is, and who presides over it, that the two counselors whom you have this day approved should be the other members of the Quorum of the First Presidency.[9]

The announcement that David's counselors in the First Presidency would be Stephen L Richards as first counselor and J. Reuben Clark as second counselor had brought an audible gasp from the congregation as the Saints realized that J. Reuben Clark, who had served up to this point as first counselor, was now to become second counselor.

David explained that "one guiding principle in this choice would be to follow the seniority in the Council" of the Twelve, though "not as an established policy." He reassured the congregation that there had not "been any rift between" himself and President Clark and that this was not to be considered a "demotion" of any kind. David assured those present that "President Clark is a wonderful servant" of the Lord and "had demonstrated . . . his ability" that very day in conducting the sustaining of Church leaders in solemn assembly.[10] Then David said of his two counselors: "They are two great men. I love them both, and say God bless them, and give you the assurance that there will be harmony and love and confidence in the Quorum of the First Presidency as you have sustained them today."[11] J. Reuben Clark then stood and publicly accepted the position as second counselor, eloquently proclaiming, "In the service of the Lord, it is not where you serve but how."[12] If President Clark felt the surprised public perception that his becoming second counselor was a demotion, he muted any such reaction. He also eased the transition by scrupulously declining to allow President Richards to defer to him.[13]

Though President McKay had elaborated on his reasoning for putting Stephen L Richards in as first counselor, for those who knew of David and Stephen L's relationship, no elaboration was necessary.

President Richards was David's closest friend.[14] There had been a special bond between the two men since Richards's call to the Twelve in 1917. The two men's views were identical in many areas.[15] Just like Jonathan and King David of old, "the soul of [Stephen] was knit with the soul of David, and [Stephen] loved him as his own soul" (1 Sam. 18:1). When President McKay was told of Stephen's death on May 19, 1959, he wept and reminisced, "He was as dear to me as a brother. A true and loyal friend. A wise counselor with one of the greatest minds in the Church. Oh! how I shall miss him."[16] Once when David was speaking about the martyrdom of Joseph Smith, he mentioned the selfless offer of Willard Richards, the father of Stephen L, to die in the Prophet's place. It seemed to David that Stephen had shown him the same sort of kinship.[17]

On April 12, David met for the first time as prophet, seer, and revelator with the newly sustained First Presidency and Quorum of the Twelve. Standing before them, he uttered what he had felt in his heart since the passing of President George Albert Smith:

> You see weaknesses in me whom you have chosen as president. There are things which displease you. Will you please be free to come to me, just as a brother, and tell me of those things when they come. I want you to feel that you can come into my presence in the office, on the street, or wherever it is, and say just whatever is in your heart. That door is always open to members of this council and the General Authorities. If there is a meeting [going on], if [your business] is essential, then, whatever you have in your mind, you interrupt [the meeting], because there is nothing that can have more importance than what you brethren would like to have. If you wish to wait a few minutes, if we have a meeting, that is all right, but you need not wait. Please come there and feel that our relationship—I am speaking of the presidency as well—our close relationship is the most sacred in all the world, and your matters are of most importance.[18]

PORTRAIT OF A PROPHET

Though seventy-seven years old, an age when most men had retired, David's hazel-brown eyes were still clear and intense as he conducted Church business. His hair was white. His "voice was still firm, but far from overbearing or pressing." His rate of speaking slowed and his volume decreased, giving him a more dignified, gentle tone of delivery, "although the content was . . . just as potent as that of [his] predecessors" and as it had been during his earlier apostolic ministry.[19] His personal grooming was impeccable. Some thought of him as being "a little bit of a showman" in his appearance. "None of the other General Authorities would dress like he did in a white suit or a flowered shirt," even when visiting the Pacific. Such dress was not typical of David either, but he adopted it occasionally.[20] Soon after David became president of the Church, single-breasted suit coats became fashionable, replacing the more traditional double-breasted style. This was one fashion trend that David did not follow. Double-breasted jackets became his trademark style until later in his presidency, when he lost weight and his old suits no longer fit.[21] A well-dressed, six-foot-one-inch-tall man "weighing two hundred well-proportioned pounds," David cut "an imposing figure."[22]

The media began to report that no other LDS president had looked more like what they imagined a prophet to look like than David O. McKay.[23] David's appearance and warm, outgoing personality were what everyone expected from a prophet of God.[24] *Life* magazine, for example, reported that he was "a saintly seventy-seven-year-old Apostle,"[25] and *Newsweek* commented that "Jack Mormons see President McKay as a very different administrator. They expect that, vigorous as he is at seventy-seven, he will keep the church clear of politics, gradually withdraw it from the business field, and concentrate on converts."[26]

As a prophet, President McKay's personality resulted in some interesting leadership techniques. He apparently found it difficult to tell a General Authority directly when he had done something inappropriate. For instance, when one of the Brethren took twenty

Newly called President of The Church of Jesus Christ of Latter-day Saints, April 1951. Official Church photograph.

Always learning, David O. McKay reads in his office, 1963.

minutes during general conference when he was supposed to speak only for ten, taking ten minutes from David's allotted time, that General Authority spoke only four more times in the next ten years, though most Brethren spoke twice a year.[27] At the same time, President McKay's leadership style often lent itself to helping those in difficult circumstances. If one of the General Authorities was giving a presentation that was not going well or was headed in the wrong direction, David would try to save the presenter from embarrassment by suggesting, "Can we postpone this until our next meeting?" Before then, David "would either get with that person, or get someone to get with him and help him to do what needed to be done to make it acceptable and presentable." By so doing, David saved the self-esteem of those involved. His uncanny knack of saying a humorous statement at the right time and place consistently relieved tense moments. Even as the prophet, David continued to be a good listener. When he entered a room, no one needed to be told that they were in the presence of a great man; he radiated the fact.[28] He was "not a dandy, or a dude, or an aristocrat, but a true gentleman," and his common practice of standing for anyone who entered a room showed his respect for all human beings. But he was not stuffy or reserved. "He laughed a lot; he was warm and generous."[29]

TO HUNTSVILLE AND BACK

Though David's title and position in the Church changed in 1951, much of his daily schedule did not. David still got up as early as 4:00 A.M. and was in his office by 5:30.[30] He knew that his early morning schedule was something of a rarity. Once, his doctor offered to set an early morning appointment so that David could get to his own office on time. The doctor was expecting that would mean about eight or nine o'clock in the morning. David "said that was a fine idea and he would see him at ten minutes after four!"[31] David had always risen early, learning the habit on the farm from his father; farming was always in his blood. There were times, even as the prophet, when he would get up early, put in a few hours on the farm

David O. McKay in Huntsville, October 12, 1957.

in Huntsville, and still arrive at his office by 8:00 A.M., where he would work a full day. "For him, even an hour on the farm was worth the trouble of the drive" because he felt rejuvenated.[32] Many thought this practice worked, for during the first decade of his presidency he was in fine health and "would never take any medications, not even an aspirin."[33]

On most days when he did not go to Huntsville, his procedure was to drive to the office early in the morning, dictate letters, drive home to 1037 East South Temple for a meal with Emma Ray, and then return to the office.[34] At Church headquarters, David "sat in a plain leather swivel chair [at] an oblong glass-covered table" where he took care of various business, pausing for lunch—"his preference was a beef-steak, rare." After lunch he would take a brief nap and then dispatch other responsibilities until early in the evening, when he would go home and dine with Emma Ray. "The range of business that passed through his hands was enormous—from the selection and assignment of Church personnel to the location of a federal office building in Salt Lake City; from decisions in Church investments to religious education; from the affairs of the Church-owned Beneficial Life Insurance Company to those of the Church-operated Hotel Utah; from bills before the Utah legislature to his speech at the Church conference."[35] Utah's population was 70 percent Latter-day Saint, so the Church's position carried a great deal of weight. David was not "a heavy-handed theocrat," but occasionally he would "flex the Church's muscle on such issues as opposition to liberal liquor statutes or in support of . . . right-to-work laws. A [proposal] to sell whiskey by the drink was easily defeated" after the LDS prophet spoke against it.[36]

But David was not a man to misuse his public influence, as he demonstrated a number of times in relation to his tendency to exceed the speed limit on his frequent drives to and from Huntsville. He was known as "a speed demon."[37] Even as the prophet, he loved to drive fast and was always "heavy on the pedal."[38] Pulled over by the highway patrol on numerous occasions, David often would not be given a ticket when the police recognized him, although he would chide, "I want a ticket. I broke the law!"[39] One morning, David went up early to Huntsville to ride one of his horses and was in a hurry afterward to get back to an important meeting at the Church Administration Building by 8:30. He was speeding down Harrison Boulevard in Ogden when "he saw a red light flashing behind him." He stopped and waited for the traffic officer to come up to the car. When the officer saw who the driver was, he said, "Oh, I'm sorry; I didn't realize it was you." David said, "Young man, if I was going one mile over the speed limit, you give me a ticket. You do your duty." He was issued his ticket. The next morning, when he arrived at the office, there were about fifteen copies of the *Ogden Examiner* waiting for him. Printed on the front page was the headline, "Mormon Prophet Gets Citation." Church employees who lived in Ogden had put them on his desk, some expecting him to call the *Ogden Examiner* editor and tell him "a thing or two." David did call him, but instead of chastising the editor, he thanked him. "I have been reading the article about me in your paper. I wanted to thank you. You have been able to straighten up a lot of people around here who think that I am slowing up."[40]

David was always in a hurry to get to Huntsville, where he could continue to participate in the activities he had loved as a boy; indeed, the child in him came out at Huntsville. On a snowy day in the dead of winter, David's son Lawrence drove his parents to their cottage in Huntsville and shoveled a narrow path from the car to the cottage door. The way was still slippery as Lawrence walked behind David and tried to steady him. All of a sudden, David slipped and fell into Lawrence, and they both landed in the snow, "laughing [their] heads off" as they rolled in it. David also loved to get fresh milk in Huntsville from Guernsey cows such as he had in his boyhood home and have bread and milk for supper.[41] Whether from frolicking in the snow or drinking fresh milk, Huntsville seemed to have a positive effect on the prophet. People would remark that President McKay looked "visibly better" and renewed after a visit to his hometown.[42]

David O. McKay loved to drive. He was known as a "speed demon."

David O. McKay on his birthday, September 8, 1961,
at Huntsville farm with Sonny Boy.

More than any other activity, David loved to spend time with his animals in Huntsville, especially the horses. He loved new foals. When Lady, a large sorrel mare, was expecting to foal, David instructed his foreman weeks beforehand to let him know the moment she gave birth. The little colt appeared just before noon one day. David was in a meeting with Church leaders when Clare Middlemiss, his secretary, received the message. When the meeting recessed for lunch, she passed along the information. David left immediately. "I'll be back in time to start the next meeting," he told Clare as he went. "I may be a few minutes late, but I'll be back." The prophet "sped up to Huntsville, inspected the newborn, smiled like a proud father, then raced back to his office, arriving only a couple of minutes late for the afternoon meeting."[43] David observed the newborn colt as he grew, intrigued by the way he "followed his mother [Lady] around as though he had been trained so to do." He named the horse Sonny Boy. "In the months and years ahead, David . . . would derive enormous satisfaction in training and riding Sonny Boy,"[44] eventually making of him a "fine saddle horse."[45] As David's favorite animal, Sonny Boy became as well known in the Church as any General Authority.

Not all of David's horses were as easy to break as Sonny Boy, but David was never discouraged. He would often instruct, "You keep enough control but give them enough line." David never had to chase a horse; they came to him willingly, as he taught them.[46]

David had no patience with those who were unkind to animals. "One day one of his sons reported that the blacksmith had hit [one of the McKays' horses] with a ball-peen hammer because the mare wouldn't stand still when she was shod. The intensity of [David's] agitation was evident, though he controlled his tongue and temper. That blacksmith no longer shod any of the McKay horses."[47] An instance of David's kindness toward all animals "occurred one summer when a swallow built her nest in the saddle house next to the barn. . . . [David] left the window open on purpose so she could get in and out to tend her nestlings. One afternoon, [another family member] saw that the window was open and closed it. She mentioned the event in our casual family conversation, and Father promptly traversed the mile between the house and [the barn] to reopen the window for the frantic little mother."[48] In view of such kindness, it was not surprising that David had a way with almost all animals.

One animal, however, never learned to like David: a Jersey bull named Jerry. One time, when David was helping his sons with the chores, he sternly commanded the bull to stop pawing the ground. Instead, as David's son Lawrence related, Jerry "put his head down and charged. Father sprinted for the fence, but Jerry hit him in the middle of his back. Father's hat went flying, and, distracted, Jerry hesitated long enough for our hired man and me to chase him away." David, although still shaken from the attack, "jumped on a horse, roped Jerry, and dragged him bellowing to the chute where our local expert dehorned him." Although he was safer to be around without his horns, the operation did nothing to improve to Jerry's disposition; he had to be kept in a pen ten feet high.[49] Even with these precautions, one day Jerry got out and was on the road when David spotted him in his headlights. David drove Jerry home by nudging him, none too gently, with the large metal bumper on the front of his car. Each time Jerry stopped moving, David would nudge him again. The technique got Jerry home, but it solidified his dislike; he bellowed whenever he saw David's car.[50]

Unlike Jerry, David's dogs—Billy and Winnie, two purebred collies—adored him and often accompanied him back and forth from Huntsville, riding on the running boards of the car. When they saw David getting ready to go, they would frisk and bark until David would say, "All right," and then they would leap aboard. Another sheepdog, Spike, won David's heart by resting his paw on David's arm while they were driving in the car.[51]

David continued to speed to Huntsville and back. When he rode his horses he "always wore a pair of Indian beaded gloves." In his hurry, David would frequently lose them, "and they would always turn up at the store in Huntsville after someone had found them."

The people of Huntsville knew him well, and often he greeted them by name, though it had been more than fifty years since he had been a resident of the small community. One day a Huntsville resident and cousin of David's named Earl Barnes "greeted him with a cigarette in his mouth. He was sure that [President McKay] would correct him; but [David] simply said, 'Hello Earl! Aren't those mountains beautiful?' Earl was so 'whipped' by that experience that he quit smoking anyway."[52]

With David's notoriety, it became more impossible for him to find privacy and solitude in Huntsville or Salt Lake City; hence, the McKays sought respite in Laguna Beach. As early as April 27, 1951, David and Emma Ray left by train for California to stay in "a modest beach cottage on Emerald Bay," fifty miles south of Los Angeles.[53] George Albert Smith had purchased it right after World War II. David "had been inclined to dispose of the property" when he became the prophet, but after he visited it he changed his mind.[54] As the occasion permitted, he and Emma Ray would head for Laguna Beach "for a few days of freedom from the constant pressures . . . at Church headquarters."[55] At the beach house, David would sit at the front window in the late afternoons and meditate as he watched the ever-moving sea. Emma Ray would again have the luxury of cooking, and together the two would shop for groceries in anonymity.[56] It was a contrast to life in Salt Lake City, where people would flock around David whenever he went out onto the street. In fact, a decision was made early in his presidency to prohibit David from going out because he was "so popular that he could not get to where he was going."[57]

A DEVOTED SECRETARY

David's secretary also tried to guard him from unnecessary well-wishers. When David became the prophet, Clare Middlemiss had been his secretary for more than eleven years. A recently returned missionary and graduate from a business college, Clare had begun to work for David in 1935, a year after he was called as second counselor in the First Presidency. At the time, Clare had not been personally acquainted with David and she was not anxious to take a new position. On her first day in David's office, she said, "President McKay, this is way beyond my expectations." David replied simply, "Well, I want you to know that I feel fortunate to have you as my secretary." From that moment on, the two of them had a close relationship. Clare often remarked that she had never heard David utter a cross word, "even to the Brethren when they were in meeting, when things came up that probably could have caused a little irritation." He always remained in good humor. On one such occasion she said to him, "President McKay, how do you do it? I can't be that way." David answered, "Sister, you must learn to control your feelings. I learned many years ago, when I felt a surge of anger or retort coming over me, to put my tongue way back in my mouth and clamp my teeth down on it, and not to say an unkind and hurtful thing. Every time that I did that, I found that it was easier the next time to control my feelings." After that conversation, Clare watched him, and whenever his tongue went back in his mouth she smiled inwardly. Few knew the incredible problems, pressures, and irritations that he dealt with because, as she said, "he always had a smile on his face."[58]

Through trial and error, Clare became adept at typing President McKay's sermons. At first it was difficult because of his practice of quoting liberally from poets and philosophers. He had memorized many of these, and his custom was to recite the first line to Clare and have her fill in the rest. One of the very first funeral sermons she helped him prepare contained Robert Burns's line: "the best-laid schemes of mice an' men gang aft a-gley." Clare could not comprehend "gang aft a-gley" on the dictaphone. She "desperately listened over and over again to those words . . . but could not distinguish them." Knowing that time was growing short, she engaged in a frantic search for the poem. She eventually found it, but from that point on she began "compiling and indexing all the poems and quotations used by President McKay" so as not to be caught short again. Over the years she collected several loose-leaf books of quotations,

David O. McKay, late 1949.

President McKay with secretary Clare Middlemiss, 1952.

and by the time David became the president of the Church, "at a moment's notice," Clare was able to supply any quotation he asked for.[59]

Frequently people would ask Clare what impressed her most about the prophet. On one occasion she replied:

> It is almost impossible to find words to portray the depth and breadth of his lofty character. There is a spirituality radiating from him that is ofttimes felt even by the stranger who visits him. He keeps himself spiritually tuned to heavenly things. His benevolent kindness and warm sympathy to those who are suffering or who are bereaved, his sincerity and friendliness, his interest in people, and love for children, are dominant characteristics. His liking of people, his instinctive ability to understand the other person's viewpoint, his belief in the sacredness and importance of each individual, make him a little short of a genius at personal relationships. His charm is legendary. When he enters a room or takes his place at the pulpit, wherever it may be, a ripple of emotions seizes those present. They catch his glow, his love of life and community. He is beloved and revered by true members of the Church everywhere. His humility is altogether genuine. He is a true prophet of God.[60]

Those who worked with President McKay found that Clare sometimes acted as a sentry and determined who got to see the prophet, allowing access to people she favored. Because Clare felt David was without guile, she believed he did not recognize when people were taking advantage of him, so she personally tried to control the heavy flow of visitors into and out of his office.[61]

THE PROPHET AND THE PUBLIC

As the prophet of the Church, David received a constant flow of dignitaries. Among the first, on October 6, 1952, was Harry S. Truman, president of the United States, campaigning for the Democratic presidential candidate. Closely following him on October

General Dwight D. Eisenhower, presidential candidate, with David O. McKay
at the Church Administration Building, October 10, 1952.

10 came Republican presidential candidate General Dwight D. Eisenhower. David gave both men "the same cordial treatment." It was after Eisenhower won the election and became the United States president on January 20, 1953, that an unusual request came to the prophet: Ezra Taft Benson, a member of the Quorum of the Twelve, was asked by President Eisenhower to be his secretary of agriculture. Because of the Political Manifesto of 1896, Elder Benson asked for President McKay's permission. After prayer, David gave Elder Benson his blessing in accepting the appointment.[62] As price controls, food controls, and farm subsidies became heated issues during President Eisenhower's second run at office, Elder Benson came under fire from his own party. He called President McKay for advice and counsel. After listening to Elder Benson's concerns, David asked one question: "Do you think you are doing what is right?" When Elder Benson answered, "Yes!" President McKay said, "If you think you are doing what is right, you continue to do what you are doing. My old Scottish grandfather taught me that when that cold, snowy wind is blowing and you are out in it, you can't do anything about it; you just turn up your coat collar and let her blow. That is what I am telling you to do. If the press and people are getting after you and you know that what you are doing is right, you just turn up your coat collar and let her blow. You have my love and my blessings."[63] Ezra Taft Benson was the only member of Dwight D. Eisenhower's cabinet to serve the entire eight years.

With Elder Benson serving on the cabinet, not wanting the Church to appear one-sided in any political persuasions, David was delighted in 1958 when another member of the Twelve, Elder Hugh B. Brown, was invited "to give the keynote address at the Democratic state nominating convention. . . . Because of Elder Brown's certified credentials as a Democrat, [David] saw in this invitation an opportunity to make an important statement . . . : 'Since some think we are one-sided in politics, . . . it might be a good thing for him to accept this assignment and let the members of the Church know that both political parties are represented in the Church.'"[64]

David's influence infused business circles as well. He had a lasting effect on business leaders, who streamed through the office of the First Presidency on a daily basis. One such visitor was Walter Ruether, one of the greatest and most famous labor leaders in America at the time. He found David to be modest, gentle, and humorous. Later that same day at a University of Utah luncheon, Ruether said of his interview with the prophet of God:

> I have never had an experience like this. I have never met someone like that. I do not believe that our generation will ever produce a man like that. . . . I [have] had the great honor of meeting perhaps the greatest leaders of the world from many countries, and many wonderful people, but I['ve] never met a man like President McKay.[65]

As seen in Ruether's experience, David had a certain presence that made a lasting impression on those who came in contact with him. When President McKay was asked to present a seminar at an educational convention in southern California, he came into a huge room during a cocktail hour. "Everybody was . . . having drinks and chatting. It was very noisy. . . . President McKay walked in with his striking white hair . . . the perfect image of a mature, intelligent individual," and all around the room it could be heard, "Who is that man? What is he doing here?" Without people even knowing who he was, David's "image and his presence captured the attention of people."[66]

When people met him, many felt they were talking to a prophet. One legendary event took place when President McKay visited New York. When "the regular [news] photographer was unable to go, . . . in desperation the United Press picked their crime photographer—a man accustomed to the toughest type of work in New York." The crime photographer took "a tremendous sheaf of pictures" of President McKay, whereas he was originally supposed to take just two. When his boss chastised him for wasting his time and photographic materials, "the photographer replied very curtly [that] he would gladly pay for the extra materials, and they could even dock him for the extra time" that he had taken. The photographer added, "When I was a little boy, my mother used to read to me out of the Old Testament, and all my life I have wondered what a prophet of God must really look like. Well, today I found one."[67]

Other members of the press soon found the McKay charm irresistible as well. David seemed perfectly relaxed in the media's presence. Once when President McKay was asked by then stake president David B. Haight to dedicate a new chapel in San Mateo, California, a *Deseret News* reporter accompanied the McKays. The reporter had a tape recorder with him so that he could record everything the prophet said. When David B. Haight and his wife met President McKay and Emma Ray on the train, Elder Haight was amazed at David's calm demeanor and warm, friendly manner, even though the press was taping every word he said.[68]

Common folk were as taken with the prophet as were members of the press. David "was very sensitive and deferential toward women," and he hoped his example would help others do the same. One day the prophet was waiting for a red light in his white Buick at the intersection of South Temple and State Street. David "was in the intersection, almost, ready to go west as soon as the light turned in his favor." A female pedestrian was walking north in the crosswalk but had traveled only halfway when "the light changed and trapped her in the middle of the street. She didn't know what to do. She looked left; she looked right;" and then she looked over at President McKay's car. With a gesture of his hand, he motioned for her to pass, and the lady passed against the light. By the time she had crossed, the light had changed again, and the driver behind David was honking his horn. David "opened the car door, stepped out, turned toward the impatient driver [behind him] and tipped his hat to him, . . . got in the car, and . . . drove away."[69] Such incidents became legendary in the Church.

Members of the Church thronged around him at all the general conferences.

On one particular day, hordes of [people] stood ten deep at the roped-off door at the rear of the tabernacle. Out came the president, protected but unaided. With peerless charm he stretched up both arms and waved to the hundreds who stood on tiptoe just to watch him enter his car. All of a sudden under the rope ducked a four-year-old lad. He darted for the president before the aides could stop him. Still smiling at the throng, the prophet felt the tugging of the little fellow at his side. . . . With some effort . . . , David helped the boy up into his . . . arms. . . .

"Well, young man, how are you today?"

"Just fine," the boy answered with no embarrassment.

"How old are you?"

"Four."

"And what are you going to do when you grow up?" The quiet words were asked with grandfatherly interest.

"Go on a mission."

"That's fine."

With a chuck under the chin and a special smile the prophet set down the boy to the relief of family and aides.[70]

As a leader, David took hold as prophet, seer, and revelator and had an effect not only on the individual lives of those Saints whom he met on a regular basis, but also on the daily lives of other Latter-day Saints through his teachings. It was during his first presidential decade that David made incredible efforts in the areas of travel, education, and missionary work as the Church experienced unprecedented growth.

NOTES TO CHAPTER 9

1. Conference Report, April 1951, 157.
2. Francis M. Gibbons, *David O. McKay: Apostle to the World, Prophet of God* (Salt Lake City: Deseret Book, 1986), 272.
3. Gibbons, *Apostle to the World,* 273.
4. Conference Report, April 1951, 182.
5. David O. McKay Diary, McKay Papers, MS 668, box 9, folder 2, Manuscript Division, University of Utah Marriott Library, Salt Lake City; Gibbons, *Apostle to the World,* 273.
6. Conference Report, April 1951, 181.
7. Ibid.
8. Ibid., 157.
9. Ibid.
10. Ibid., 151.
11. Ibid.
12. Ibid., 154.
13. D. Michael Quinn, *J. Reuben Clark: The Church Years* (Provo, UT: Brigham Young University Press, 1983), 126.
14. Glen L. Rudd, interview by Mary Jane Woodger, February 8, 1996, Salt Lake City, McKay Research Project, College of Education, Brigham Young University, Provo, UT; transcript in author's possession.
15. Quinn, *J. Reuben Clark,* 126.
16. Gibbons, *Apostle to the World,* 401.
17. David O. McKay, London Temple Dedication, Fourth Session, September 8, 1958, McKay Scrapbook, no. 154, MS 4640, LDS Church Archives, Salt Lake City.
18. David O. McKay, Council Meeting, April 12, 1951, McKay Scrapbook, no. 122.
19. Richard N. Armstrong, *The Rhetoric of David O. McKay, Mormon Prophet* (New York: Peter Lang, 1993), 116.
20. Gunn McKay, interview by Mary Jane Woodger, July 28, 1995, Provo, UT, McKay Research Project, College of Education, Brigham Young University; transcript in author's possession.
21. Keith Terry, *David O. McKay: Prophet of Love* (Santa Barbara, CA: Butterfly, 1980), 140.
22. Alden Whitman, "Missionary President," McKay Scrapbook, no. 110.
23. Rudd interview.
24. David B. Haight, interview by Mary Jane Woodger, August 20, 1996, Salt Lake City, McKay Research Project; transcript in author's possession.

25. *Life,* April 23, 1951, 121; quoted in Richard N. Armstrong, *The Rhetoric of David O. McKay, Mormon Prophet* (New York: Peter Lang, 1993), 6.

26. *Newsweek,* 16 April 1951: 92; quoted in Armstrong, *The Rhetoric of David O. McKay,* 6.

27. Hartman Rector Jr., interview by Mary Jane Woodger, October 1997, Salt Lake City, McKay Research Project; transcript in author's possession.

28. Robert L. Simpson, interview by Mary Jane Woodger, December 30, 1996, St. George, UT, McKay Research Project; transcript in author's possession; Loren C. Dunn, interview by Mary Jane Woodger, October 11, 1995, Salt Lake City, McKay Research Project; transcript in author's possession; Marion D. Hanks, interview by Mary Jane Woodger, October 1995, Salt Lake City, McKay Research Project; transcript in author's possession.

29. Hanks interview.

30. Whitman, "Missionary President."

31. Lou Jean McKay Blood, interview by Mary Jane Woodger, August 8, 1995, Provo, UT, McKay Research Project, College of Education, Brigham Young University, Provo, UT; transcript in possession of author.

32. David Lawrence McKay, *My Father, David O. McKay* (Salt Lake City: Deseret Book, 1989), 57.

33. Blood interview.

34. "She Has Gift of Understanding," *Deseret News,* January 24, 1970, Church News section.

35. Whitman, "Missionary President."

36. Ibid.

37. Rudd interview.

38. Gunn McKay interview.

39. Jack Newey, interview by Mary Jane Woodger, September 1, 1995, Salt Lake City, McKay Research Project; transcript in author's possession.

40. Simpson interview.

41. Newey interview.

42. Gunn McKay interview.

43. Terry, *Prophet of Love,* 139.

44. Gibbons, *Apostle to the World,* 291.

45. Terry, *Prophet of Love,* 139.

46. Edward and Lottie McKay, interview by Mary Jane Woodger, July 30, 1995, Salt Lake City, McKay Research Project; transcript in author's possession.

47. George R. Hill, interview by Mary Jane Woodger, October 28, 1995, Salt Lake City, McKay Research Project; transcript in author's possession.

48. David Lawrence McKay, *My Father,* 59.

49. Ibid.

50. Barrie McKay, interview by Mary Jane Woodger, August 15, 1995, Salt Lake City, Utah, McKay Research Project; transcript in author's possession.

51. David Lawrence McKay, *My Father*, 59–60.

52. Gunn McKay interview.

53. Gibbons, *Apostle to the World*, 282, 284.

54. Terry, *Prophet of Love*, 197.

55. Gibbons, *Apostle to the World*, 284.

56. Terry, *Prophet of Love*, 198.

57. Barrie McKay interview.

58. Clare Middlemiss, Interview with KSXX Radio Station, January 20, 1970, McKay Scrapbook, no. 110.

59. Notes from Remarks by Clare Middlemiss at the U.S. Circuit Conference, Hotel Utah, McKay Scrapbook, no. 77.

60. Sacrament Meeting of Ogden Sixtieth Ward, South Ogden Stake, Ogden, UT, Program Dedicated to President McKay in Honor of His Ninety-Second Birthday, McKay Scrapbook, no. 81.

61. Quinn interview.

62. Gibbons, *Apostle to the World*, 312–15.

63. Haight interview.

64. Gibbons, *Apostle to the World*, 373.

65. Quoted in Hanks interview.

66. Simpson interview.

67. Arch L. Madsen, "In Memories of a Prophet," *Improvement Era*, February 1970, 72.

68. Haight interview.

69. Thomas S. Monson, interview for David O. McKay School of Education, October 7, 1996, Salt Lake City; video in author's possession.

70. Terry, *Prophet of Love*, 195.

CHAPTER 10

PROCLAIMING THE TRUTH

You and I have the responsibility of taking advantage of these new and great opportunities to preach the Gospel, of making real new visions, and of bringing into the lives of Latter-day Saints and members of the world more blessed opportunities to know the way of truth.

—David O. McKay[1]

As President McKay took over the reins of the Church presidency, an impression that had accompanied him for a long time now came to the forefront. When he had been a missionary in Scotland, he had felt an inkling that the Church he had grown up experiencing as a local, Utah, and intermountain organization was going to expand during his lifetime. His missionary experiences taught him that the rock cut out of the mountain without hands that Daniel had prophesied about so long ago was beginning to roll, that the gospel truly would fill the whole world (see Dan. 2:34–35). This idea began to sprout even more on his world tour in 1921. He knew it was not by chance that he was the Apostle chosen for that experience.

Now, as he became the Lord's mouthpiece, those inklings would receive full development. President McKay's desire and objective was to give the Church a new, international image. As he looked upon this task, he realized that his responsibilities lay in three areas: First, he knew he needed to be among the people, and to do that he would need to travel. His travels would be more extensive than those of any previous prophet, a feat made possible by the advances in transportation the 1950s brought. Secondly, he knew that more temples needed to go to where the people were. Third, he knew that the Church was ready to take education to its people. As the prophet, seer, and revelator, he would be the impetus for providing that education.

A PROPHET AMONG THE SAINTS

President McKay's first trip as president of the Church was to Palmyra, New York. Here he attended the Hill Cumorah Pageant, which had been produced since 1937. Rumors had circulated that the pageant would be shut down because of the Korean War, but as the prophet watched the Hill Cumorah Pageant, he became "one of its staunchest supporters." In a statement to the press, he lauded the pageant's professionalism by saying: "There is nothing amateurish about it."[2] With President McKay's support, the Hill Cumorah Pageant grew and flourished, becoming a wonderful tool in attracting men, women, and children to the gospel.

President McKay returned home and just a few days later "was stricken with an attack of vertigo so severe that it was almost impossible for him to stand without support." After being released from the hospital, the prophet remained ill for a month. With such a setback, it is possible that he wondered if his desires to travel, meet the people, and internationalize the Church would still happen. He wrote in his journal on September 27: "I am feeling pretty well. . . . However my nervous system is still impaired and I am fully conscious of the fact that I must not over-do until I am stronger."[3]

President McKay's health gradually improved until he was able to travel again. As he globe-trotted, the *Deseret News* Church News section carried reports of his day-to-day experiences, and the Saints followed their prophet's activities with great interest. "Such travels brought him into personal contact with kings and queens, presidents and premiers, prime ministers and ambassadors," and, most importantly, Church members.[4] Traveling in the 1950s to areas where the Saints' population

President McKay and his wife leaving for a mission tour, 1955.

David O. McKay with Greek Orthodox Church leaders, 1962.

was most concentrated, he made trips across the world, including Europe, Latin America, New Zealand, and the South Seas.[5]

In 1952, President McKay's nine-country visit to the European missions included England, Scotland, the Netherlands, Denmark, Norway, Sweden, Germany, Switzerland, and France. On the way to Europe, arrangements had been made in New York for David and Emma Ray to stay at the Waldorf Astoria in "a lavish tower suite." When he walked into the suite, he "promptly instructed the travel agency to secure much more modest accommodations for the rest of the trip. 'It would be ridiculous for the Church to receive this kind of exclusive treatment in Europe,' he commented."[6]

The McKays had a successful European tour, often being able to visit with royalty and heads of state, including "an invitation to a garden party at Buckingham Palace given by Queen Elizabeth" and audiences with the queen of Holland, king of Sweden, and president of Finland.[7] While in England, President McKay also visited the Lord Mayor, who quoted Robert Burns during his remarks but forgot some lines. Because President McKay was able to finish the lines for him, the Lord Mayor was impressed with his knowledge of Scottish poetry.[8] During their visit to the Netherlands, President and Sister McKay were granted an audience with the queen. The queen offered the McKays cigarettes and tea, which they politely refused. The queen said to him, "Mr. McKay, do you mean to tell me that you won't have a little tea with the queen of the Netherlands?" President McKay replied, "Would the queen of the Netherlands ask me to do something that I have taught 1.3 million people not to do?" The queen answered, "Mr. McKay, you are a great man. I wouldn't ask you to do that." While "nibbling at the cookies, [President McKay] took the opportunity of explaining the Word of Wisdom." When the scheduled time was up, the McKays stood to leave, but the queen said, "Oh, so soon? Why, I have all the afternoon free."[9]

Although President McKay rarely had much preparation time while in Europe, he "never gave the same sermon twice."

> Instead, he drew on his well-stocked memory and understanding of gospel principles to . . . [tailor] his addresses to each national audience and [delight] his hearers with appreciative quotations from their own literature. In England, he quoted Charles Dickens's appraisal of Mormon emigrants aboard the *Amazon* as "the pick and flower of England." In Berlin, he quoted Goethe; in Paris, Victor Hugo.

President McKay also made an effort to schedule meetings for servicemen, of whom he said, "They're missionaries, too." Through his travels, he learned to speak through a translator and gave at least thirty-two interviews to the media in his European tour alone.[10] In nine weeks, President McKay visited nine countries and held nearly fifty meetings.[11]

While in Berlin, Germany, on June 29, 1952, a miraculous event took place. Arrangements were made for a meeting in the Mercedes Palast Theater, the largest hall in north Berlin. Prior to the meeting, President McKay received word of a Church member from behind the Iron Curtain who had lost her husband and eldest son under communist rule and had been, for five years, confined to her bed.[12] She had heard that President McKay was coming to Berlin, and being unable to travel herself, she sent her son and daughter, ages ten and twelve, to go to the conference with this hope: "I know if I send my children to shake hands with President McKay, and then they come home and take my hand—if I can hold their little hands in mine—I know that I shall get better."[13] During the meeting, President McKay asked the mission president to point out the two children among the thousands assembled in the building.

> Anticipating meeting them, [he] took a new handkerchief, and when that little girl and boy came along, [he] went to them and shook their hands, and said, "Will you take this handkerchief to your mother with my blessing?" [He] later learned that after [he] had shaken hands with them, they would not shake hands with anyone else . . . until they got back to their mother.[14]

When President and Sister McKay returned to Salt Lake City, Emma Ray wrote to the mission president's wife "to find out how the mother of the two little children was getting along." She replied:

> This sister thanks the Lord every day for the blessing and the handkerchief which President McKay sent through her two children, and she has the faith that she will fully recover, and I believe so, too. Immediately after the children came home, her feet and toes began to get feeling in them, and this feeling slowly moved up into her legs, and now she gets out of bed alone and seats herself on a chair, and then, with her feet and the chair, works all the way around to the kitchen sink, where she has the children bring her the dishes to wash, and other things, and is very thankful that she is able to help now.[15]

President and Sister McKay often kept up an incredible pace during his tours. David Lawrence and his wife, Mildred, often accompanied them and worried about their health. The demands on the prophet, who was in his late seventies, were excruciating. For instance, in Wales, the prophet and Emma Ray had traveled all day and arrived just in time for

> a missionary meeting where he spoke, and then he and [Emma Ray] attended a Welsh musical. After that, the mission president asked if he would consider visiting a sick elder in the hospital who would otherwise not see him. Mildred and [David Lawrence] remonstrated, "You just can't keep this up. It's already midnight." With even greater gentleness and a good deal of firmness, he reminded [them,] "This is what I'm here for if they have to carry me out on a slab."[16]

It was President McKay's practice always to shake hands with everyone present. His son Llewelyn would groan "when someone would ask for [President McKay's] autograph because other people then took up

David O. McKay at a ground-breaking ceremony for a chapel.

the idea and within a few minutes a long line formed." During a 1953 tour, President McKay dedicated a meetinghouse at Chapel Hill, England. Immediately after the closing prayer, a line formed. At the front of the line was a little girl about nine years old who asked Llewelyn, "May I have President McKay's autograph?" Llewelyn reported,

> [I] began to find excuses, not knowing that my father was just behind me overhearing the conversation. [President McKay] put his hand on my shoulder and said, out of the children's hearing distance, "My boy, never hurt or disappoint a child. Children are more sensitive to praise, to criticism, and to recognition than we realize. I can take the time to sign these few autographs—it means a lot to these youngsters and I wouldn't disappoint them for anything."

> He then turned to the little girl and jokingly asked, "Do you think I can write plainly enough so you can read it?"

> The young girl . . . became flustered. At that moment, President Reiser [the British Mission president] interrupted to ask a pressing question. . . . When President McKay turned . . . to begin writing autographs, the girl had disappeared.

> I have never seen my father more upset. "Llewelyn," he called, "please find that little girl in the blue dress. I'm sure she has the impression that I didn't wish to sign her book. She misinterpreted my remarks. You must find her. She must not go home with this false impression!"

> Before long, branch presidents and mission presidents were looking for a little girl in blue, but all search was in vain.

> During the drive back to London, [President McKay] mentioned the incident again. One of the elders riding with us said, "We think we know who the little girl is, and the branch president in

the village where she lives is going to inquire and will phone you tonight in London."

Sure enough, a telephone call came that night, and . . . [President McKay] instructed:

"Tell that little girl I am sorry I missed her at New Chapel, and that I have asked the branch president to send her book to me by mail to Salt Lake City; I will sign my autograph and mail it directly back to her."

And he did![17]

Fulfilling a promise he had made in 1921 to visit every mission of the world, President and Sister McKay left Salt Lake City on January 2, 1954 (the day of their fifty-third wedding anniversary), on a journey that would make him the first president of the Church to "visit missions in South Africa and South and Central America." These visits "would mark completion of an official visit by President McKay to every existing mission of the Church."[18] As their plane landed in Johannesburg, they were greeted by a joyous crowd singing with all their hearts "We Thank Thee, O God, for a Prophet" and "Come, Come, Ye Saints." The following day, 450 people gathered for two conference sessions of the Transvaal District. After the session, President McKay personally greeted each person in attendance.[19]

President McKay met with government officials and the United States ambassador to the Union of South Africa while in Pretoria, and he held a three-day conference in Capetown, with missionaries from the surrounding territory attending. At all of the meetings, "every word spoken was heard in deepest silence, and with the greatest interest and reverence. It is difficult to get a full appreciation of the meaning of this visit of the Prophet of the Lord to these remote places. The people had longed for such a contact for so many years, but had felt little hope that it would ever materialize."[20]

President McKay took advantage of his time in South Africa to teach the people. While in a meeting at Johannesburg on January 10, he taught the children with an illustrative story about the value of character.

> "What am I holding in my hand?" (President McKay exhibiting a glass of water.)
>
> Answer: "A glass of water."
>
> "What kind of water?"
>
> Answer: "Pure water."
>
> "What is this I hold in my hand?" (exhibiting a fountain pen) (hands) "Look at those thinkers!"
>
> Answer: "A pen."
>
> "A pen is right. And what do you think is in that pen? You tell me, young man."
>
> Answer: "Ink."
>
> President McKay: "I am going to take that glass of pure water and put just one drop of ink in it—I think I shall put not even a drop in it, but I shall bring this pen, with ink in it, in contact with that pure water. Now watch." (President McKay inserted the pen and moved it about a bit and the ink spread from the pen into the water.) "Now what kind of water is in the glass?"
>
> Answer: "Impure water."
>
> "Yes, I have polluted that water. Should you like to drink it now?"

Answer: "No."

"No, for I have put ink in that water and made it impure."

"How many of you have a little baby boy or girl at home?" (hands) "I see. Do you know that that little baby is just as pure and sweet as that pure water I had in the glass; and that it has just come from the presence of our Heavenly Father? . . .

"Now, imagine that sweet little baby before you this morning, just as that glass of water. . . . Will you tell me what might enter that baby's life if you would pollute it, just as that ink polluted the water?"

Answer: "Death."

"No, death is not such a terrible thing as we think it is. I want to know, while that little baby is in life here what might go into his soul that could pollute it as that ink did the water."

Answer: "Evil."

"Evil is right. Now, will you specify some things which are evil."

The children then talked of the Word of Wisdom violations, stealing, lying, and other things that would pollute their souls just as much as the ink had polluted the water. President McKay had masterfully taught a great lesson by showing them his demonstration of ink in water.[21]

President McKay's devotion to the spiritual program of his visit to South Africa was evidenced on the final day of the conference in Capetown, which was devoted to a ten-hour testimony meeting, breaking only shortly for lunch and two ten-minute breaks. On this visit to South Africa, President McKay made personal contact with virtually every member of the Church, going so far as to visit an LDS woman who was hospitalized in Capetown.[22]

As he had done in South Africa, President McKay took opportunities in South America to meet with various dignitaries. In Buenos Aires, he accomplished what was considered to be impossible by meeting with the Argentine leader, Juan D. Peron. President Peron proved to be quite gracious and displayed

> "a surprising interest and knowledge" of the Mormon religion. The discussion shifted from one topic to another until President Peron learned of a huge Sunday conference to be held by the mission.
>
> "Where are you holding your conference?" Peron asked in Spanish.
>
> "At the Consejo de Mujeres," the mission president, Lee Valentine, replied.
>
> Peron shook his head. "It's too small," he declared. Instead, he suggested the Cervantes, the second largest theater in the country.
>
> President McKay accepted the kind offer. After the interview, "Argentina's Saints were thrilled at it, for they realized this was a diplomatic step forward for the Church."[23]

In 1955, President McKay completed a 45,000-mile journey to the Pacific such as he had previously taken in 1921. During his first visit, he had felt that the country of Fiji was not yet prepared for the gospel. By 1955, Fiji was ready. Leaving on January 4, 1955, President McKay and his party headed for Nandi, Fiji. As the plane neared the country, the group was told there was a hurricane headed

David O. McKay leaves for a mission tour, January 1955.

from Suva, Fiji, so the airplane stopped on the island of Canton for refueling. For three hours, the hurricane swirled north of Fiji. "Then came news from puzzled officials that the hurricane was no longer a threat. . . . For some reason the hurricane had reversed its course and was heading back toward Nandi and would precede them." By the time they arrived in Nandi, the route was clear, though "the black flags [were] still flying in warning of an approaching hurricane." The group learned that the storm had literally done the impossible and reversed its course. President McKay remarked, "Something very unusual happened this day."[24]

The deviant action of the hurricane brought about much discussion in Fiji. "Weather officials explained in detail the abrupt change of the storm's path, but could offer no explanation for it, and called the typhoon 'The Screwball.'" However, favorable changes in weather conditions during President McKay's trip were not unique to that particular incident. There were violent storms that miraculously ceased at the last minute, as well as other phenomena that enabled him to continue his trip and hold open-air meetings. "President McKay always anticipated good weather, and occasionally referred to some lack of faith on the part of those who worried."[25]

Because of the weather delays, President McKay and his party were forced to stay in Suva, Fiji, a day longer than planned. While the McKays were doing a little shopping, they met two missionaries and a local elder, Cecil B. Smith. President McKay had previously been "unaware that there were missionaries or members of the Church residing in Suva, and no arrangements had been made for a meeting. However, as soon as President McKay learned at this chance meeting that there were members of the Church on the island, he immediately set aside a time" to hold a meeting at the home of Brother Smith. Twenty-eight members of the Church attended. "For thirty-three years, [Brother Smith] had kept this little flock together, and now the Prophet of the Lord and his wife were . . . in his home."[26]

From Fiji, the party went on to Tonga and then Samoa. President McKay recalled a frightening incident:

> Just as I got off the launch that carried us from the sea plane to the wharf, Ray, while waiting for delays incident to landing requirements, sat down in a chair. It tipped back unexpectedly, and she falling helplessly struck her head on the bench, her left elbow and coccyx [tail] bone on the cement floor.

> I was several feet from her . . . [and] when I reached her side, she was in a sitting posture holding her head in both hands evidently in intense pain, tears rolling down her cheeks.

There was no evidence of a fracture or broken skin, but Emma Ray's pain concerned President McKay greatly. He "held her head and offered a silent prayer . . . [telling] the Lord he could not finish the work he had been sent to do if [Emma Ray] were not healed. As soon as he took his hands off her head the intense pain left and she was able to continue her journey . . . [though] her back and elbow [were] painfully bruised."[27]

President McKay was instrumental in healing others also. Often "he would go to the hospital to administer, . . . [going] from one room to another . . . [and] do what he could until . . . he would come home [exhausted] and just drop on the bed."[28] There were even times when merely shaking hands with the prophet brought healing. Sister Nina Penrod, who was severely afflicted with arthritis, shook hands with President McKay and "felt a shock, and she wondered if others might have heard the sound that accompanied the shock which had seemed very loud to her. . . . She felt elated because something wonderful had happened to her, for her arthritis pains were all gone." After a short rest, she was able to reach "each arm up her back touching her shoulder blades," an act she had not been capable of for years.[29]

Not all visits with the sick resulted in physical healing; President McKay also rejoiced in spiritual healings that took place. On his trip to the South Pacific, he and Emma Ray visited a leper colony. One man particularly affected by the dread disease had heard one of the other afflicted men testify that Jesus Christ had again spoken in this dispensation to Joseph Smith. This man became completely converted, though his body remained affected by leprosy. In the services at the leper settlement that the McKays visited, "that man stood up in the audience and said, 'This disease has affected my hands and other parts of my body, but I am glad it came to me because it has been the means of hearing and receiving the blessings of the restored gospel.' [President McKay] could not keep the tears from rolling down [his] cheeks because of the testimony of this afflicted man."[30]

While in Samoa, "President McKay and his party met all the high chiefs." They took a drive to Sauniatu, the place where he had given the memorable apostolic blessing thirty-four years before. In what must have been a touching sight for the prophet, "there were several carloads of Saints, six buses filled with visiting Saints, and a large number of others already waiting for [them] in the village. As [they] crossed the bridge, [they] beheld the beautiful *David O. McKay Monument,* freshly painted in white, showing a beautiful gold plaque" commemorating what had happened there years before.[31]

On this trip, President McKay also visited New Zealand and Australia. In New Zealand, desiring to bring the full blessings of the restored gospel to the Saints there, the prophet searched for an appropriate site to build a sacred edifice. The New Zealand Saints, along with members in other lands, would soon have in their own country a temple of the Lord.

BRINGING TEMPLES TO THE PEOPLE

For President David O. McKay, few other assignments were as important as building temples. Prior to his administration, there had been eight temples—four in Utah and one each in Arizona, Idaho, Canada, and Hawaii. President McKay followed the inspiration to bring temples to Saints in other lands, an undertaking that required the often challenging tasks of selecting and acquiring a suitable site. Before President McKay's first European tour, the Lord had inspired him to know that Europe was now ready for a temple.[32] Bern,

Switzerland, was selected as a central location for all of Europe, and President McKay took the opportunity while there to look for a temple site. Visiting several spots in the city on June 11, 1953, President McKay's company had stopped to refuel when he "pointed up to the hills above the little town of Zollikofen and said, 'That would be an ideal location for a temple.' President Bringhurst [the Swiss-Austrian Mission president] agreed, adding, 'but it's not available. We can't get it.'" Another site near Bern was chosen, but the property "was tied up in a complicated estate settlement. . . . All of the heirs had to consent to the sale, and one firmly refused because 'land in Switzerland is not expandable.' After several months, the best choice, the property at Zollikofen, suddenly became available for half the price; and, with the consent of the First Presidency, President Bringhurst promptly closed the deal."[33]

Looking forward to the dedication of the new temple in Switzerland, and now New Zealand, there needed to be a way for a single presentation to accommodate the diverse languages spoken by the members. President McKay gave the assignment to Gordon B. Hinckley, who, after fasting and praying in the Salt Lake Temple, was inspired to put part of the temple ceremony on film. After a year of many long hours spent trying to produce a film that would "be a fitting representation of that sacred work," the English-language film was completed. It was then produced in various other languages and prepared in time for the dedication of the Swiss Temple.[34]

On September 11, 1955, President McKay dedicated his first temple as prophet, seer, and revelator in Bern, Switzerland. During the dedication, he remarked that he could feel the presence of "former presidents and Apostles of the Church," including Joseph F. Smith, who had prophesied forty-nine years earlier in the city of Bern that "temples would be built in diverse countries of the world."[35] He dedicated his second temple—the Los Angeles Temple—on March 11, 1956, fulfilling another earlier prophecy by Brigham Young in 1847: "In the process of time the shores of the Pacific may yet be overlooked from the temple of the Lord."[36]

The year 1958 was a significant year for President McKay in that he dedicated two temples—the New Zealand Temple on April 20 and the London Temple on September 7. The dedication of the London Temple was difficult for President McKay. He had been experiencing cloudy vision in his right eye earlier that year, and Dr. Richard W. Sonntag operated to remove a cataract, a complicated procedure at the time. President McKay didn't expect that his eye would recover overnight, but "at the same time, he did not anticipate the more than two months of discomfort and apprehension the surgery produced. He was hospitalized for six days; and it was almost two weeks before the stitches were removed."[37]

By the end of June, everyone thought that he would be able to return to normal, but on June 27, still ill, he recorded in his journal, "Not so well today. Very nervous and tired. Eye sore and inflamed. Hard to see." He also had a new lens put in his glasses, which brought about new problems and further upset him. By July 12, however, things began to look up: "Each day I am a little better able to see with my operated eye." Finally, on August 11, Dr. Sonntag examined President McKay's eye and diagnosed him with 20/20 vision with glasses and "gave [him] permission to drive and go about [his] business as usual."[38]

With the doctor's authorization, President McKay was able to go ahead with the original plan of dedicating the London Temple in the first week of September. Emma Ray had planned to go with him but unexpectedly became ill and "was hospitalized the last day of August with a deep-seated lung congestion." His journal records the loneliness he felt leaving Emma Ray behind: "For the first time during twenty-three years on a trip of any length, I was deprived of the loving companionship of Sister McKay. Although feeling better, she does not feel equal to make this brief, busy trip to attend dedicatory services of the London Temple."[39]

When he finally got to London, President McKay was delighted to find that, per his directions, an ancient oak tree had been preserved. When he had originally found the site for the temple in London, he was informed that the tree was at least 450 years old, and had been growing when Columbus discovered America. He gave specific instructions that the tree "be preserved."

Workmen at the site . . . later named it the "David O. McKay Oak." A special plaque was inscribed and placed on the trunk of the tree as a tribute to the durability of the tree and comparing the life of President McKay to the strength of this oak.[40]

The dedication of the London Temple caused such an interest among the people that the *Daily Express,* one of London's newspapers, commented, "Other churches in Great Britain would do well to take note of the response by the public created during the public viewing of the new London temple."[41] As President McKay read this article, he could not help but contrast it with the many negative editorials he had read while he served as European Mission president. With the Lord's help and direction, the Church was becoming more accepted and international.

LIFTING THE MEMBERS THROUGH EDUCATION

As these temples began to bless the global Church membership, President McKay focused on another goal: to bring education to the people. When he became the prophet in 1951, one of his first official acts was to establish a college in Hawaii. At the groundbreaking of the Church College of Hawaii in February 1955, he prophesied:

From this school, I'll tell you, will go men and women whose influence will be felt for good towards the establishment of peace internationally. Four hundred and fifty million people waiting to hear the message over in China, a noble race. . . . I don't know how many million over in Japan. You prepare to go and carry that message. Three hundred and fifty million down in India. We have scarcely touched these great nations, and they're calling today.[42]

The Polynesian Cultural Center was also established under President McKay's direction. Located adjacent to BYU–Hawaii, the forty-two-acre cultural theme park was designed to be part living museum and part entertainment. President McKay avowed that visitors' experiences at the Polynesian Cultural Center would continue to influence their lives afterward.[43]

Under President McKay's guidance, growth in Church education was significant. In the last ten years of his administration, enrollment of students in institute and seminary classes increased from 67,000 to 162,000.[44] Originally, seminaries had operated in local schools on a released-time basis, meaning a building was constructed near high schools and students were released during the regular school day to attend. As Latter-day Saints spread outside of the Intermountain West, released-time was not possible, so early morning and home study seminary programs were established.

According to President Thomas S. Monson, President McKay was also "primarily responsible for the great expansion that took place on the campus of the Brigham Young University. He wanted everyone to be well educated, both in the humanities, the law, other disciplines, and religion was never to be neglected. He almost put his personal imprimatur on each of the buildings."[45] He had a strong belief in what could be accomplished through supporting the development of Brigham Young University. "Because of its combination of revealed and secular learning," the First Presidency wrote in 1957, "Brigham Young University [was] destined to become, if not the largest, at least the most proficient institution of learning in the world, producing scholars with testimonies of the truth who [would] become leaders in science, industry, art, education, letters and government."[46] The Church College of Hawaii, Ricks College in Idaho, and the Church College of New Zealand also grew in enrollment and physical size under President McKay's direction. Besides these larger schools, the Church also established elementary and high schools in Tahiti, Samoa, Tonga, Chile, and Mexico.[47]

Through President McKay's hands, the Lord brought the Church into the forefront of international society. At the end of the 1950s, no longer were the people of the Church thought of as [odd]. The reverse was true. Howard Hughes was filling his executive offices with returned missionaries or other LDS men who met the standards of the Church. Other business magnates recognized the integrity of Mormon men—for instance, the vice president of a Procter and Gamble Company division at Los Angeles who had needed a group of trainees for management positions had called the LDS Church for a list. . . . The image blossomed. No one fostered that image more than President McKay, and he did so with a dignity that spelled "class." Polished, yet never losing his natural simplicity, refined by the cultivation of true nobility, he neither said, nor intimated, nor even thought evil of others. His manner of open alignment with honorable men everywhere amassed dividends.[48]

In addition to gaining the respect of many in the world, all of this brought heavenly smiles upon the Church as President McKay entered his second decade as prophet, seer, and revelator.

NOTES TO CHAPTER 10

1. Conference Report, April 1936, 58.
2. Harold I. Hansen, "Cumorah's Lonely Hill," 1986, typescript, 67; copy in author's possession.
3. Francis M. Gibbons, *David O. McKay: Apostle to the World, Prophet of God* (Salt Lake City: Deseret Book, 1986), 285.
4. "President Assisted Expansion," *Deseret News,* January 18, 1970, McKay Scrapbook, no. 110, MS 4640, LDS Church Archives, Salt Lake City.
5. Alden Whitman, "Missionary President," McKay Scrapbook, no. 110.
6. David Lawrence McKay, *My Father, David O. McKay* (Salt Lake City: Deseret Book, 1989), 218–19.
7. Llewelyn R. McKay, *Home Memories of David O. McKay* (Salt Lake City: Deseret Book, 1956), 261.
8. Edward and Lottie McKay, interview by Mary Jane Woodger, June 30, 1995, McKay Research Project, College of Education, Brigham Young University, Provo, UT; transcript in author's possession.

9. David Lawrence McKay, *My Father,* 225; see Susan Arrington Madsen, *The Lord Needed a Prophet* (Salt Lake City: Deseret Book, 1990),149–50.

10. David Lawrence McKay, *My Father,* 219–20.

11. Ibid., 218.

12. Keith Terry, *David O. McKay: Prophet of Love* (Santa Barbara, CA: Butterfly, 1980), 118–19.

13. David O. McKay, *Cherished Experiences from the Writings of President David O. McKay,* comp. Clare Middlemiss (Salt Lake City: Deseret Book, 1955), 149–50.

14. Ibid., 150.

15. Ibid., 150–51.

16. David Lawrence McKay, *My Father,* 221.

17. Llewelyn R. McKay, *Home Memories,* 133–35.

18. Jeanette McKay Morrell, *Highlights in the Life of President David O. McKay* (Salt Lake City: Deseret Book, 1966), 129.

19. Ibid., 131.

20. Ibid., 131–32.

21. David O. McKay, *Cherished Experiences,* 178–81.

22. Morrell, *Highlights,* 132–33.

23. Terry, *Prophet of Love,* 127.

24. Ibid., 130.

25. Morrell, *Highlights,* 179.

26. David O. McKay, *Cherished Experiences,* 43–4.

27. David O. McKay, January 20, 1955, McKay Scrapbook, no. 39; and "Incident of an Accident and Almost Immediate Healing of Sister McKay," McKay Scrapbook, no. 131.

28. Richard N. Armstrong, *The Rhetoric of David O. McKay, Mormon Prophet* (New York: Peter Lang, 1993), 13.

29. David O. McKay, *Cherished Experiences,* 156–57.

30. David O. McKay, Remarks, Papeete, Tahiti, January 19, 1955, McKay Scrapbook, no. 143.

31. David O. McKay, *Cherished Experiences,* 69–71.

32. Terry, *Prophet of Love,* 119.

33. David Lawrence McKay, *My Father,* 224.

34. Sheri L. Dew, *Go Forward With Faith: The Biography of Gordon B. Hinckley* (Salt Lake City: Deseret Book, 1996), 177–78.

35. Terry, *Prophet of Love,* 147.

36. Morrell, *Highlights,* 161.

37. Gibbons, *Apostle to the World,* 361.

38. Ibid.

39. Ibid.

40. Morrell, *Highlights,* 203.

41. Ibid., 206.

42. David O. McKay, *Groundbreaking Dedicatory Service, The Church College of Hawaii, February 12, 1955* (Laie, HI: The Church of Jesus Christ of Latter-day Saints, 1955).

43. Vernice Wineera, "Culture and Church at the Polynesian Cultural Center," *Voyages of Faith,* ed. Grant Underwood (Provo, UT: Brigham Young University Press, 2000), 210.

44. "President Assisted Expansion," *Deseret News,* January 18, 1970; McKay Scrapbook, no. 110.

45. Thomas S. Monson, interview for David O. McKay School of Education, October 7, 1996, Salt Lake City; video in author's possession.

46. Letter from the First Presidency to All Stake Presidents, 4 November 1957, Adam S. Bennion Papers, L. Tom Perry Special Collections, Brigham Young University Harold B. Lee Library, box 9, folder 9, p. 2.

47. "President Assisted Expansion," McKay Scrapbook, no. 110.

48. Terry, *Prophet of Love,* 182.

CHAPTER 11

A RADIANT PERSONALITY

There is no power so potent, no power so effective in influencing the lives of others, as Personality. *It is not just an influence, but many times is an inspiration.*

—*David O. McKay*[1]

As President McKay entered the second decade of his tenure as prophet, it became evident that his personality had infused itself into the lives of Church members in a remarkable way. One of President McKay's constant teachings was about the radiation of personality. He often taught, "We inherit certain traits from our parents, our grandparents, and so on, which help to form our own personalities. Through the proper development of these traits, *each of us can become an inspiration to others.*"[2] In another address he commented,

The effect of your words and acts is tremendous in this world. Every moment of life you are changing to a degree the life of the whole world. Every man has an atmosphere or a radiation that is affecting every person in the world. You cannot escape it. Into the hands of every individual is given a marvelous power for good or for evil. It is simply the constant radiation of what a man really is. Every man by his mere living is radiating positive or negative qualities. Life is a state of radiation. To exist is to be the radiations of our feelings, natures, doubts, schemes, or to be the recipient of those things from somebody else. You cannot escape it. Man cannot escape for one moment the radiation of his character. You will select the qualities that you will permit to be radiated.[3]

PERSONAL INFLUENCE AMONG CHURCH LEADERS

As an exemplar of this teaching, the radiation of President McKay's personality imprinted itself at Church headquarters and beyond. His personality especially influenced the General Authorities whom he called. When President McKay called Thomas S. Monson as a new member of the Twelve on October 4, 1963, Elder Monson was just thirty-six years old. President McKay's heart softened as he remembered the same call coming to him at almost the same age. He could empathize when Elder Monson seemed stunned for a moment before accepting the call.[4] Among the counsel President McKay gave his new associate were these words: "There is one responsibility that no one can evade. That is the effect of one's personal influence."[5]

Elder Monson surely must have known by then that President McKay was a wonderful example of a man who radiated kindness, warmth, and compassion. Once, before his call to the Twelve, Elder Monson visited President McKay in his office. He noticed a picture hanging on the wall and said, "Well, that's a beautiful framed painting, President McKay. Is that of your ancestral home in Huntsville?" President McKay laughed and replied, "Let me tell you about that picture. . . . A sweet little lady came in [and] gave that to me a week or two ago, and she said, 'President McKay I have spent the entire summer painting your ancestral home.'" President McKay went on, "You know . . . I never had the heart to tell her she'd painted the wrong home. She'd painted the house next door, but I thought about it, and I said to her, 'My dear, the home you had painted is the home next door, but in reality, that was the home I would see when I would lie on the bed in my ancestral home and gaze out the screen porch to that beautiful scene of the home you painted. You were inspired to paint that home.'"[6]

David O. McKay, seated. *Standing, left to right:* Alvin R. Dyer, Hugh B. Brown, Nathan Eldon Tanner, Joseph Fielding Smith, Thomas S. Monson, and LeGrand Richards.

Thomas Monson soon saw firsthand other personality traits and characteristics of the prophet. After his first meeting in the temple as a General Authority, Elder Monson ate lunch with the rest of the Quorum and the First Presidency. President McKay sat at the head of the table with a counselor on either side, and the members of the Twelve sat around the square table in order of seniority. Because Elder Monson was the junior member, he ended up sitting just one person away from President McKay. The prophet's conversation must have surprised the young Apostle. In a chatty manner during the meal, President McKay turned to him and said, "Brother Monson, welcome to our luncheon table." He then matter-of-factly said, "I read an interesting article in the *Reader's Digest* this month, entitled 'I Quit Smoking.' Did you happen to read it?" Luckily, Elder Monson had read it earlier on an airplane. He responded, "Yes, President McKay. I read the article. That man had the right idea." President McKay replied, "Yes, the author had the right idea, but she was a woman, not a man." "Whoops!" thought Elder Monson. He was amazed at the prophet's candor and memory for details. Then President McKay asked, "Brother Monson, do you think that bar none William Shakespeare really wrote the sonnets attributed to him?" Elder Monson thought, "Where is this conversation going? I'm a business major." But he replied, "Yes, I do. I think he wrote them." President McKay then smiled and continued, "So do I, Brother Monson, so do I. Do you read Shakespeare?" "Occasionally, occasionally, President." "What is your favorite work of Shakespeare?" "Henry VIII, President." "And what is your favorite passage from Henry VIII?" "President, I think my favorite passage was the lament of Cardinal Wolsey when he said, 'Had I but served my God with half the zeal I serve my king, he in mine age would not have left me naked to mine enemies.'" "Oh I love that passage," President McKay said. "Brother Monson, would you pass the potatoes, please?" Elder Monson passed the potatoes in a hurry. He was running out of his Shakespearean background but felt that Heavenly Father let him recall what he needed to during his conversation with the prophet.[7]

Another man who experienced President McKay's unique leadership personality was Gordon B. Hinckley. When Elder Hinckley came into the office, President McKay asked him to sit right across the desk where he could be close to him. President McKay then congenially disclosed that he wished to present Elder Hinckley's name in general conference the next day as an Assistant to the Quorum of the Twelve. Elder Hinckley remembered the piercing eyes, the strong face, and the feeling he had that President McKay was looking right through him.[8]

Another General Authority called by President McKay was Loren C. Dunn. President McKay had known Elder Dunn's father, who had been a stake president in Tooele, Utah, for twenty years, and he expressed the great respect he had for Loren's father. Elder Dunn affirmed his praise and told President McKay that his father was the greatest man he had ever known. President McKay then gave Elder Dunn an interesting challenge, "You've spoken respectfully and lovingly of your father. We want you to serve in this calling in such a way that it will bring honor to your family and [be] acceptable to your father as well."[9] Those words had a great effect on Elder Dunn. Elder Dunn mentioned that President McKay "used my love and respect for my father as a means of challenging me to do my best and serve valiantly."[10]

Sometimes interviews with President McKay were nonverbal but nonetheless conveyed a feeling of esteem for the individual. Robert L. Simpson had such an experience when he first met President McKay. Elder Simpson had served as a missionary in New Zealand and had flown back to the country for the dedication of the temple in 1958. Upon meeting Elder Simpson, President McKay put out his right hand, but he pulled him in close, put his left hand on Elder Simpson's shoulder, and looked into his eyes. For Elder Simpson, it was "a magical moment."[11] He expected President McKay to start a conversation, but President McKay did not say anything; he just looked at him with eyes that "penetrated [his] very soul." After about forty or fifty seconds, President McKay simply said, "I am pleased to know you."[12] Several months later, Elder Simpson received a call from President McKay, wherein President McKay said the following: "Brother Simpson, based on our personal interview in the New Zealand Temple, I feel impressed to call you to preside over the New Zealand Mission. How soon can you leave?"[13] There had been no words or questions between them in the temple, yet for President McKay, it had been a personal interview.

According to Marion D. Hanks, one of the pleasant aspects of any interview with President McKay was that while one was with him, one had "the full attention—the eyes, ears, the interested heart—of a great man." However, Elder Hanks went on to say that President McKay's questions could be forthright and intensive. He remembers President McKay asking him such things as, "Are you fully loyal to your family?" "Are there any improper involvements or alliances outside your home?" "Are there any unresolved problems in your life?" Yet President McKay asked those questions in such a kind and gentle manner that Elder Hanks could not help but answer in kind.[14]

One other interview became a poignant moment in the life of Elder Hanks. He met with the prophet before leaving for Vietnam. The prophet wanted him to take a message to the six thousand LDS servicemen in the war. During the interview, President McKay was very interested in Elder Hanks's plans and prospects for his trip. As the interview ended, President McKay reached out and touched Elder Hanks lightly on the knee and instructed, "Tell them [the servicemen] of this exchange of love."[15] President McKay was expressing his love for all of those men serving in the military. Elder Hanks recalled, "He wanted that love, . . . respect and affection to be communicated to them through me from him."[16]

Though the cares of the Church must have weighed heavily upon him, President McKay never lost his sense of humor. For example, during one general conference in 1962, when two of the younger members of the Seventy had given outstanding addresses, President Hugh B. Brown nudged President McKay and said: "President McKay, I believe this Church is going to carry on after you and I are gone." President McKay turned to President Brown and asked, "Gone where? I am not going any place. . . . Where are you going?"[17]

CLOSE ASSOCIATIONS IN THE FIRST PRESIDENCY

In 1959, President Stephen L Richards passed away. President McKay knew President Richards's personality, strengths, and friendship that he enjoyed so much could never be replaced; however, President McKay found that the Lord wanted Henry D. Moyle to fill the vacancy. Moyle, an Apostle since 1947, was a hard-driving, powerful entrepreneur who brought new talents and strengths to Church leadership. He was ordained the second counselor in the First Presidency on June 12, 1959. Moyle's bishop at the time was George R. Hill, a relative of President McKay's. When President McKay called Henry D. Moyle, Bishop Hill asked President McKay if he thought he could work with such a strong-minded individual. President McKay replied, "I have never had a horse that I couldn't break to the bit, nor have I ever worked closely with anyone who did not give me total, loyal support."[18] President Moyle's driving, ambitious personality came at a time when it was dearly needed, because soon after the death of Stephen L Richards, President J. Reuben Clark's health began to deteriorate rapidly, as he was nearing ninety years old. President Clark asked President McKay to release him months before his death, but President McKay did not. Instead, to alleviate some of the stress of the highly demanding calling, President McKay ordained Elder Hugh B. Brown to serve as his third counselor in the First Presidency in June 1961. Hugh B. Brown, originally from a farming town in Alberta, Canada, before becoming a member of the Quorum of the Twelve, had previously practiced law with J. Reuben Clark Jr. after returning from military service in World War I. During the Second World War, Elder Brown had been called by the First Presidency to serve as coordinator for the hundred thousand LDS servicemen stationed in Europe.[19] When President Brown was called as an additional counselor in the First Presidency, he was dumbfounded. President McKay reminded him, "Brother Brown, . . . the right of nomination does not rest in you, but in me; and you are the nominee!"[20]

David O. McKay and J. Reuben Clark met as long-standing friends in Clark's home for the last time to discuss matters of Church business in 1961. There President McKay found President Clark "slumped down in a wheelchair with a shawl wrapped around his shoulders." President Clark began to cry when he saw the prophet. President McKay knew that President Clark would be unable to attend the next general conference. He also noticed that President Clark "did not pay much attention to details." President Clark would simply affirm, "Whatever you Brethren have decided I approve!"[21] They reminisced about their days together until David had to leave. J. Reuben Clark passed away on October 6, 1961.

After President Clark's death, Hugh B. Brown became the second counselor. The First Presidency remained stable until one night in the fall of 1963 when, on a Church ranch in Florida, President Moyle died of a heart attack. Just a few weeks later, on October 4, 1963, Hugh B. Brown, an Apostle since 1958, was ordained as first counselor in the First Presidency and N. Eldon Tanner was ordained as second counselor. President Tanner became a great asset to the Church and to the three succeeding prophets under whom he served. He was a man of great intelligence and was widely recognized as such throughout the world. After working in public education administration, Tanner had served in government, become the president of a petroleum company, been the director of a bank, and supervised the construction of a pipeline that ran across Canada.[22]

In the autumn of 1966, President McKay called Thorpe B. Isaacson into the First Presidency. Professionally, Elder Isaacson had served for years on multiple boards for institutions of higher learning, and within the Church he had served as a General Authority since 1946, first as a counselor in the Presiding Bishopric and then as an Assistant to the Twelve.[23] At the same time he called President Isaacson, President McKay also called Joseph Fielding Smith as another counselor. President Smith had been an Apostle since the age of thirty-three in 1910 and brought much knowledge and experience to the First Presidency.[24] The addition of two new counselors was approved by the Council of the First Presidency and Quorum of the Twelve on October 28, 1965, and the new counselors were set apart the next day.

During the first meeting of the expanded First Presidency, held on November 9, President McKay shared his reasons for calling the additional counselors:

> I am not so well as I used to be and called you brethren as counselors in the First Presidency to help carry the work. I pray the Lord's blessings to attend us in this quorum of the First Presidency. It is nothing new in the Church. The Prophet Joseph Smith had several counselors; President Brigham Young had seven at one time I think; and this will constitute the quorum of the First Presidency. I should like to meet regularly with you and take up matters . . . as the occasion requires.[25]

Alvin R. Dyer was also called as an additional counselor in the First Presidency in April 1968.[26] Interestingly, Elder Dyer had been ordained an Apostle in 1967 but not as a member of the Quorum of the Twelve. During the ordination, President McKay told Elder Dyer he was "making him a watchman on the tower over the consecrated lands of Missouri."[27] After becoming an Apostle, Elder Dyer began buying property in Missouri and apprising President McKay of all developments.[28] Though President McKay's First Presidency contained additional counselors and various personalities over the years, it was always his personality and decisions that came to the forefront.

PERSONAL INFLUENCE IN THE PUBLIC SPHERE

It was not just Church leaders that became enamored with President McKay's personality and decisiveness; political leaders constantly made trips to see President McKay and Salt Lake City.

During the 1960 presidential campaign, both Richard M. Nixon and John F. Kennedy visited with President McKay. Both presidential candidates knew that President McKay could, though he would not, affect the balance of any vote in the Intermountain West.[29] Most especially, Lyndon B. Johnson became captivated by President McKay's personality. President McKay received a phone call from President Johnson on January 25, 1964, two months after he took office.[30] "President McKay, you will not remember me, but I visited you twice in Salt Lake City." President McKay quickly replied that he did remember him. Then said President Johnson: "President McKay, I need some strength and advice from you. Could you come to Washington for an hour's consultation with me—any time next week? Come at your convenience; I shall meet your time, President McKay."[31] Plans were then made for President McKay to make a trip to the nation's capital the following week. When President McKay arrived at the White House on January 31, President Johnson explained why he had called him. He said he always felt inspired when he was in President McKay's presence. The cares and concerns of his office were becoming increasingly heavy to bear, and he felt he needed help. President Johnson said that when he was a boy, he could rest his head on his mother's shoulder; now he needed another shoulder to rest on, and he looked to President McKay. He wanted advice from President McKay. President McKay thought for a moment and then said that he knew that the president was an honorable man. Then President McKay advised: "Let your conscience be your guide. Let the people know that you are sincere, and they will follow you."[32]

Favorable media accounts of President McKay's activities increased the number of dignitaries wanting to visit with him. Many of them came away realizing David O. McKay was one of the singular men of his generation. Norman Vincent Peale, one of the most significant motivational speakers, authors, and clergymen of the twentieth century, was one who visited with the prophet. Peale said that even at the age of ninety-one, President McKay's "delight in things bubbled over in his laughter, his optimism, his warm and ready smile, and

David O. McKay visits President Lyndon B. Johnson at the White House in
Washington, D.C., January 31, 1964.

President David O. McKay at the National Congress of Parents and Teachers, where he was awarded a life membership "in recognition of devoted and distinguished service to children and youth," June 20, 1961.

especially in the prayer with which our visit ended." As Peale stood up to leave President McKay's office, President McKay slipped his arm through his and, "in fatherly tones, voiced thanks for human friendships, for the saving love of Christ, for the privilege of being his disciples."[33] Peale exhibited a reaction to President McKay that was common, observing:

> I found him not only an obviously great person, but a warm, loving man. My several conversations with him left me with the impression of a great mind with an unusual grasp of affairs both religious and secular. At the same time, he was good company and told me a number of amusing incidents. I recall his genial laugh and rare good humor. On my last visit he was feeble, but when my wife entered the glorious room in which he received visitors, I was touched by his gracious courtesy as he strove to rise. I at once urged him to remain seated, but he replied, "I always stand in the presence of a lady." He was a true gentleman of the fine old school.[34]

On December 29, 1968, a Gallup poll listed David O. McKay as one of the most admired men, along with Norman Vincent Peale. The question the poll takers asked was, "What man that you have heard or read about living today in any part of the world do you admire most?" In the religion category, President McKay was the second man on the list—quite an honor for a leader of a small church. (The Church at that time had only two and a half million members.)[35] Being chosen was a testament of his warmth, kindness, and compassion.

Producer Cecil B. DeMille, a longtime friend of David's, wrote in his autobiography, "There are men whose very presence warms the heart. President McKay is one of them. I spoke from the heart when, in the middle of a commencement address I was giving at Brigham Young University, I turned to him on the platform, and said, 'David McKay, almost thou persuadest me to be a Mormon!'"[36] Many believe that it was in honor of their friendship that DeMille held the world premiere of his movie *The Ten Commandments* in Salt Lake City.[37]

PERSONAL INFLUENCE IN THE CHURCH

A new image for the Church was embodied in the personage of David O. McKay.[38] His image was also infused into Church programs and the hearts of people being drawn to the Church. In 1960, President McKay had prophetically stated, "The time has come for many thousands of people in Europe to accept the teachings of the Church." Eight years later Alvin Dyer said in an interview, "In two years 50,000 persons joined the Church. This was in direct fulfillment of Mr. McKay's prophecy."[39]

The Lord was using President McKay's personality to bless Church programs. In fact, an article in the *Deseret News* reported that during his tenure

> visitors' centers have been built to replace former bureaus of information. Extensive programs have been developed for world affairs and national and local exhibits. These have been supplemented by tours throughout the United States, and into both Canada and Mexico by the Tabernacle Choir. The choir's records have become best sellers. Church periodicals have continued to match the membership growth of the Church. A new publication called the *Unified Magazine* was created to meet the needs of the non-English-speaking members of the Church.[40]

No program had more far-reaching effects on the Church members' lives than the correlation program, introduced in 1961. Correlation centered on the home and declared it as the "basis of a righteous life." As President McKay introduced the correlation program, he explained that the auxiliaries were to "aid the home and its programs, giving special aid and succor where such is necessary."[41] The program was designed to assist individual Church members in taking advantage of all the Church's resources and activities.

Elder Gordon B. Hinckley of the Quorum of the Twelve presents President McKay with a pen sketch by Henry K. Jacubowski of the Brazilian Mission, January 24, 1969.

Correlation emphasized four priesthood programs: home teaching (which replaced ward teaching), missionary, genealogy, and welfare.[42] On the ward level, a priesthood executive committee (PEC) and a ward correlation council (ward council) were formed in 1964. In 1965, "the Family Home Evening Program was developed, complete with structured programs, lessons, and activities, as part of the direction correlation took. A lesson manual for every family in the Church [began to be] prepared annually."[43]President McKay also made changes to the structure of priesthood leadership. The *Deseret News* reported "the creation of the body of priesthood leaders known as Regional Representatives of the Twelve. . . . Sixty-nine men were appointed to receive counsel and instructions relative to the priesthood programs in specific areas from the Council of the Twelve. These regional representatives, in turn, conduct the leadership training of stake officers and ward bishoprics [at] regional meetings."[44] President McKay also felt inspired to ordain members of the First Quorum of the Seventy to be high priests. He explained that these ordinations were necessary so that Presidents of the First Quorum of the Seventy could more fully carry out their assignments from the Twelve. With growing needs of Church administration, the First Presidency also announced they would construct the thirty-eight-story Church Office Building in the early 1960s.[45]

In all of these developments, President McKay constantly used humor and lightheartedness as part of his leadership style. Even when things seemed to go wrong, the prophet remained calm. For instance, when it was found that someone had absconded with some Church funds, President McKay was approached about taking action. His reply was, "A dog does not know he is a dog unless he has fleas. Don't worry about it. These things happen."[46] However, on other occasions, if necessary, President McKay took appropriate action, always believing in decorum and order. There once was a Scout leader who took his troop on an outing in a truck that was unlicensed. On the trip the truck's brakes failed, and several Scouts were killed. The Scoutmaster was devastated and wanted to speak to President McKay.

President McKay decided not to see the Scoutmaster because he did not want to condone improper action.[47] President McKay expected everyone to go through correct procedures and gently reproved those who did not. By way of illustration,

> At one time the Ogden Knitting Mills had a contract with the Church to make the temple garments. The owners were either non-members or inactive. Someone suggested to Church leaders that it was inappropriate for these people to be handling [temple] garments. The Church took away the contract and the company faced financial ruin. S. Dilworth Young [a member of the First Council of the Seventy] knew the owners. . . . As Elder Young was walking down the street he spotted the prophet and mentioned the problem to him. David O. McKay listened and said that what had happened was wrong. He then said, "I'll take care of it but next time you go through the quorum." David O. McKay reinstated the mill's contract. S. Dilworth Young learned a lesson. He said, "I don't care if the temple falls down, I won't ever go straight to the prophet again."[48]

President McKay was careful about what he said and did and expected the same of other Church leaders. He knew if he so much as whispered to a child, what he said could be told around the world. He knew there would be public stories about private things, and he used his image, position, and popularity to send out the right kind of messages effectively. President McKay was also very concerned about the efficiency of those at the Church Administration Building. Few individuals were as well known for punctuality as President McKay, and he taught others this trait. One time when President McKay was visiting a stake, the stake president started the meeting one or two minutes late. President McKay mentioned to him that if he as the stake president told the Saints he would start at a certain time, he should keep his word. At the next meeting, the stake president started two minutes early. Afterwards President McKay told the stake president that starting early was not appropriate either; one should do what they say they are going to do.[49]

In everything he did and in every decision that he made, President McKay had one constant guide. When one of his sons asked him how he handled the awesome responsibilities associated with the Church, President McKay's answer was simple: "Whenever I have to make a decision on Church matters I do so as if right soon after I would have to explain my actions to Christ himself."[50] Thus, while President McKay may have left an imprint on the Church with his personality, he acted on weightier matters only with divine approval. For example, though some said that the black Church members would never get the priesthood in this life, President McKay held that "there is no doctrine that holds Negroes under a divine curse," but rather that it was just a practice "which we expect to change."[51] However, the Lord did not inspire President McKay to make the change. Even when the Church came under deep criticism for the policy, to the point that hostile actions were exhibited against Brigham Young University teams,[52] President McKay held firm that the Lord would let the prophet know when He was ready to open the door; that He would tell him if the time was right. Though the Lord did not give a revelation to President McKay during his presidency to change the policy, a revelation was received almost twenty years later by one of President McKay's successors, President Spencer W. Kimball.

Matching his dedication in waiting for revelation was President McKay's lifelong commitment to the principle of free agency. Elder Loren C. Dunn spoke of this firm commitment. "He had great respect for a person's free agency. He was very careful not to cross the line of free agency. However, . . . he also established perimeters of conduct in such a way that everybody knew what it was the Lord, the Church, and President McKay expected them to do. At the same time, they had the freedom to act as they saw fit. What he did was never in a forceful way," but rather "in the context of recognizing and respecting a person's free agency, nevertheless, being absolutely firm as far as where the guidelines and rules were."[53]

David O. McKay's personality allowed him to be comfortable whether in a humble home or a queen's palace. A little child was as important to him as heads of state.[54] President McKay's bright vision for the Church radiated from him. He "didn't always have the answer, but he knew that the answer was out there someplace." He surrounded himself with great, intelligent men whom he trusted and then had them find out answers and bring them back to him.[55] President McKay's administrative style brought the Church into international recognition during the 1960s and distinguished him not only as a Church leader, but also as a world leader.

NOTES TO CHAPTER 11

1. "The Radiation and Influence of a Powerful Personality," *The Instructor,* August 1969, 265 (original emphasis).
2. Ibid. (original emphasis).
3. Conference Report, October 1969, 87.
4. Francis M. Gibbons, *David O. McKay: Apostle to the World, Prophet of God* (Salt Lake City: Deseret Book, 1986), 410.
5. Thomas S. Monson, "Your Personal Influence," *Ensign,* May 2004, 20.
6. Thomas S. Monson, interview for David O. McKay School of Education, October 7, 1996, Salt Lake City; video in author's possession.
7. Ibid.
8. Gordon B. Hinckley, interview for David O. McKay School of Education, October 7, 1996, Salt Lake City; video in author's possession.
9. Loren C. Dunn, interview by Mary Jane Woodger, October 11, 1995, Salt Lake City, McKay Research Project, College of Education, Brigham Young University, Provo, UT; transcript in author's possession.
10. Ibid.
11. Robert L. Simpson, interview by Mary Jane Woodger, December 30, 1996, St. George, UT, McKay Research Project; transcript in author's possession.
12. Ibid.
13. Ibid.
14. Marion D. Hanks, *The Gift of Self* (Salt Lake City: Bookcraft, 1974), 221.
15. Ibid., 222.
16. Marion D. Hanks, interview by Mary Jane Woodger, October 1995, Salt Lake City, McKay Research Project; transcript in author's possession.

17. Hugh B. Brown, "Dedicatory Program: Clark Library, Smoot Administration Building, Physical Plant Building," October 10, 1962, *BYU Speeches of the Year* (Provo, UT: Brigham Young University, 1962), 13.

18. George R. Hill, interview by Mary Jane Woodger, October 28, 1995, Salt Lake City, McKay Research Project; transcript in author's possession.

19. Arnold K. Garr, Donald Q. Cannon, and Richard O. Cowan, eds., *Encyclopedia of Latter-day Saint History* (Salt Lake City: Deseret Book, 2000), 146.

20. Gibbons, *Apostle to the World*, 403.

21. Keith Terry, *David O. McKay: Prophet of Love* (Santa Barbara, CA: Butterfly, 1980), 169.

22. Garr, Cannon, and Cowan, *Encyclopedia of Latter-day Saint History*, 1221.

23. Ibid., 555.

24. Ibid., 1133.

25. David O. McKay diary, November 9, 1965; cited in Gibbons, *Apostle to the World*, 413.

26. Garr, Cannon, and Cowan, *Encyclopedia of Latter-day Saint History*, 310.

27. Hartman Rector Jr., interview by Mary Jane Woodger, October 1997, Salt Lake City, McKay Research Project; transcript in author's possession.

28. Gibbons, *Apostle to the World*, 414.

29. Terry, *Prophet of Love*, 182.

30. Jeanette McKay Morrell, *Highlights in the Life of David O. McKay* (Salt Lake City: Deseret Book, 1966), 262.

31. Ibid., 262.

32. Ibid., 264–66.

33. Norman Vincent Peale, *Guideposts* (Carmel, NY: Guidepost Associates, 1965), 12–14; cited in Richard N. Armstrong, *The Rhetoric of David O. McKay, Mormon Prophet* (New York: Peter Lang, 1993), 7–8.

34. Personal communication between Richard N. Armstrong and Norman Vincent Peale, November 10, 1977; cited in Armstrong, *The Rhetoric of David O. McKay*, 14.

35. Gibbons, *Apostle to the World*, 420; and Lou Jean McKay Blood, interview by Mary Jane Woodger, August 8, 1995, Provo, UT, McKay Research Project; transcript in possession of author.

36. Cecil B. DeMille, *The Autobiography of Cecil B. DeMille*, ed. Donald Hayne (Englewood Cliffs, NJ: Prentice Hall, 1959), 433.

37. Armstrong, *The Rhetoric of David O. McKay*, 8.

38. Ibid., 14.

39. Alden Whitman, "Missionary President," McKay Scrapbook, no. 110, MS 4640, LDS Church Archives, Salt Lake City.

40. "President Assisted Expansion," *Deseret News,* January 18, 1970, McKay Scrapbook, no. 110.
41. Ibid.
42. Ibid.
43. Ibid.
44. Terry, *Prophet of Love,* 170.
45. Glen L. Rudd, interview by Mary Jane Woodger, February 8, 1996, Salt Lake City, McKay Research Project; transcript in author's possession.
46. Ibid.
47. Barrie McKay, interview by Mary Jane Woodger, August 15, 1995, Salt Lake City, Utah, McKay Research Project; transcript in author's possession.
48. Gunn McKay, interview by Mary Jane Woodger, July 28, 1995, Provo, UT, McKay Research Project; transcript in author's possession.
49. Richard L. McKay, Address given at the David O. McKay Honor Day Celebration at Ogden LDS Tabernacle, September 29, 1968, McKay Scrapbook, no. 99.
50. Whitman, "Missionary President."
51. Richard O. Cowan, *The Church in the Twentieth Century: The Impressive Story of the Advancing Kingdom* (Salt Lake City: Bookcraft, 1985), 193.
52. Dunn interview.
53. Barrie McKay interview.
54. Simpson interview.

David O. McKay as prophet during the 1960s.

CHAPTER 12

THE IDEALS OF A PROPHET

What you sincerely in your heart think of Christ will determine what you are. . . . No person can study this divine personality, can accept His teachings without becoming conscious of an uplifting and refining influence within himself.

—David O. McKay[1]

As President David O. McKay taught the Latter-day Saints, it seemed that his teachings began to revolve around slogans, sayings, or quotes that became part and parcel of his presidency once he said them. Whether or not these sayings originated with him, all were eventually attributed to him.

"WHAT-E'ER THOU ART, ACT WELL THY PART"

The first slogan he became known for came from his mission experience in 1898 in Scotland when he saw a quote on a stone arch that said, "What-E'er Thou Art, Act Well Thy Part." President McKay felt that if the Saints would act well their part in their responsibilities, the work of the Lord would go forth. The prophet helped Church members realize that the most important factor in acting well their part was for individuals to understand their stewardship before Christ.

Some of the most memorable ideas on the topic come from instruction he reportedly gave to workers at the Church's physical facilities.

> Someday you will have a personal priesthood interview with the Savior Himself. If you are interested, I will tell you the order in which He will ask you to account for your earthly responsibilities.

> First, He will request an accountability report about your relationship with your wife. Have you actively been engaged in making her happy and ensuring that her needs have been met as an individual?

> Second, He will want an accountability report about each of your children individually. He will not attempt to have this for simply a family stewardship but will request information about your relationship to each and every child.

> Third, He will want to know what you have done with the talents you were given in the preexistence.

> Fourth, He will want a summary of your activity in your Church assignments. He will not be necessarily interested in what assignments you have had, for in His eyes the home teacher and a mission president are probably equals, but He will request a summary of how you have been of service to your fellow man in your Church assignments.

> Fifth, He will have no interest in how you earned your living but if you were honest in all your dealings.

> Sixth, He will ask for an accountability on what you have done to contribute in a positive manner to your community, state, country, and the world.[2]

President McKay speaking at general conference during the 1960s.

President McKay greeting students at a BYU devotional assembly, May 18, 1960.

"WITHIN THE CHAMBERS OF THE SOUL"

President McKay expected Church members to control their thoughts and actions. Mastery of self was to be highly valued. He once declared, "In self-mastery, there is no one great thing which a man may do to obtain it; but there are many little things by observing which self-control may be achieved; and a subjecting of the appetite to the will, and a refusal to satisfy desire are two of these little things."[3]

On another occasion President McKay instructed, "The hardest battles of life are fought within the chambers of the soul. A victory on the inside of a man's heart is of far more worth in character building than a dozen conquests in the everyday battle of business, political, and social life."[4] For President McKay, spirituality was "the consciousness of victory over self and of communion with the Infinite. Spirituality impels one to conquer difficulties and acquire more and more strength. To feel one's faculties unfolding and truth expanding in the soul is one of life's sublimest experiences."[5]

At the heart of the prophet's teachings on self-mastery was the principle of agency, which President McKay described as a "measuring rod by which the actions of men, of organizations, of nations may be judged."[6] On many occasions as the president of the Church, he insisted that agency was "God's greatest gift to man" and absolutely necessary for progress.[7] For President McKay, however, the principle of agency was coupled with the principle of responsibility. He directed that "man's responsibility is correspondingly operative with his free agency. . . . and that is the effect not only of a person's actions but also of his thoughts upon others. Man radiates what he is, and that radiation affects to a greater or less degree every person who comes within that radiation."[8]

"EVERY MEMBER A MISSIONARY"

From his early days as a prophet he began to be characterized as "the Missionary President." President McKay tried to personify missionary persuasion. As Richard N. Armstrong wrote, "The 'every member a missionary' responsibility was generally understood in the

LDS Church, but it remained for [President] McKay to not only institutionalize it, but to popularize it."[9] In 1958, President McKay referred to a program he had introduced when he was European Mission president in 1923 and added that his message that day was "every member—a million and a half—a missionary." From that moment on, the "every member a missionary" motto was stamped in the minds of devoted members, and soon after the media also began using this motto to distinguish his presidency.[10]

President McKay supported the message by improving missionary programs. He introduced the first proselytizing plan for missionaries in 1952. This plan, entitled *A Systematic Program for Teaching the Gospel,* grouped gospel teachings into six discussions. In 1961, under his presidency, the first worldwide mission presidents' seminar was scheduled, allowing leaders to share their experiences with one another. To further improve the missionary program, language training schools were instituted at Brigham Young University, Ricks College, and the Church College of Hawaii at Laie.[11] Under President McKay's "Every Member a Missionary" program, the Church seized an opportunity to construct a pavilion at the New York world's fair. The project cost a great deal, but the possibilities of introducing and sharing the gospel were too great to be ignored.[12] Missionaries manned the pavilion to answer the questions of fairgoers, and they were able to show a feature film called *Man's Search for Happiness.*[13]

President McKay's marked attentiveness to missionary work "inspired a remarkable upward surge" that continued to increase over the second half of the twentieth century.[14] In writing about President McKay's missionary efforts, Alden Whitman gave these statistics: "In a decade the number of missionaries was quadrupled . . . and the number of annual converts rose from 12,000 to 180,000. . . . Conversions were [especially] accelerated in Latin America and the South Seas."[15]

"NO OTHER SUCCESS CAN COMPENSATE FOR FAILURE IN THE HOME"

In 1935, President McKay gave the Church another motto. This slogan, "No other success can compensate for failure in the home,"

David O. McKay with his grandchildren and daughter, December 21, 1957.

originated in a book he had read many years earlier entitled *Home: The Savior of Civilization.*[16] This line became a watchword during his presidency and is still associated with the name of David O. McKay. More than any other subject, President McKay felt inspired to address family principles.

President McKay's talks frequently dealt with courtship, marriage, family, home, and parenting. He often spoke of his parents, family, upbringing, and beginnings in a small rural town as an ideal way of life and frequently portrayed his mother, Jennette Evans McKay, as an example worthy of emulation. He esteemed all women from his experiences with his own mother. President McKay advised, "The best time for the child to learn . . . rules of conformity is between the ages of three to five. If the parents do not get control of the child during those ages, they will find great difficulty in getting control later."[17] President McKay loved children and felt that they were a nation's greatest asset.[18] He believed that "next to eternal life, the most precious gift that our Father in heaven can bestow upon man is His children."[19] His background as an educator came into play as he shared his expertise and prophetic vision with parents. On one occasion he reminded parents, "In teaching children, it should ever be kept in mind that 'Behavior is caught, not taught.' Example is more potent than precept. Parents have the duty to be what they would have their children become in regard to courtesy, sincerity, temperance, and courage to do right at all times."[20]

President McKay often spoke about marriage. In some of his conference addresses he spoke about the love he felt for his children and Emma Ray. His marriage of over sixty years became the model union for future generations of Church members. He admonished the Saints, "Let us teach youth that the marriage relation is one of the most sacred obligations known to man, or that man can make."[21] He was considered a wonderful example of how a husband should treat his wife.[22] He explained that a good husband is also a "true gentlemen," and that a true gentlemen is "open, loyal, true, . . . honorable, . . . and faithful to himself, others, and God."[23]

More than any other prophet, David O. McKay talked about courtship and dating. He advised, using Benjamin Franklin's adage, "During courtship, keep your eyes wide open; but after marriage, keep them half shut."[24] In his teachings, President McKay answered questions that many young people continue to ask, such as, "How do I know when I am in love?" He gave the following counsel:

> If you meet a girl in whose presence you feel a desire to achieve, who inspires you to do your best, and to make the most of yourself, such a young woman is worthy of your love and is awakening love in your heart.

> I submit that, young men, as a true guide. In the presence of the girl you truly love you do not feel to grovel; in her presence you do not attempt to take advantage of her; in her presence you feel that you would like to be everything that a Master Man should become, for she will inspire you to that ideal. And I ask you young women to cherish that same guide. What does *he* inspire in you?[25]

President McKay taught that after marriage, couples should continue to court in order to have a happy, fulfilled union. He instructed, "Young people, marriage is a relationship that cannot survive selfishness, impatience, domineering, inequality, and lack of respect. Marriage is a relationship that thrives on acceptance, equality, sharing, giving, helping, doing one's part, learning, and laughing together."[26] President McKay taught that responsibilities in the home should become the center of the Saints' lives: "Mothers, fathers, treasure sacredly and sense keenly your responsibility to the child during those first five plastic years of its life."[27] His sermons often discussed the sanctity of marriage and the home as he called on parents to spend more time with their children and to teach them about character and integrity. He promised that "pure hearts in a pure home are always in whispering distance of heaven."[28] He called the home the

The McKays on their golden wedding anniversary, January 1951.

"cell-unit of society," and declared that "parenthood is next to Godhood."[29] Emphasizing family home evening, he prophesied: "The strength of a nation, especially of a republican nation, is in the intelligent and well-ordered homes of the people. If and when the time comes that parents shift to others or to the state the responsibility of rearing their children, the stability of the nation will be undermined and its impairment and disintegration will have begun."[30]

Prophetically, President McKay knew that an attack on the family was imminent, and he prepared Church members accordingly. He warned, "When family life disintegrates, the foundation and bulwark of human society is undermined."[31] By the time divorces became more prevalent during the 1960s and 1970s, President McKay had already defined the Church's stand on divorce as follows:

> Except in cases of infidelity or other extreme conditions, the Church frowns upon divorce. . . . A man who has entered into a sacred covenant in the House of the Lord to remain true to the marriage vow is a traitor to that covenant if he separates himself from his wife and family just because he has permitted himself to become infatuated with the pretty face and comely form of some young girl who flattered him with a smile. Even though a loose interpretation of the law of the land would grant such a man a bill of divorcement, I think he is unworthy of a recommend to consummate his second marriage in the temple.[32]

TEACHING THROUGH HUMOR

While such sobering warnings were necessary, President McKay also infused humor into his teachings, and some of his most memorable anecdotes centered on the family. When he would begin talking about courtship and finding the right partner, he would often share one of his favorite Scottish stories.

> The problem of choosing a proper, congenial mate is very vital. In regard to this I suggest in general that you follow the advice of

David O. McKay in his office on his eighty-fourth birthday.

Sandy, the Scotchman, but not his example. His friend MacDonald came to Sandy and said, "I'm verra much worried, Sandy. I dinna ken [I don't know] whether to marry a rich widow whom I do not love, or marry a puir lass [poor lass] of whom I'm verra fond."

And Sandy said, "You'd better follow the promptin's o' yer heart, MacDonald."

"All right," said MacDonald, "I'll do it. I'll marry the puir lass."

"In that case," said Sandy, "would you mind giving me the address of the widow?"[33]

Speaking at a fireside, he told a joke about one wife's cooking that went like this: "A young woman . . . said to her husband, 'I know my cooking isn't good. I hate it as much as you do; but do you find me sitting around griping about it?'" President McKay then informed his congregation:

Griping after marriage is what makes for unhappiness. A wise mate learns to control the tongue. . . . Do not speak the complaining word; just walk outdoors. I once heard of a couple who never had a quarrel, for they decided that whenever one lost his or her temper he or she would go out and take a walk. He spent most of his time walking.[34]

Another Scottish story he loved to tell was about Jock. President McKay would begin:

Too many of us are like that Scotsman of whom I told you, who had lost his wife by death, and his neighbor came in, gave comfort, and said what a good neighbor she had been, how thoughtful of others, what a good wife she had been to Jock, who was mourning. Jock said, "Aye, Tammas, Janet was a guid woman, a guid neighbor as you say; she was a' you say an' mair. She was aye a guid, true wifey tae me, and I *cam' near tellin'* her sae aince or twice."

On another occasion, instructing parents, he said: "You wonder why one child is so different in disposition from another. . . . The first babe had no brothers to tease him; the tenth babe perhaps had nine."[35]

President McKay reminded the Saints, "Don't be afraid to laugh. . . . A person without a sense of humor misses much of the joy of living!"[36] Perhaps that was one of the main reasons people delighted in hearing President McKay speak; he was entertaining. His charm and sparkling wit awakened friendship, and he was always ready to tell or hear a good story. President McKay believed, "A good laugh is a panacea for many ills." He frequently said, "Every time a man laughs he takes a kink out of the chain of life."[37] He emphasized that The Church of Jesus Christ of Latter-day Saints was a happy church to belong to and that obeying was an appendage to love.[38] Part of President McKay's love included a great power to lift people. President Gordon B. Hinckley described that power in this manner: "At the pulpit, [he would stand] tall and stately . . . lifting his hand to that vast congregation as he spoke words that inspired and lifted and made everyone there want to live a little better as a Latter-day Saint."[39]

THE IDEALS PROPHET

Part of that inspiration had to do with one of President McKay's most prevalent themes, that of higher ideals. David O. McKay was an idealist. Some thought he might have been too idealistic, but ideals and aspirations are what the prophet gave the Saints as a beacon to follow. He once wrote:

If every man born into the world would have as the beacon of his life ideals, how much sweeter and happier life would be! With such an aim, everyone would seek all that is pure, just, honorable, virtuous, and true—all that leads to perfection; for these virtues he would glorify whoever seeks to glorify God. He would eschew that which is impure, dishonorable, or vile.[40]

President McKay gave the Saints aspirations, a "yearning for something high and good, an exalted desire."[41] As Elder Henry B. Eyring recalled, President McKay's teachings "tend[ed] to be around the notion of holding up very high ideals. . . . He was able to hold up lofty ideals in a way that attracted young people and helped them feel that it [was] possible to aim very high."[42]

President McKay pointed the Saints toward the Savior and urged them to let the ideals He taught shape their lives. He taught, "What you sincerely in your heart think of Christ will determine what you are, will largely determine what your acts will be. No person can study this divine personality, can accept His teachings without becoming conscious of an uplifting and refining influence within himself."[43] The prophet urged the Saints to seek the "abundant life," which was "obtained not only from spiritual exultation, but also by the application of the principles that Jesus taught to daily life."[44] As President McKay neared the end of his earthly life and mission, he both taught and exemplified the ideal that following Christ brings individuals joy, happiness, and supreme satisfaction. He became the personification of the ideals he taught.

NOTES TO CHAPTER 12

1. Conference Report, April 1951, 93.
2. Statement of President David O. McKay given at a meeting in his apartment in the Hotel Utah to a group of brethren responsible for physical facilities in the Church, reported by Cloyd Hofheins in a talk to the seventies quorum of Provo Utah Oak Hills Stake, May 16, 1982; cited in Stephen R. Covey, *The Divine Center* (Salt Lake City: Bookcraft, 1982), 54–55.
3. David O. McKay, "On Fasting," *Improvement Era*, March 1963, 156.
4. David O. McKay, "Sylvester Q. Cannon," *Improvement Era*, August 1943, 465.
5. Conference Report, October 1969, 8.

6. Conference Report, October 1965, 7.
7. Conference Report, April 1950, 32.
8. Ibid., 33–34.
9. Richard N. Armstrong, *The Rhetoric of David O. McKay, Mormon Prophet* (New York: Peter Lang, 1993), 75.
10. Ibid., 75.
11. "President Assisted Expansion," *Deseret News,* January 18, 1970, McKay Scrapbook, no. 110, MS 4640, LDS Church Archives, Salt Lake City.
12. Keith Terry, *David O. McKay: Prophet of Love* (Santa Barbara, CA: Butterfly, 1980), 170.
13. Shaun D. Stahle, "Not That We're Back, It's That We're Still Here," *Church News,* June 12, 2004.
14. Armstrong, *The Rhetoric of David O. McKay,* 78.
15. Alden Whitman, "Missionary President," McKay Scrapbook, no. 110.
16. James Edward McCulloch, *Home: The Savior of Civilization* (Washington, D.C.: The Southern Cooperative League, 1924), 42; quoted in Conference Report, April 1935, 115–16.
17. David O. McKay, "Home . . . and the Strength of Youth," *Improvement Era,* August 1959, 583.
18. David O. McKay, Utah White House Conference on Child Health and Protection, April 7, 1931, McKay Scrapbook, no. 2.
19. General Sunday School Conference, October 2, 1949, McKay Scrapbook, no. 14.
20. Conference Report, April 1935, 114.
21. David O. McKay, *Pathways to Happiness,* comp. Llewelyn R. McKay (Salt Lake City: Bookcraft, 1967), 113.
22. Hartman Rector Jr., interview by Mary Jane Woodger, October 1997, Salt Lake City, McKay Research Project, College of Education, Brigham Young University, Provo, UT; transcript in author's possession.
23. Ohio Conference Minutes, November 29, 1926, McKay Microfilm, reel 8, no. 498, Church Archives.
24. David O. McKay, "Ideals for Courtship and Marriage," *Improvement Era,* February 1960, 110.
25. "As Youth Contemplates an Eternal Partnership," *Improvement Era,* March 1938, 139 (original emphasis).
26. David O. McKay, "Ideals for Courtship and Marriage," 110.
27. David O. McKay, *Pathways to Happiness,* 115.
28. McCulloch, *Home: The Savior of Civilization,* 42; quoted in Conference Report, April 1964, 5.
29. David O. McKay, *Pathways to Happiness,* 117.
30. Ibid., 117, 3.

31. Conference Report, October 1947, 119.

32. David O. McKay, "The Home Front," *Improvement Era,* November 1943, 657.

33. David O. McKay, "Temple Marriage," *Deseret News,* February 27, 1952, Church News section.

34. David O. McKay, "Ideals for Courtship and Marriage," 110.

35. Conference Report, October 1960, 115.

36. David O. McKay, "Relief Society Conference," *Relief Society Magazine* 18 (1931): 349.

37. Llewelyn R. McKay, *Home Memories of David O. McKay* (Salt Lake City: Deseret Book, 1956), 165.

38. Ibid.

39. Lou Jean McKay Blood, interview by Mary Jane Woodger, August 8, 1995, Provo, UT, McKay Research Project; transcript in possession of author.

40. Gordon B. Hinckley, interview for David O. McKay School of Education, October 7, 1996, Salt Lake City; video in author's possession.

41. David O. McKay, "Peace and Goodwill," *Improvement Era,* December 1955, 893–94.

42. General Session of Thirtieth Annual Convention of Primary Association Officers in Barrett Hall, University of Utah, Salt Lake City, June 10, 1932, McKay Scrapbook, no. 2.

43. Henry B. Eyring, interview by Mary Jane Woodger, August 13, 1996, Salt Lake City, McKay Research Project; transcript in author's possession.

44. Conference Report, April 1951, 93.

45. David O. McKay, *Gospel Ideals* (Salt Lake City: Deseret News Press, 1957), 151.

President McKay with his grandson Johnny McKay.

CHAPTER 13

BELOVED PROPHET

I never think of death. I only think of life.

—*David O. McKay*[1]

Even at the end of his life, President McKay was an optimist. On the occasion of his ninetieth birthday, he said, "I never felt better in my life and I mean it. . . . The only thing that worries me is that I get tired after working eight or ten hours a day."[2] Truly, the few years that lay ahead were relatively happy ones. By the time President McKay entered his tenth decade, he was seen by the Saints and others around the world as the ideal: the ideal religious leader, the ideal missionary, the ideal educator, the ideal father, the ideal grandfather, the ideal husband, and the ideal follower of Jesus Christ.

Into the last years of his life, President McKay continued to enjoy his favorite pastime—horseback riding. Concerned for President McKay's health, his doctor had forbidden him to ride, but President McKay ignored his doctor's advice. President McKay's nephew, George Richard Hill, related the tale of how he one day "helped Llewellyn catch and saddle Sonny Boy." George then

> led Sonny Boy to [President McKay's] door yard to let him mount, not knowing how we could gracefully assist him. President McKay stood by the horse momentarily, patted him fondly on the neck, and then placed his foot in the stirrup and

vaulted into the saddle like an eighteen-year-old. When the two
of them returned from a glorious ride, [President McKay's]
comment . . . as he dismounted was, "George Richard, don't you
tell the doctor I rode Sonny Boy."[3]

President McKay continued to enjoy this indulgence, but he
would eventually realize that he needed to slow down in his final years.

On May 7, 1963, he and Llewelyn went [to Huntsville] for a
horseback ride. As the saddle blanket was placed on Sonny Boy,
the horse became frightened and bolted. "I was knocked down
and pulled along the ground for about a block," wrote the
Prophet. "However, he stopped and I was not hurt. We finally
saddled him and he was his usual self and I had a very good ride
on him which I enjoyed thoroughly." When [President McKay]
returned home, he was silent about the incident, not wanting to
trouble Sister McKay, who, he was certain, "would have worried
a great deal about it."

Any worry [President McKay] spared his wife at the time was
merely deferred, as this entry of June 27 [1963] implies: "I was
so tired when I got home that I alarmed members of the family
who were there. I could hardly talk and they became very much
concerned." Then, for the first time, we perceive a hint that
David O. McKay had discovered his own mortality. "I know that
I have used up my reserve energy . . . and that it is foolish for me
to go on this way, working such long hours without rest and
sometimes without food."[4]

In November 1963, President McKay also suffered a mild stroke
that left his legs weak and his speech impaired. "Intermittently
medication prescribed by his physician tended to make him drowsy
and lethargic. But his mind was not impaired. His perceptions and
mental faculties . . . enable[d] him to perform ably the essential role

President McKay at April 1962 general conference.

of his prophetic office. The counselors were able to handle the ongoing affairs of the Church," while the prophet made the decisions that deviated from standard procedures.[5]

In order to reserve his energy, President McKay borrowed portions of his previous addresses in composing his new ones.[6] His thoughts had changed very little over the course of his life, and his ideals were timeless. For the next few years, President McKay continued to speak in general conference, but by October 1966, his legs had become so weak that he required a stool to sit on to deliver his talk. From that point, members of his family, usually his son Robert, would read the talks for him. He wanted to attend all the sessions of conference, but because his physician suggested otherwise, he watched some from his apartment.[7] Even amidst physical limitations, President McKay's mind always remained "very fertile." He paid attention to what was going on in the world and in the Church.[8] In 1969, he was delighted with the moon landings, speaking of them in his last address. He was also fascinated with the astronauts, including Colonel White, whom he had met personally.[9]

Concerned with President McKay's health, those close to him would often try to relieve him of responsibilities. Soon after his ninety-sixth birthday, his secretary, Clare Middlemiss, visited with him about the upcoming conference and asked, "'Do you want to turn this over to someone else, your counselors, and let them prepare this now?' He said, 'Say, young lady, who's the president of this Church? . . . We'll go on as usual.'"[10]

He was adamant that his age not become an issue in his leadership or the enjoyment of his life. President McKay often chided those who tried to save his energy: "Don't ever mention that a man of my age shouldn't be doing such things." He could say such things because "he *was* doing them, he would continue to do them until his last breath."[11] President McKay insisted on "still driving a car until the last year of his life."[12] President McKay "disliked the very appearance of old age and," before being confined to a wheelchair, he "would not be seen hobbling about in public with a cane," though he used one privately.[13] In his presence, he would not allow the subject of age to even be discussed. And when the subject was broached, he deflected such comments with humor. He would tell others, "It's awful to grow old, . . . but I prefer it to the alternative."[14]

When he had to be assisted, he would respond with humor. After his stroke, when one of his legs would give out, he quipped, "One thing that I cannot stand is disobedience, and my leg is being very disobedient right now."[15] Once when the prophet was ailing and President Lyndon B. Johnson commented on how good he looked, he replied, "I haven't an ache or a pain. . . . I am just plain sick."[16] Another time he joked, "How do you know when your youth has been spent? When your get [up] and go has got up and went."[17] Occasionally, President McKay would visit welfare farms with the Brethren. On one particularly hot day, he turned to the rest of the Brethren and optimistically suggested, "Isn't it good to get this warmth in your bones?"[18] President McKay's humor never subsided.

In the last few years of his life, President McKay spent most of his days in the Hotel Utah apartment where the McKays had lived since they moved from their South Temple home in July 1960. "The apartment was adequate in size. Its living room was long, housing a large sofa and comfortable chairs scattered about tastefully." Beyond the dinner table sat twin apple-green chairs, where President McKay and Emma Ray would sit holding hands as they watched a television program together. "The housekeeping details [were] managed by the Hotel Utah," and "Gabrielle Baruffol, or 'Gabby,' their French-Swiss housekeeper, fussed about them with the singular pride of a mother hen. Short, stocky and lovable, . . . her job was to carry the physical burden of the most ideal couple of the church, and she did so with gusto."[19]

One of Gabby's daily tasks was to help Emma Ray dress. She would see "that the tiny lady looked presentable—hair combed, makeup applied, and a lovely dress and shawl or sweater worn." Even with Gabby's help, President McKay was still adamant that he be allowed to be a gentleman. During each meal, the same ritual was

A birthday kiss for Emma Ray, June 21, 1963.

repeated. "Moving with difficulty across the room to the dining table, he would refuse to allow anyone else to hold Emma Ray's chair as she was seated for meals. Slowly setting aside his cane and grabbing the dining table to steady himself, then just as slowly releasing his hold on the table for a firm grip on the back of her chair, he looked down at his sweetheart. Emma Ray smiled as her noble husband pulled back her chair." With exertion of energy, Emma Ray would slide herself "carefully into the waiting seat. He struggled to push her forward." Afterward he insisted on making it to his own chair, pulling it out, easing himself down, and scooting the chair up to the table. "Gabby stood near, . . . longing to be of help. But [President McKay] had a fierce desire to remain the gentleman Emma Ray had married."[20]

Though his body became old and slower, those characteristic gentlemanly manners never left David, and throughout the Church, President McKay was still known as the ideal gentleman. In his later years, even when confined to a wheelchair, he continued to try to rise when a woman entered the room.[21] Each week, before "being taken in to the temple for [his] weekly meeting," President McKay "would taxi his wheelchair up in position to [Emma Ray's] wheelchair. And then he would lean to the left and she would lean to the right and they would have a kiss for each other. And then he'd say, 'Alright, I'm ready to go.'"[22]

On one of the McKays' last wedding anniversaries, a photographer came to the apartment to take pictures. He "lined [the McKays] up and got everyone out of the way. At the critical moment as the photographer snapped the picture, [Emma Ray's] little hand moved [David's] big hand up to her lips and kissed it. As that happened, President McKay wept and sobbed."[23] Such images found their way into the *Church News* and into the hearts of the Saints.

Ever learning, David was alert, even to the last. In one of the last leadership meetings President McKay attended at the age of ninety-six, he turned to his fellow General Authorities and said, "Brethren, I went to the temple yesterday, and I learned something new. I learned it myself."[24] Elder Boyd K. Packer remembered, "Here he was, the prophet—an Apostle for over half a century and even then he was learning, he was growing. His expression 'I think I am finally beginning to understand,' was greatly comforting to me."[25]

Until the last week of his life he was still receiving official guests and conducting Church affairs.[26] The last Christmas Emma Ray and David spent together, a violin teacher from Ogden brought twenty young children to see the prophet. As the violins played "We Thank Thee, O God, for a Prophet" and "I Need Thee Every Hour" (one of President McKay's favorites), President McKay was overwhelmed and tears rolled down his face.

Not long before he passed away, while reading him letters of support from members of the Church, his secretary asked, "'President McKay, you still love life, don't you?' He put his head back, and he said, 'Oh yes. I never think of death. I only think of life.'"[27]

His final illness began about 11:30 P.M. on Saturday, January 17, 1970. He resisted falling into a coma, but on Sunday, January 18, with Emma Ray by his side, he slipped from this life, dying of acute congestion of the heart.[28] On the day he died, the five hundredth stake of the Church was formed. One can imagine this great prophet slipping through the veil and there seeing what he had seen fifty years earlier in the Apia, Samoa, harbor, even the City Eternal. One can imagine David walking toward the beautiful white city, joining the "great concourse of people approaching the city." One can see his white hair matching a flowing white robe. One can imagine him approaching the Savior, whose radiance would beam on the countenance of David O. McKay, who had truly been born again.

LOVINGLY REMEMBERED

President McKay's body lay in state for three days while "tens of thousands of [mourners] lined the sidewalks around the Church Administration block, waiting to file past the body of the man they had known and loved."[29] Loyal Saints, slowly moving past the casket, could be seen as a human river honoring the prophet who had become for them a fountain of righteousness.[30] At his funeral, Elder Harold B. Lee suggested that "that person who has lived best, is he

President David O. McKay waves to a young girl
in Wilmette, Illinois, May 6, 1962.

who in his passing, has taken up [the] most hearts with him." During those days of mourning in 1970, it became clear that President McKay had taken many hearts with him. That ability to capture hearts had come not "by studying books about religion, [or] . . . attending a theological seminary," but through David O. McKay's relationship with God.[31] The prophet's influence had imprinted itself on the hearts of those who had known him as their prophet for nineteen years. A great spirit had come to preside and had now had fulfilled his mission.

The public press, radio, and television media lauded David O. McKay's accomplishments during the days between his death and funeral, including the development of the Church welfare system and his emphasis on family home evening.[32] When President McKay left mortality, over half the membership of the Church had known no other prophet. In April 1951, when David O. McKay was first sustained, the Church had just over one million members. By the final night of President McKay's life in January 1970, the Church's size had increased to 2.8 million. President McKay's missionary zeal had reaped rich rewards. The year he became the prophet, convert baptisms had numbered 14,700; by 1968 the number had risen to 64,021. Missionary forces had grown likewise; full-time missionaries increased from 5,500 to 13,000, and the number of missions grew from 43 to 88.[33]

This prophet, known for his emphasis on education, had also directed the expansion of Brigham Young University through the construction of over eighty major new buildings. Enrollment at the school during his presidency quadrupled from 5,086 to 24,144. During his watch, "the Church Colleges of Hawaii and New Zealand were opened; five schools were opened in Santiago, Chile; 36 elementary and two high schools were started in Mexico; and others were completed at Pago Pago and Tahiti."[34]

No previous prophet had seen such growth; but more than that, on a personal level, David O. McKay had become the "epitome of goodness in the minds of millions of people throughout the world."[35]

Quoting an editorial from the *Deseret News,* Joseph Fielding Smith said that during David O. McKay's life, "wherever he passed, men lifted their heads with more hope and courage. Wherever his voice was heard, there followed greater kindness among men, greater tolerance, greater love. Wherever his influence was felt, man and God became closer in purpose and in action."[36]

During the funeral that was held on January 22, 1970, in the Salt Lake Tabernacle, many of his associates paid him the highest of compliments. One accolade, given by President Hugh B. Brown, was that David O. McKay had "lived as nearly as it is humanly possible for a man to live a Christlike life." President Brown declared there was more to David O. McKay than just his sermons. "Those who listened to him," he said, "felt there was something finer in the man than anything he could say."[37] President Brown then shared something that David O. McKay had once said: "If even the simplest principles of the Savior's teachings had been observed, history would have been changed."[38] Through observing the simplest principles of the Savior's teachings, President McKay had changed the course of The Church of Jesus Christ of Latter-day Saints, its members, and the world. The small, intermountain Church had become an international organization. Quoting again from the *Deseret News* editorial, President Joseph Fielding Smith added, "If ever a man of modern history left this world better for having lived in it, that man was David O. McKay."[39]

In his eulogy, President Harold B. Lee stated, "None of us will ever forget the touchstone of his soul, which was the secret of his nobility, when he declared, 'What you think of Christ will determine in large measure what you are. That man is greatest who is most Christlike.'" Turning his attention to Emma Ray, President Lee promised, "He won't be far away from you, Sister McKay. He will be waiting. I think he can't be long without you over there. He probably knows that you won't want to be long without him. He will be waiting. Have no fear. Be of good peace, and that time will come and that glorious reunion where time is no more, where there will be no tears, no sorrow."[40] True to that promise, the glorious reunion of the "ideal couple" took place just ten months later, when Emma Ray Riggs McKay quietly passed away on November 14, 1970.

Even with the passing of his wife, President David O. McKay was not soon to be forgotten. As President Brown remarked, "When a great man dies, for years the light he leaves behind him lies on the paths of men."[41] Now, decades after David O. McKay left mortality, the love, teachings, and light of his life continue to be an inspiration and a profound influence for good in the paths of men and women throughout the world.

NOTES TO CHAPTER 13

1. Quoted in Clare Middlemiss, Interview with KSXX Radio Station, January 20, 1970, McKay Scrapbook, no. 110, MS 4640, LDS Church Archives, Salt Lake City.
2. David O. McKay, quoted in Don Reed, "President McKay at Ninety Proud of Church Gains," *Ogden Standard-Examiner,* September 8, 1963, 1.
3. George R. Hill, interview by Mary Jane Woodger, October 28, 1995, Salt Lake City, McKay Research Project, College of Education, Brigham Young University, Provo, UT; transcript in author's possession.
4. Francis M. Gibbons, *David O. McKay: Apostle to the World, Prophet of God* (Salt Lake City: Deseret Book, 1986), 368.
5. Ibid., 417.
6. Richard N. Armstrong, *The Rhetoric of David O. McKay, Mormon Prophet* (New York: Peter Lang, 1993), 123.
7. Gibbons, *Apostle to the World,* 419.
8. Marion D. Hanks, interview by Mary Jane Woodger, October 1995, Salt Lake City, McKay Research Project; transcript in author's possession.
9. Middlemiss, Interview with KSXX Radio Station.
10. Ibid.
11. Keith Terry, *David O. McKay: Prophet of Love* (Santa Barbara, CA: Butterfly, 1980), 156 (emphasis added).
12. Ibid., 208.
13. Ibid., 200.
14. Ibid., 200, 208.

15. Robert L. Simpson, interview by Mary Jane Woodger, December 30, 1996, St. George, UT, McKay Research Project; transcript in author's possession.
16. Gibbons, *Apostle to the World,* 379.
17. Boyd K. Packer, interview by Mary Jane Woodger, July 9, 1996, Salt Lake City, McKay Research Project; transcript in author's possession.
18. Simpson interview.
19. Terry, *Prophet of Love,* 199–200.
20. Ibid., 200–201.
21. Richard McKay, interview by Mary Jane Woodger, 1995, Salt Lake City, McKay Research Project; transcript in author's possession.
22. Thomas S. Monson, interview for David O. McKay School of Education, October 7, 1996, Salt Lake City; video in author's possession.
23. Hanks interview.
24. Simpson interview.
25. Boyd K. Packer, *The Holy Temple* (Salt Lake City: Bookcraft, 1980), 263.
26. "David O. McKay, Mormon Leader, Is Dead at Ninety-Six," *New York Times,* McKay Scrapbook, no. 110.
27. Middlemiss, Interview with KSXX Radio Station.
28. Ibid.; and "David O. McKay, Mormon Leader, Is Dead at Ninety-Six," McKay Scrapbook, no. 110.
29. "Rites Laud Life of Late Prophet," *Deseret News,* January 24, 1970, Church News section.
30. See Joseph Fielding Smith, "'One Who Loved His Fellowmen,'" *Deseret News,* January 24, 1970, Church News section.
31. Harold B. Lee, "'He Lighted the Lamps of Faith,'" *Deseret News,* January 24, 1970, Church News section.
32. Ibid.
33. "President McKay Guided Church during Phenomenal Growth," *Deseret News,* January 24, 1970, Church News section.
34. Ibid.
35. "Rites Laud Life of Late Prophet."
36. Quoted in Smith, "'One Who Loved His Fellowmen.'"
37. Hugh B. Brown, "'God Makes a Giant among Men,'" *Deseret News,* January 24, 1970, Church News section.
38. Quoted in ibid.
39. Quoted in Smith, "'One Who Loved His Fellowmen.'"
40. Lee, "'He Lighted the Lamps of Faith.'"
41. Brown, "'God Makes a Giant among Men.'"

ABOUT THE AUTHOR

D R. MARY JANE WOODGER is an Assistant Professor of Church History and Doctrine at Brigham Young University. Born and raised in American Fork and Salt Lake City, Utah, Dr. Woodger has always had a great love for teaching. After obtaining a B.S. in Home Economics Education, Dr. Woodger taught Home Economics and American History for a number of years in Salt Lake City, where she received the Vocational Teacher of the Year Award from the Jordan School District. In 1992, she completed her M.Ed. at Utah State University. In 1997, she received from Brigham Young University an Ed.D. in Educational Leadership, with a minor in Church History and Doctrine.

In 1998 Dr. Woodger was honored by Kappa Omicron Nu with an Award of Excellence for her dissertation research entitled "The Educational Ideals of David O. McKay." Dr. Woodger has authored and coauthored numerous articles on doctrinal, historical, and educational subjects. These articles have appeared in various academic journals as well as venues for the LDS audience, including the *Journal of Book of Mormon Studies, Deseret News Church News,* and *The Religious Educator.* Her current research interests include twentieth-century Church history, Latter-day Saint women's history, and Church education.